SPEAKING OF LIFE

COMMUNICATION AND SOCIAL ORDER

An Aldine de Gruyter Series of Texts and Monographs

Series Editor

David R. Maines, Wayne State University

Advisory Editors

Bruce Gronbeck • Peter K. Manning • William K. Rawlins

SPEAKING OF LIFE

Horizons of Meaning for
Nursing Home
Residents

Jaber F. Gubrium

ALDINE DE GRUYTER
New York

About the Author

Jaber F. Gubrium is Professor in the Department of Sociology at the University of Florida. He has conducted research on the social organization of care in diverse treatment settings, including nursing homes, physical rehabilitation, caregiver support groups, and family counseling. His continuing fieldwork on the organizational embeddedness of social forms serves as a basis for comparative interpretive ethnography and a sociology of description.

Professor Gubrium is the editor of *Journal of Aging Studies* and the author of *Living and Dying at Murray Manor*, *Oldtimers and Alzheimer's*, *Analyzing Field Reality*, and *The Mosaic of Care*. His recently coauthored books (with J. Holstein) *What is Family?* and *Constructing the Life Course* present constructionist approaches to domestic order and the life course.

ALDINE DE GRUYTER
A division of Walter de Gruyter, Inc.
200 Saw Mill River Road
Hawthorne, New York 10532

This publication is printed in acid-free paper ∞

Library of Congress Cataloging-in-Publication Data

Gubrium, Jaber F.
    Speaking of life : horizons of meaning for nursing home residents
/ Jaber F. Gubrium.
        p.   cm. — (Communication and social order)
    Includes bibliographical references and index.
    ISBN 0-202-30481-7 (alk. paper). — ISBN 0-202-30482-5 (pbk. :
alk. paper)
    1. Nursing home care.   2. Nursing home patients.   I. Title.
II. Series.
RC954.3.G83   1993
362.1'6—dc20
                                                                93-28591
                                                                CIP

Manufactured in the United States of America

10 9 8 7 6 5 4 3 2 1

FOR THE STORYTELLERS

Jake Bellows
Rebecca Bourdeau
Lula Burton
Mary Carter
Ruby Coplin
Martha Gilbert
Karen Gray
Sue and Don Hughes
Myrtle Johnson
Bea Lindstrom
Jane and Tom Malinger
Julia McCall
Jane Nesbit
Opal Peters
Betty Randolph
Peter Rinehart
Lily Robinson
Roland Snyder
Alice Stern
Celia Turner
Rita Vandenberg
Grace Wheeler

Contents

Foreword

There has been only one paradigm shift during the past century in sociological thought that has meant much. That was when, under the influence of Thomas and Znaniecki's *Polish Peasant* research, instinct theories were forever replaced by social ontologies. Genetics was out, social forces and social processes were in, and sociology flourished as a result.

But a weariness now permeates the field. Formula sociology (do a survey, run some statistics, test a model), which also flourished, worked well for awhile, but we now understand that it worked best as an ideological and administrative practice. It went a long way toward legitimating sociology, but in the process it ironically became an orthodoxy that retarded scholarship. And so now, with the limits of the orthodoxy reached, the discipline is tired.

That disciplinary weariness has created an intellectual space that is now being filled by the renewed vigor of interpretive approaches. On its surface, this renewal looks like a second major paradigm shift: witness the rise of cultural studies, both American and European; the collage of postmodernist and poststructuralist debates, the increased attention to narrative the rhetoric; the wide-spread advocacy of multi-method research designs, the broader base of interactionist scholarship throughout the social sciences, let alone the increased blurring of genres that Geertz wrote about. I suspect, though, that there is more continuity and less of a shift in these approaches than one might think. What we have is merely a sharper and more articulate framing of ideas, perspectives, and concepts that have been around for decades and that these new framings have mobilized a new energy, excitement, and set of promises.

Jay Gubrium has represented a central and sustaining voice in and of that continuity. He has brought imagination, intellect, and an admirable tenacity to his scholarly endeavor, and he has justly become internationally known for his qualitative research is gerontology. When others were torturing the details of topics such as the demographic conditions for the emergence of nursing homes, Gubrium was publishing *Living and Dying at Murray Manor* and providing a masterly account of the living among the dying. When others sought to chart sequences along the life course, he told us of the biographies and lived experiences that cut across those sequences. For over twenty years, he has reminded us that sociology ought to study what people actually do; that people are creatures who communicate through symbols and are part of the very environments they create, and that their essence (in Dewey's sense of the term) rests in a selved, ongoing, and always partially formed inter-subjectivity. Science, with its methods and theories, and policy, with its attempts to structure human contact, must both eventually make their peace with these human conditions.

With the publication of *Speaking of Life*, Gubrium enters the apparent paradigm shift, sometimes called the interpretive turn, sometimes the narrative turn. In so doing, he exemplifies the continuity of scholarship in which these "turns" are grounded. He emphasizes meaning, context, time, reasonable accounts, the normalcy of inconsistency, and emotionality, which have been the bread and butter of interpretive, qualitative research all along. But he sharpens these traditional issues by emphasizing narrativity and what he calls horizons of meaning. He focuses attention on lifelong biographical linkages among nursing home residents that can be rendered only in the form of life narratives. Within these narrative renditions, horizons of meaning are discovered: worry, disappointment, regret, death, hope, joy. The nursing home is not a mere set of role arrangements, nor merely a setting containing people who can tell life narratives. Rather, it is like any other site of human collectivities— storied, transacted, layered with ambiguity, permeated by contingency, and ultimately, given life through perspectives of interpretation.

Gubrium takes these sorts of things seriously in giving us a realist narrative of nursing home residents' lives. He brilliantly accomplishes the task he sets out upon by providing stories to residents' faces, but I think he really goes further by telling us that there must be faces to the sociological storyteller. For, indeed, our professional accounts are the only *one* narrative version subject, like all stories, is to group conventions of storytelling. Here, he warns us of the undesirable consequences of conceptual dogma, of the inhumane and impractical implications of univocal policy, of the inevitable reactivity in social research, of the observed and rendered fact that nursing home residents are not always "residents'" when they talk to us. In *Speaking of Life*, Jay Gubrium speaks again of life among the dying. But, he also speaks of the continuity of interpretive research and thereby contributes a considerable dose of energy to our tired discipline.

David R. Maines

Acknowledgments

It is the narratives of those whose experience we study that make it possible to do social science. This book is dedicated to the men and women, resident in nursing homes, whose stories form the basis of what I have written. I am deeply grateful to them for affording me and my assistant both the time and the pain to convey the meanings of their lives and care in residence.

Carol Ronai, my doctoral student, assisted in the interviewing. She was an invaluable source of insights and efficiently moved the project along. I thank the University of Florida's Institute for Community Studies for administering the project, whose staff competently completed the transcriptions and managed the narrative material.

A number of colleagues and friends read the manuscript and made helpful comments. My good friend and collaborator Jim Holstein, with whom it is always a pleasure to work, identified strengths and weaknesses and in his invariably supportive manner advised me how to improve and sharpen the presentation. Florida colleague Anne Wyatt-Brown brought a critical humanist's eye to the text and informed me of the many ways in which what I had to say paralleled literary themes. David Maines, this book's series editor, offered useful advice.

Sharon Kaufman's research on the aging self and Robert Rubinstein's work on personal meaning have been sources of inspiration. I have extended some of their insights into the nursing home setting. Suzanne Gubrium, Steve Golant, R. Satyanarayana, and Camille Van Kirk were most encouraging throughout the project. As usual, my loving daughters, Aline and Erika, pummeled me with approving sarcasm. And, last but not least, the people I worked with at Aldine—Richard Koffler, Arlene Perazzini, and Mike Sola—were a first-rate editorial and production team.

The larger study of which this project was a part was supported by a two-year grant from the National Institute on Aging (R01 AG07985).

Introduction

Quality assurance has become a leading goal of health care delivery, the effect of public alarm over the high cost of care and the aim of offering the best care for the fewest dollars. One outcome has been the development of systems of quality management to assess quality on several fronts, from the quality of care provided to the resulting quality of life for care receivers.

This is increasingly evident in long-term care. In the past, nursing homes were besieged by journalistic exposes of poor-quality care; the leading assault now is being rationalized into the formal documentation of the quality of care provision and the quality of life for residents. A quality assurance industry is emerging to design assessment instruments, offer data management services, and monitor results and compliance activity.

Yet, for all the alarm and rationalization, few are asking what the subjective meaning of quality of care and quality of life is for those whose lives are affected. In contrast to the relatively short stays of hospital patients, nursing home residents are typically "long stayers" and, for better or worse, are likely to encounter the nursing facility as a final household. Matters of home, family, interpersonal ties, life history, self-worth, dependence, disappointment, and destiny confront residents in ways irrelevant to hospital patients or other short-stay care receivers. The matters significantly mediate the meaning of quality of care and quality of life.

This book examines the subjective meaning of the nursing home's quality of care and quality of life. A sample of residents has been given the opportunity to tell their stories, to speak of life and to convey in their own terms the meaning of the qualities in their facilities in relation to the significant matters of long stays. Meanings are presented from residents' points of view, revealing where and, if so, how in their lives the qualities figure in. It is a bottom-up rather than a top-down look and shows how what may be administratively deemed the qualities of care and life do not reflect what the qualities appear to be to care receivers.

The thesis is that the qualities are narratively organized by horizons of meaning: Residents convey the meaning of the quality of care and quality of life in terms of the differential linkages they make with lifelong experiences. For example, for residents whose horizons show them to be "worried to death" or who demonstrate otherworldly linkages, such as being engrossed with "lovin' the Lord," the quality of the facility's care is not as significant as it is for residents whose horizons articulate a vigilance for equity and justice in interpersonal relations. Among the former residents, the quality of care is at worst a source of daily irritations and at best a gamut of mere comforts. Against the horizon of vigilance, however, the quality of care becomes an all-consuming matter.

This thesis relates to a long-standing theoretical concern with how experience is given voice in everyday life, part of a broader interest in the sociology of description. For many years, the interest focused empirically on how organizations condition the way participants convey experience. For instance, ethnographic material gathered in fieldwork in a nursing home called Murray Manor was interpreted to reveal that a single nursing home, in practice, was three different "worlds" of living and dying. I argued then that differences in attitudes, sentiments, and behavior among administrators, frontline workers, and residents could not be understood unless their respective worlds were taken into account (Gubrium 1975). Recently, I have turned this around a bit theoretically to highlight participants (in this case, nursing home residents) as more active conveyers of meaning, less conditioned by circumstances than taking circumstances into account in telling their stories. It has not been a complete turnabout, inasmuch as residents' narratives are not viewed as conveyed with total disregard for leading orientations to the qualities of care and life, the special circumstances that distinguish residents from each other, and the broader experiential significances of long-term care and stays in a nursing home. But it is a definite turn to narrative as grounds for interpretation.

As far as possible in the following chapters, I present residents' stories in their own voices. Overall, the reader will not find the stories particularly gripping. They are only occasionally vividly packaged or poignantly ironic. Some are dishearteningly sad; others are glib or comical. Reading them, from chapter to chapter, is an emotional roller coaster. A few of the stories are repetitive, digressive, even confused. Yet they are categorizable into narrative types, revealing the storytellers to be meaningfully oriented in different ways to matters of life and care. Their tellers link the present qualities of care and nursing home life with experiences long past and with what is foreseen well beyond the days ahead. Mundane as the stories are, they inform the reader that quality of life and quality of care, in residents' voices, are not so much rationally assessable conditions, as they are horizoned, ordinary, and biographically active renderings of lifelong experience.

CHAPTER

1

Faces without Stories?

Twenty years ago, I completed fieldwork that led to the publication of *Living and Dying at Murray Manor* (Gubrium 1975), an ethnography of a nursing home. I can't say that horizons of meaning for nursing home residents or more particular concerns such as the quality of care and the quality of life were uppermost in my mind at the time. If anything, these matters were simmering at the sidelines of research focused on life worlds within institutional settings. It would be in the course of studies that followed much later that the matters' subjective meaning for residents would become the full-blown project reported here. Even so, the project has critical roots in the earlier work, which is where I will begin.

The fieldwork for the ethnography had an unexpected yet propitious start. Trained as a survey researcher and having just finished a study of life satisfaction among noninstitutionalized elderly, I planned to investigate the ingredients of life satisfaction for elderly in nursing homes. Methodologically, the plan seemed straightforward enough: Take the concepts and the skills learned in the community study and apply them in the nursing home setting.

But I had never set foot in a nursing home, and I knew no one who was resident in one nor anyone who worked there. The research literature on the social organization of nursing homes was meager. Anthropologist Jules Henry (1963) provided a comparative view of a hospital and two nursing homes. He called one of the nursing homes "hell's vestibule" because it offered residents filth and neglect. A few articles by sociologists were forthcoming, such as Elizabeth Gustafson's (1972) paper on the moral career of the nursing home patient and Charles Stannard's (1973) on the social conditions for patient abuse in a nursing home. Fiction writer May Sarton's (1973) eloquently written and touching account, *As We Are Now*, of seventy-six-year-old protagonist Caro Spencer's experience as a resident in a rural nursing home called Twin Elms was a year from publication.

From the media, I had gotten a quite negative sense of what nursing home life was like. There were the frequent exposes of poor nursing

1

home care I read in newspapers and magazines and watched on television public affairs programs. I could hardly mention my new research interest without being told things such as "Those awful places you read about," "I would never put my mother in one of them," and "That's the end of the road."

It all suggested that I take a look for myself, to get a firsthand view of the situation within which my survey questions were to be asked. I contacted seven nursing homes and arranged to speak with the administrators about my research plans, especially the need to spend time in a few homes to get a handle on the rhythms of everyday life and caregiving. The administrators expressed interest in the study, but some were understandably wary of my intentions because of what one called the "bad press" nursing homes were getting.

One administrator, whose name I fictionalized as Mr. Filstead in *Living and Dying at Murray Manor*, showed the kind of concern that I later realized was an ethnographer's dream. Filstead prided himself on being research-oriented and hoped to effect improved living conditions not only for the residents of his facility, which became Murray Manor, but for nursing home residents everywhere. He admired the aim of getting a firsthand view before launching the survey. I recall him explaining that things can't be "just labeled as all bad or all good and leave it at that, like you read in the papers." I had mentioned how I felt about the need to understand the complexities of life satisfaction and wanted to avoid rushing to judgment about what would be asked in a survey. I admired Filstead's commitment to the welfare of residents and his decided preference for seeing "all sides" of circumstances.

Inviting me to "take a look" at Murray Manor, Filstead eased my way into various units, introducing me to the floor staff and some of the residents. I soon found myself comfortably ensconced at nurses' stations, walking unit floors, visiting residents' rooms, sitting and chatting in lounges, participating in the activities area and in occupational therapy, and sharing meals with residents and the staff. On the floors, I became acquainted with the enduring tension between caring and completing a job. Off the floors, I was invited to participate in the activities of those whom I eventually called "top staff," which included the administrator, director and assistant director of nursing, the medical director, the in-service coordinator, the social worker, the activity supervisor, an occupational therapist, a chaplain, and the dietitian. I made a special point of attending patient care planning conferences, the purpose of which was to review residents' conditions with the aim of setting short- and long-term goals for their care.

Interacting with top staff, floor staff, and the residents, I began to think that their daily lives and worlds offered quite different perspectives on the meaning of care and caregiving. It occurred to me that a single nursing home might be three different organizations in practice, depending on the point of view. I actually used the term *worlds* to convey the difference because the term suggested something separate and distinct, yet equally compelling. What top staff saw as good and efficient caregiving, floor staff could consider "just getting the job done." What a resident felt was time well spent chatting with a friendly aide, from the aide's point of view could be less time to complete other duties.

The idea that whatever went on in the nursing home had to be understood within the context of particular worlds informed my growing inclination to turn the planned nursing home survey into a different project. I presented the idea to Filstead of conducting what I described as an "in-depth" sociological study of a single nursing facility. It needed doing, I explained, because the social organization of work and life in such settings had not been documented. It wasn't long before Filstead formally welcomed me to "join the team." So began the research for *Living and Dying at Murray Manor* and the background work for a study of the subjective meaning of the qualities of care and life.

RETRIEVED KNOWLEDGE

Twenty years later, there is a literature presenting the complexities. The accounts have documented knowledge that could not have been retrieved by the conventional survey or quality assessment. A cross-cultural view is offered by Jeanie Kayser-Jones (1981), who compares two facilities, one in California and the other in Scotland, to show the cultural mediations of life satisfaction and quality of care. Anthropologist Renee Shield (1988) describes how everyday life and care at the Franklin Nursing Home, a Jewish facility, are affected by ethnicity and the cultural contradictions of orienting to the environs as both a home and a hospital. Joel Savishinsky (1991) illustrates meanings and losses, memories and symbols, through the voices of individual residents, comparing his material with other nursing home ethnographies. Sociologist Tim Diamond's (1993) book, *Making Gray Gold*, based on his observations as an employed nurse's aide, tells of the broad-based complications of care work, beset as it is by the competing pressures of corporate profit-making, residents' needs, and the separate domestic experiences of the aides themselves. Other studies, equally insightful, add to our understanding (see Johnson and Grant 1985; Savishinsky 1991, chap. 1).

It is important to consider the kind of knowledge retrieved by nursing home ethnography. First, ethnography gives us anything but a static view of care, life, and death in the nursing home. Actually participating in the setting under study, the observer is witness to the practical fate of residents' and staff members' responses to events. Time spent with residents, for example, has a way of showing how what is said about the quality of care on one occasion can contradict what is said on another, even while the responses may be equally reasonable expressions in their separate contexts. In this regard, varied as they are, the narrative linkages made by residents in the following chapters are in-depth interview meanings, just as, say, standardized quality of care assessments are measurement-situated accounts.

When a frail elderly resident comments in the morning to an inquiring charge nurse that she, the resident, is well taken care of, compliments her assigned aide for the quality of her care on the afternoon of the same day, and later in the evening tearfully complains to a visiting daughter that the quality of care in the facility leaves much to be desired, time and context have a way of sorting the difference. We have an empirical basis for entertaining the possibility that the concern as addressed to a charge nurse or an aide is different in kind, not just degree, from the concern expressed to a daughter. In the former context, we may learn that what is at stake is continued good relations with staff members, while in the latter, it may be an interpersonal history of emotional blackmail.

Second, ethnography retrieves point of view in the documentation of experience. I have tried to underscore this by using the terms *story* and *version* to illustrate how an event takes on different meanings when examined from the viewpoints of separate parties or witnesses (Gubrium 1991). Listening to stories about an event such as a resident's alleged hostility suggests that the event necessarily comes in different versions because those who tell their stories do so in connection with their particular ties to, and interests in, the event. The hostility toward others that is warranted as perfectly reasonable from the standpoint of the resident who wishes "peace and quiet" during the night and believes peace and quiet to be a matter of residents' rights, may be seen as a sign of confusion and agitation, possibly dementia, by staff or family members worried about the resident's lucidity. Ethnographically, there is nothing contradictory about the difference, natural as it is to its points of view.

Consideration of viewpoint sheds critical light on the growing interest in quality assurance in health care. The nursing home industry is responding to nursing home reform legislation that makes quality of care and quality of life targets of national policy (Institute of Medicine 1986). An important feature of quality assurance is that care deal with the psychosocial needs of residents, which purports to take account of the whole person, not just physical health and functional capacity.

Resident assessment systems for nursing homes are in use or under development nationwide (see, for example, Morris et al. 1990; *NHCMQ*

Training Manual 1991). The knowledge retrieved by ethnographic research makes it evident, however, that such systems, which produce information in the form of so-called minimum data sets and other standardized measures, are applied without regard to viewpoint. They can hardly uncover differences in the interpretation of quality that emerge when viewpoint is taken into account. The systems are constructed from one-dimensional, typically administrative, definitions of quality. Their assessment instruments are designed accordingly and portend subjectively biased outcomes from the start.

Researchers Rosalie and Robert Kane (1988) caution those who would enter especially into the assessment of social functioning without taking its complexity into account. Well aware of the subjective, cultural, interactive, perspectival, and otherwise exceedingly general nature of the concepts of social health and social functioning, the Kanes write:

> Rhetoric about "treating the whole person" pervades today's medical world, especially primary-care fields. Nevertheless, holistic person-centered health care remains a vague ideal. The term holistic, which is rarely well specified, connotes caregivers who are mindful of the patient's physical, emotional, and social circumstances when making a diagnosis or recommending a course of action. Providers with this philosophy are expected to remember that patients are not diseased objects but people with families who live in communities and who view their health needs in the larger context of their social structure and personal life. . . . The hallmark of long-term care is a fusion (and sometimes a confusion) of health and social care. . . . Finding an efficient and accurate way of assessing the social well-being of elderly patients is a formidable challenge. (p. 133)

The Kanes' (1988) own pioneering research in the area has shown how varied the meanings of quality of care and quality of life can be when point of view is considered. Comparing the views of social workers and nursing home administrators in a different study, Betsy Vourlekis and her associates (1992) found that while there is consensus on priority psychosocial needs, there are different understandings of how psychosocial needs are to be met. Such findings lead us to ask, Whose view of quality is the basis of assessment?

Third, ethnography displays subjective complexity, avoiding the reduction of experience into undifferentiated scores such as a summary index of personal initiative. Anyone who has taken the time to observe people and listen to what they say knows that consistent behaviors, thoughts, and feelings are hardly more in evidence than behavior at odds with itself, sea changes of mind, and mixed emotions. Personal initiative, for example, has stories associated with it, which if we listened to carefully would show initiative to be a matter of judgment, sensitive to discretionary comparisons with others, the subject's earlier life, and expectations for his or her future.

Ordinary caveats conveyed in formal interviews and in casual conversation highlight the complications. Cautionary utterances made by respondents, such as "it depends," "I've never thought about that before," "thinking ahead," "talking about it makes me . . . ," and "compared with earlier in life," indicate experience (and data) in the making and reflect matters that are far from the simple traits of individuals. Meaning is not necessarily made on the spot, but is mediated by comparative, retrospective, and prospective considerations.

The interpretive contingencies and narrative complications of social functioning have a way of making rather shallow the sorting of conduct, attitudes, and sentiments into either/or, yes/no, agree/disagree, or more or less. Such response options register the mere surface of the qualities of care and life. To represent this in the rationalized form of indexes, scales, or Likert-type responses (strongly agree, agree, neutral, disagree, strongly disagree) is to render subjective complexity invisible. As researchers, we diversely construct, deliberate over, debate, and periodically reformulate our own ideas about the lives we study. Why should we suppose that those studied don't do likewise?

A NARRATIVE TURN

A mark of the newest ethnography is that the many faces seen in a field setting have their own stories. Whether the setting is a small, nonliterate society, a retirement community, a household, or a nursing home, fieldwork is increasingly a matter of documenting narrative and its organization.

The history of ethnography shows considerable variation in the extent that story and narrative are taken as metaphors for orienting to the field. Whether anthropological or sociological, early ethnography tended to ignore native authorship. In realist styles of writing, ethnographers wrote more or less colorfully of the social organization of this or that people, community, or other recognizable grouping with little regard for point of view (Geertz 1988; Van Maanen 1988). There has been a decided turn to authorship and narrativity in recent ethnography, indeed to the writing of ethnography itself (Clifford and Marcus 1986; Atkinson 1990; Clough 1992; Maines 1993; Maines and Ulmer 1993). Especially pertinent in the new ethnography is the way the style of ethnographic writing shapes the reader's response to the experiences and worlds written about. We are apt now to be told as much about the story behind ethnographers' own faces as about the stories of those studied.

This book does not represent as radical a turn, but it does take the nursing home resident's life narrative or story of life as a point of departure for uncovering the subjective meaning of the nursing home experience in relation to the life as a whole (see Kaufman 1986; Rubinstein 1988, 1989, 1990, 1992). Thinking back on the Murray Manor fieldwork in this way, I would say that my observations did orient to stories of work and life there as authored out of different perspectives. The concept "worlds" helped me to interpret a nurse's aide's story, for example, as grounded in the local experiences of a rather different author (and world) than the story, say, of an administrator or a resident. I did not evaluate the different stories for their comparative accuracy in depicting events in the life of the nursing home, but rather accepted them as perspectives and documented them from their separate angles.

Yet, if the role of field-worker as participant observer does lend itself to the storied representation of everyday life, in the versions and from the points of view life can be conveyed, participant observation's decided attention to setting and interaction makes it partial to stories about the present, even while it does not ignore stories about the past. At Murray Manor, my observations were centered on what was inferred from, done, or said about the daily events, thoughts, and feelings of staff members and residents, not on the subjective meaning of such matters in the context of a concerted interest in lifelong experiences. I was not as much concerned, for example, with how the nurse's aide's personal history, especially her family, class, or ethnic background, related to her feelings about what I called the "bed-and-body" work she was responsible for completing. Rather, as participant observer, I approached the aide's story as a narrative of current social relations with co-workers, employers, residents, and family members. Residents' stories were heard likewise, as narratives about living and dying at Murray Manor.

Taking the role of in-depth interviewer in this latest project and focusing on subjective meaning helps to uncover lifelong biographical linkages and locate them in relation to interpretations of current experience. What can be learned about the meaning of the resident's nursing home situation when it is examined in the context of his or her life narrative? How does a life story inform the relevance of care quality? The questions turn us to an alternative sense of story, one less centered on the present—nursing home living—than broadened to take account of meaning in relation to life as a whole.

Whether in the short or the long run, residents do bring life experiences with them to the facilities in which they live. They do not cease being Roland Snyder, Martha Gilbert, Ruby Coplin, Jake Bellows, Lula Burton, Alice Stern, Grace Wheeler, Julia McCall, or Karen Gray after checking in. They are not just more or less sick, alert, oriented, and ambulatory, but in their words "as well as can be expected for a man who's been ill much of my life," "not as confused as most of them are here," "feeling more at home than ever before," and "crying my eyes out because it's come to this," among other expressions that communicate what life has become in relation to what it was. It is these linkages that are now my concern.

BIOGRAPHICALLY ACTIVE RESPONDENTS

The narrative turn relates to a new perspective on an important concept. Sociologists commonly categorize those researched in terms of *roles*. Theirs are not individual studies of Jake Bellows, Julia McCall, Alice Stern, and others, but of their place and experience in the world as, say, frail elderly or nursing home residents. Sociologists trace patterns in role relationships, for example, the relationship between marital status and nursing home residence or between gender and caregiving. More complicated relationships may be investigated, such as the connection between gender and caregiving in historical context or in rural and urban comparison. Regardless of the relationship studied, experience is analytically appropriated to role, not to the individual. The concept role is used to explain the experience of those who occupy roles, as in the finding that the nature of caregiving is explained by the fact that it is centered in women's experience.

Concepts can be a disciplinary hazard. Anthropologists instinctively think in terms of culture to organize their observations, even while they differ among themselves on its connotation. Psychologists readily use the concept of the person, even if some colleagues prefer a less global notion. Sociologists are inclined to view experience in terms of roles, although they recognize alternative senses of the concept. The hazard comes in mechanical application, usage that does not stop to consider how experience will be conveyed in the process. This prompted Herbert Blumer (1969) somewhat reluctantly to reflect on the possibility of a science without concepts. Assuring his reader that such a science was inconceivable, Blumer still complained of concepts that unnaturally colored the empirical world or concepts so set in stone as to endure long after they proved empirically useful.

The concept role as applied by gerontological specialists can be particularly mechanical. Does the specialized purview serve to present the experiences of the later years chiefly in terms of the elderly role, as anthropologist Sharon Kaufman (1986) asks in her study of the self in aging? Kaufman shows how elders, allowed to tell their stories in their own terms, categorically transcend age as a framework for conveying experience. More to the point, are the lifelong experiences of the nursing home resident primarily understood according to the parameters of institutionalization? Does twelve-year nursing home resident Julia McCall, for instance, convey details of her life solely from the perspective of the official resident? Given the opportunity to tell her story in the open format of an in-depth interview, to what roles does *she* appropriate her experience? How does her life in a nursing facility and her status as a resident color her story, if at all?

The questions direct us to residents who are biographically active, providing space from the outset for them to narrate the informing roles they deem pertinent for understanding the meaning of the past and future in relation to the present (Gubrium and Lynott 1985; Gubrium, Holstein, and Buckholdt 1994). These are respondents who are not, a priori, experientially framed as residents, whose lives are not predefined primarily in terms of institutional contingencies.

Viewing residents as biographically active is not to see them, even under the most favorable of research conditions, as purely telling the individual truths of their lives. Narrative, after all, is eminently social, conveyed by someone to another, who together collaborate in its production (Bauman 1986; Frank 1980). Knowledge of nursing home resident Lula Burton's life story requires the researcher to ask about it, and the asking itself helps to shape the story. What Burton shares responds to the request to tell her story (Wallace 1992). She may never have been asked this before, nor have considered how to organize lifelong experiences in this way. The researcher (any researcher), too, is biographically active from the start, implicated as he or she questions, frames experience, prompts, and moves on to other questions.

HORIZONS AND THEIR NARRATIVE LINKAGES

Listening to Lula Burton and others speak of the qualities of care and life is hearing more than words and deeds. Also conveyed are horizons of meaning drawn by the patterns of narrative linkages each makes with experiences in and out of nursing homes. In referring to meaning as having horizons, I take it that what residents say about matters such as the quality of care needs to be understood in relation to the linkages. It is the linkages that give the qualities subjective meaning (see Gadamer 1993; Goffman 1974; Schutz 1967).

As Chapter 8 will show, for example, the subjective meaning of the quality of care and nursing home life for Lula Burton is conveyed in her interview through repeated linkages with the special circumstance of having grown up and grown old alongside her twin sister Lily, who now shares a room with Lula in a nursing home. Against this horizon of meaning, Burton's orientation to the quality of care and nursing home life contrasts with others who lack close and continuing relationships or whose relationships have been troublesome.

Horizons of meaning divide the book into parts and chapters. Part I shows the ways in which various horizons orient residents to the qualities of care and life in the nursing home. Residents Martha Gilbert and Jane Nesbit of Chapter 3, for instance, do not just convey the chronological facts of their lives past and present, but speak of the quality of nursing home life in terms of new meanings of home. Residents Myrtle Johnson and Alice Stern of Chapter 4 not only tell us how the present situation relates to their pasts, but are repeatedly amazed that their lives have "come to this," referring to the fated emptiness of a nursing home existence.

Special circumstances, such as having a lifelong disability or living in the nursing home with a spouse or sister, further specify horizons of meaning and are the subject matter of Part II. In such cases, a significant past event, an extraordinary experience, or special relationship becomes a primary narrative linkage for the present. For example, the long-standing conversation that marriage has been for spouses who now live together intimately in a nursing facility offers a special experiential continuity that other residents, many widowed or sole survivors, do not have and contrastingly horizons their respective senses of the quality of nursing home life (see Berger and Kellner 1970).

The orientations and special circumstances presented are not exhaustive of horizons of meaning for nursing home residents. Rather, they exemplify the varied narrative linkages of experience to reveal subjective meanings of the qualities of care and life.

THE STUDY AND THE RESIDENTS

Nursing home life typically is studied for its negative impact on the person. In Colleen Johnson and Leslie Grant's (1985) overview of the effects of institutionalization, the negative impact is said to vary according to institutional "totality" (Goffman 1961), that is, with the degree of confinement and life engrossment of a setting. In that respect, a prison would seem to be more confining and engrossing of self and daily life than, say, a public school or a support group. To the extent a nursing home is a total institution, it is said to depersonalize the self. Identity and self-worth become matters of institutional definition and management (Coe 1965). A social blandness overshadows individual differences

(Gottesman and Bourstrom 1974; Watson and Maxwell 1977). Leon Pastalan (1970) has portrayed this as a loss of privacy stemming from the environmental encapsulation of personal autonomy. This combines with the estrangement and isolation resulting from a lost home and the death of kindred or withdrawal of support from significant others. According to Richard Zusman (1966), it forms a "social breakdown syndrome," which Russell Ward describes as "the individual becoming increasingly oriented to the world of the institution and isolated from the outside world, thereby losing the capacity to exist independent of the institution" (1979, p. 402).

The negative view does not reveal how residents themselves assign meaning to institutional living. To find out and to learn how lives as a whole figure in, I contacted six nursing homes recognized as comparable in the quality of the care they offered. After a series of meetings to explain the research rationale and its goals, the homes' administrators agreed to participate in the study. The administrator of one of the nursing homes contacted was on target when he offered this understanding of what I aimed to accomplish:

> I think it's a very good idea, getting these folks' life stories. Ya walk in here day after day and it's easy to think that all there is to their lives is sitting in wheelchairs, eating, sleeping, and being sick. That's pretty negative. They're just faces in the hall, without any stories. I would guess that if you took the time to listen, they'd have a lot of interesting things to say about their lives . . . not that I would want you to paint a glowing picture. I know that a lot of them are very sick, more than ever, given the current trend of things, and nursing homes have their share of problems, as you know. But residents are people too and I like the way you're going to try and bring that out—give them a chance to tell their stories.

The phrase "faces without stories" was his, but I used it effectively from then on to describe the study.

The nursing homes were located in Florida. The state's population is a mix of natives and immigrants, typically from midwestern and eastern states, which was reflected in the backgrounds of the residents who became the subjects of the study. Whether from the North or the South, many had spent childhoods in small towns or rural settings. This was a generation of people, now mostly in their seventies, eighties, and nineties, who grew up in large families. Residents commonly spoke of having had five, six, up to ten or twelve siblings. They were quick to add that many of the siblings had died and, as a result, they had experienced a great deal of sickness and death among loved ones in their lifetimes.

It is perhaps the last generation to take for granted the place of religion in daily living. Not that all the residents were religious or had become so in later life. Rather, surrounding their attitudes and preferences were everyday vocabularies that routinely referred to religious practices, the deity, and moral life, something that now seems to typify public life only on special occasions. It also is a generation for which an ethic of hard work is a matter of open pride. In the interviews, it was rare for work and its difficulties not to be mentioned, even by those who had had stable and fairly well-paid jobs.

Typical of the nursing home population as a whole, most of the residents interviewed were widowed, female, and white, with some African Americans. While a few residents had had extensive formal education, such as the rare professional and graduate degree, many had only six, seven, or eight years of schooling. This, too, was not unusual for this generation. As one resident reminded me, "We didn't much go beyond the eighth grade back then because you didn't need it and, if you wanted it and the family could afford it, you had to ride all the way across the county or into town."

Respondent selection was affected by health and communicative ability. The comatose, intermittently conscious, and demented were not interviewable. We were not prepared to interview the deaf or the alert but orally noncommunicative. Staff and family members sometimes informed us that they preferred particular residents not be interviewed because the residents were too ill for prolonged interaction. If the study sample is biased, it is toward the relatively less sick and the more communicative.

A total of fifty-eight residents completed interviews, twenty-four of whom are represented in the following chapters. Thirty-three of the fifty-eight completed interviews were with so-called long-stayers, who had resided in a facility for over a year. Twenty-two of the long-stayers had lived in their nursing home for over two years and seven for more than five years. Among the latter was Julia McCall, a twelve-year resident. All thirty-three long-stayers were interviewed once in the course of the study.

The other twenty-five completed interviews were with residents whom we followed for a year from their time of admission. I wanted to explore how horizons of meaning changed following placement, whether in a stepwise or more complex fashion. Each of these residents was interviewed within two months of admission. They were not all new to nursing home living, however. Several had been residents of other nursing homes before coming to reside in their current ones. Some of the twenty-five residents died before their second or third interviews, which were scheduled, respectively, six months and one year after the first interview. Some became too ill to be reinterviewed. Some were discharged and moved too far away to make an interview feasible. A few refused to be reinterviewed. Of the twenty-five residents followed, ten were reinterviewed six months later and, for the reasons stated, did not complete their scheduled third interview. Seven of the twenty-five completed a third interview one year after admission. Eight of the twenty-five were discharged before being reinterviewed in the nursing home, but were interviewed again following their return to the community.

THE INTERVIEWS

The in-depth interviews, conducted by myself and my assistant Carol Ronai, ranged in duration from a half hour to two hours. Each interview was flexibly focused on commonplace considerations of life in nursing homes—questions about the fate of life, daily living in the facility, the meaning of home and family, self-perception, health, aging, and death. To accent the biographical and following psychologist Jerome Bruner's (1986) practice, respondents were asked at the outset to tell their life stories, even if might seem difficult to do in a relatively short time. They were encouraged to begin wherever and however they wished. Respondents were invited to address the matters under consideration in relation to lifelong and current personal experiences. They also were asked if they had the opportunity to write their life story, what the various chapters would be about. We were especially interested in how the last chapter related to their present situation and its horizons.

However brief, beginning with the telling of a life story set two narrative precedents. It served to inform the respondents that we were interested in whether and, if so, how their lives as a whole related to their current situations. We wanted to see if the distant personal past and both the foreseeable and imagined future were narratively linked with the present qualities of care and life in the nursing home to make meaning in relation to lifelong experience. While some residents warned us that their lives weren't very interesting or claimed that there was little to tell, we nonetheless assured them that we would listen to whatever linkages they cared to make between the present and the past in speaking of their lives. Beginning with the life story also offered us an empirical basis for suggesting to the residents possible linkages between the past, the future, and the present, which we reminded them they were free to ignore or recast in their own terms.

An interview guide was constructed early on (see Appendix). The plan was to use it more as a conversational agenda than as a procedural directive. We hoped this would enhance the interview's interactive format. In some interviews, certain guide items became the crux of conversations. For instance, resident Karen Gray's background in health care administration and regulation turned many topics of conversation in her interview into quality assessment discussions. When Gray was not wearing her "personal hat," the narrative linkages conveyed in her interviews were articulated out of her professional experience (see Chapter 11). In other interviews, guide items receded into the background as residents set their own narrative agendas. The sequence in which interview guide items were asked was determined more by the flow of particular conversations than the order of their appearance in the guide.

Because residents were conceived as biographically active, their emphases were taken to be as important as guide items in shaping the interviews. The rule was to let the relevance of particular guide items be determined by the experiential linkages respondents made in the course of the interview, keeping in mind that many guide items nonetheless reflected public concerns thought to potentially bear on the lives of all residents.

The adage, No man or woman is an island, set another rule for the interview process. Previous research experience and a theoretical orientation to the social character of self and communication were a basis for encouraging respondents to compare their lives with others, especially other residents in the nursing home. We also interjected ourselves into the interviews by gently suggesting how one might feel or would think if one were in the resident's shoes or the resident in another's place. Residents were invited to agree or disagree and encouraged to describe differences, if any. The idea was to suggest and offer up contrasting narrative linkages as a basis for prompting the respondent to newly discover, elaborate upon, or demur from possible connotations of his or her experience.

These rules—from encouraging subjective relevancies to prompting subjective possibilities—provided a procedural basis for documenting the biographical activity of respondents. The rules helped to avoid conjuring up nursing home residents and the interviewers as narrative dopes (Garfinkel 1967).

Interviews were tape-recorded with the informed consent of the residents. The tapes were later transcribed and the transcripts checked for accuracy against the recordings. In the extracts presented in the following chapters, all personal names have been fictionalized except for my own informal first name (Jay) and my assistant's first name (Carol). While the residents and the interviewers referred to each other in various ways—sometimes by first names and other times more formally as Mr. or Ms. So-and-so—first names are used to identify speakers in all interview extracts. Where location or affiliation might reveal identities, pseudonyms also are used.

Before moving on to the interview material, it is important to keep in mind that the responses form life narratives, not life histories (see Bertaux 1981; Bertaux and Kohli 1984). Life histories are meant to be evaluated according to how accurately they reflect what actually happened in their subjects' lives. The truth of a life history lies less in its formulation than in its subject matter. Ideally, life histories should factually describe the lives they are about. Life narratives, in contrast, are communicated lives. The past, present, and future are linked together to assemble meaning. In our case, lives are communicated by nursing home residents in collaboration with the researcher. The life narratives in this book should be read accordingly, not in terms of whether, say, Jake Bellows actually was a stand-up comic on the road fifty weeks of the year, but in terms of how he links that experience to his feeling of being "at home" in the nursing facility, his way of conveying subjective meaning.

It also should be kept in mind that the life narratives are not personality profiles, even while long-standing personal traits and experiences are invoked by residents in speaking of life. The narratives do not convey the overall psychological designs of the lives they are about. As Jake Bellows and the other residents speak of life in the following chapters, they do so as agents considering their experiences in relation to their current living situation and in the context of an in-depth interview. What comes across is a retrospectively and circumstantially constructed rendition of the qualities of care and life, sparked by the opportunity to link together parts of experience and guided by a slate of public concerns.

PART

I

ORIENTATIONS

2

Worried to Death

The life narratives of some nursing home residents highlight worry, disappointment, and thoughts of death. Worry can be so profoundly central to the narrative as to overwhelm the life story. The mere mention of such common life themes as family and home unleashes sobs and expressions of how it may soon come to an end. In such moments, whatever is conveyed about the past, be it family, home, or some other realm, is told in relation to thoughts of death. It is difficult to imagine no longer being with one's "wonderful and warm" family, with the children one raised, with one's "dear and caring" son or daughter. It is hard to acknowledge the possibility of becoming like one of the nursing home residents who have "lost their minds" or are totally incapacitated, who are no longer themselves. The worry is as much about the loss of identity as it is about growing frailty, as much about leaving oneself and others forever as it is about dying.

Yet those who worry to death can be ready to die. For many, the unimaginable makes it too difficult to go on. It is as if they admit, in a strange twist of an ancient maxim, The examined life is not worth living. Worry is linked by some to a sense that one either has outlived or might outlive those one should not. It is a prevalent belief that, by all rights of fate, the oldest die first, the younger die next, and the youngest last. In this connection, the worried despair that they might outlive a cherished son, daughter, or younger brother or sister. They are ready to die because of this, too, as much as from what the unimaginable confronts them with.

Among the worried, the quality of care of the nursing home is a matter reckoned in a restricted framework. For some, the quality of care is hardly the problem, as adequate or fine as care is judged to be in support of activities of daily living such as eating, dressing, and cleanliness. One can be a "good eater" but nonetheless be ready to die. One can be the active participant of the Sunshine Club, a group for spreading good cheer, yet narratively convey that as marginal to the real possibility of "never getting better." For others, quality of care may be a point of constant complaint, yet hardly matter at all in relation to what they once knew. As annoying as the quality of care might be at times, it is just a matter of daily living, the "nursing home resident" role not conveying what life is believed to really be about.

Disappointment can be conveyed in relation to oneself or others. There is the disappointment of not progressing as expected in recovering from a disabling illness or accident, turning what was foreseen as a short, rehabilitative stay in a nursing home into long-term residency. In this context, the nursing home portends the end of life as once known. There also is the disappointment associated with the need for others, often adult children, to place a frail elderly parent in a nursing home because the burdens of continued home care have become unmanageable. While the need may be acknowledged by residents, lingering doubts over failed filial responsibility cause them to be disappointed in those—their children—from whom they had come to expect much more.

RITA VANDENBERG

Our first resident, Rita Vandenberg, is ready to die. She is an eighty-two-year-old divorced white female, who has diabetes, injects insulin, suffers from congestive heart failure, and is arthritic. Now living at Bayside Nursing Home, Vandenberg has resided in institutional settings for many years, the last a three-year stint in a nursing home in another state. She keeps busy in many ways, not the least of which is trying to make Bayside a home. But it is an effort overwhelmed by a story of worry for herself and especially her surviving, middle-aged son.

Vandenberg was interviewed two weeks after she moved into Bayside and again six months later. She refused to be interviewed a third time one year after we met because she was worried about getting depressed and having heart failure.

The First Interview

We began the first interview by talking about her work life, which quickly converged on her present worries.

> Jay: Everyone has a life story. Why don't you tell me a little about your life?
> Rita: Well, there's not much. I worked in the telephone company as a telephone operator before I was married. After I got married, I moved to New Jersey and had two boys. I didn't work until he [husband] passed away, after we moved to Reading, Pennsylvania. Then I got work, mostly in the steel mill.
>
> It wasn't very exciting. I did a lot of work and places just seemed to have jobs lots like. That lasted a little while and then I'd go and hunt

something else to do. But my last work was . . . as I got older, I worked in a children's home, a house mother . . . oh, about ten and a half years I think. And then after that, I couldn't take that anymore. It got on my nerves a little bit as I got older. So then I worked in a nursing school as a housemother where they were teaching the nurses. I worked there eight and a half years and I retired from there. And since that, I did nothing but go out and eat with my brother, who passed away about two weeks ago. And I lost my mother. My mother first, then my sister, and then my son. And then my brother. So I'm living too long.

But I had a nice life. I had to work. I wanted to be home all the time, but I couldn't be. Had to work for the money. And I had my son, the one in the picture over there. He was in the marines for thirty years, then he went to college, and now he's teaching. But he's not too well. Has rheumatoid and the knees must be operated on. And he has some kind of disease of the nerves. They have to cut the nerves somehow for him to walk. My other son [Tom], he died. I think Tom's dead about two years now, maybe not quite two years. He had cancer of the pancreas. He was only fifty-two, just a young fellow. [Whimpers]

Jay: I'm sorry. [Pause] So you had two sons.

Rita: They're very good to me. The one here . . . I wanted to stay up in Reading because my family's up there, my brothers and sisters. But he wanted me with him. So he brought me down to Mississippi when he lived there. I was there a little while and I got a heart attack. So then they put me in a nursing home because my daughter-in-law couldn't take care of me. Then he moved to Tennessee and I been in a nursing home up there. It was nice up there. But it was Seventh Day Adventist and there was no meat, and I like meat. But they were nice. They were good people. Three years I was up there.

I presented her with the idea of writing her life story and asked how she would divide it into chapters. She began immediately to tell me about life during the depression in New Jersey. It was a detailed, un-chaptered account of living with in-laws and raising her two sons. The sons soon became the focus of her remarks, the saddest part of which was losing one of them two years earlier. As she talked about this, she sobbed grievously.

Jay: Can I get you something? Can I get you a tissue or something?

Rita: No. I'll be all right. [Pause]

Jay: Is that better? So . . . you lost him, what . . . two years ago?

Rita: I don't believe it's quite two years. I lost my mother, my oldest sister, and my son. All within about a year. [Weeps] I lost my oldest sister. She's only a year and four days older than myself. We were very close. And then my mother. My mother was ninety-seven. And then my mother died in July. The following November my son died.

Jay: Mmm. I'm sorry. That's very difficult.

Rita: You can lose your mother, your sister, but losing my son is so [weeps] . . . well. I'll get a Kleenex. I'm sorry.
Jay: No, that's okay. [Comforting Vandenberg] I'm sorry.

We talked about the deaths and eventually returned to her early married life. Again, her sons were prominent.

Rita: I always said I could write a book. But I don't know. Having my babies was very happy. I was very happy with them. They were . . . kept me busy, because they were small. Both of them were small. Then as they grew up, there was no trouble. I didn't have trouble with them. I always can say they were good to me. And this one's still very good to me. He's not well. I wish he would be well. But he was in the marines too long. I said, "Are you sorry you stayed too long." He said, "No, Mom, I'm not." He was in Vietnam twice.
Jay: Oh, he was? About my age then.
Rita: He was a pilot of the helicopters. Got shot at a few times. So I don't know why he liked that life. That was a worry of mine.

At that point, we began to talk about the present—her life in the nursing home, her room, her roommate, daily living, and her need for privacy. She complained of the constant presence of her roommate's visiting husband. The husband, Vandenberg claimed, had no respect for privacy. He'd turn on the television while Vandenberg napped and barge into the bathroom unannounced, even ignoring a room-occupied sign that the social worker had devised to solve the problem. Yet Vandenberg felt sorry for the roommate because the roommate was helpless and bedridden, worse off than she herself was. Vandenberg complimented the nursing staff, whom she described as very friendly, remarking, "I haven't come across one I disliked at all. They call me Ms. V."

Having few complaints about the quality of care and judging the home superior to any in which she had resided, Vandenberg again spoke of her family, her life rearing two sons without benefit of husband. Mentioning her "dead" husband again, she stopped and backtracked.

Rita: So those were nice times. I had sad times, too, and I'm divorced. I told you my husband's dead. To me he's dead.
Jay: You were divorced? How long ago was that?
Rita: I was about thirty-seven. He was in the service and he was running with women and drinking. So . . . but I tell people he's really dead to me.

She described her years with him and the very few contacts she has had with him since, mainly through her sons. She was quick to point out that he hadn't been part of her life for years, someone whom she didn't care much to think about. Her thoughts promptly returned to her son's health and her own shrinking future.

I redirected the conversation to the present and her life in the nursing home, aiming to see how that figured in her story.

> *Jay:* Now that you've been here for a few weeks, does it feel like home?
> *Rita:* Yes, very much. I feel as if I'm going to be happy here. I wish I could feel better because my sugar goes up. It's over four hundred. So then they call a doctor and he says to add more insulin. But the nurse who comes and gives it says, "You might end up in the hospital." I say, "Well, I don't want to go in the hospital. This is good enough for me."
> *Jay:* So you say it doesn't quite feel like home yet? You say that it will feel like home? Or what would you say, Mrs. V?
> *Rita:* I think it will. Things are strange yet to me and I don't know many of the women. The ones that I talk to a little bit at the table and that stuff, don't make sense. And people are hard . . . I mean if they're southern, it's hard for me to understand them. [Elaborates] Now when someone talks to me, I face them so I can kind of concentrate if they talk fast. But that happens I guess when you get older.

I asked her how she felt about growing old. As sure as Vandenberg noted that she hoped to eventually make Bayside her home, she remarked that she was ready to die. Her enduring worries about her son's health combined with worry for her own health. The possibility of becoming as helpless as those around her led her to explain:

> I don't want to live to be that I can't take care of myself. I don't want to be in a wheelchair. To be helpless—that would be terrible for me. So I'm ready to go anytime. I just feel that there's nothing much ahead of me. My son's responsible for me. He comes and visits me every two weeks. He's coming this Saturday. But he's not well. I'm so worried about him. He teaches school every day and when he comes home he's on the couch. His legs feel terrible. [Elaborates] I always said this old age is for the birds. It isn't for us. [Elaborates] When I see some of these women that can't even remember anything or talk funny, or they're really lost, really lost . . . I don't want to get like that. I see these people here can't even feed themselves. They can't hold their head right. Some of them hold their head all the way back. I don't want to get like that. No, it wouldn't be living. I'd be half dead. But, don't get me wrong. They treat 'em all real well anyway.

For Vandenberg, these residents who were frail and more helpless than she was signaled her future, not the quality of care in the facility.

Six Months Later

Six months later, Vandenberg is reinterviewed by Carol Ronai, my research assistant. The looming end of Vandenberg's life—as a thing now much over—hardly enables her to retell her story. As it does for some other residents, the interview lead-in, centered on life as a whole, too vividly rehearses the central themes of being worried to death and ready to die, even while the margins of the narrative are filled with attempts to appreciate the present situation as homelike.

> *Carol:* I was wanting to talk with you again about your life.
> *Rita:*   No. [Weeps]
> *Carol:* No, we're not going to do that.
> *Rita:*   No. No. I couldn't. That's too hard. [Weeps]

Ronai tries again, asking Vandenberg to speak of life by starting with when she was born and describing her childhood. Vandenberg readily speaks at length. This time, it isn't life as a whole that comes under consideration, but specific points not necessarily formed as a grand narrative about its entirety. As in the first interview, she talks about her family in Pennsylvania and her children. The conversation soon returns to her present situation and her feelings about living at Bayside.

> *Carol:* So is this like home to you now?
> *Rita:*   Yes, a lot like home. A lot of times I wished I was in Pennsylvania cause I had my family up there. But the sister that could have taken me, she passed away. And the others, well, their husbands like trips. They take a lot of trips and I would have been left out.
> *Carol:* Sure.
> *Rita:*   And the doctor didn't want me alone. So I wouldn't want to go and interfere with no family life at all.
> *Carol:* What is it about this place that's like home?
> *Rita:*   Well, everybody seems nice. Now maybe there's somebody that don't care for you too much, but I never came across somebody like that.

Talk of the happy and sad points of Vandenberg's life eventually leads again to her son's death and, following that, to her own future. Vandenberg recalls her dead son's last words:

> You get over it cause you know that it's going to happen some day. And I'm so happy that I helped him. He [the son] called me everyday, and sometimes twice a day, even from the hospital when he was in. [Just before he died], he called and said, "I have something to tell you, but I don't want you to cry Mom." But I did.

Asked what she thinks her daily life will look like a year from now, Vandenberg remarks:

> I don't think I'll be around a year from now. . . . No, I really don't 'cause I have some bad days now. I don't tell 'em every time cause, uh, what can

they do? . . . But I can feel when my, uh, I get a thing in my heart. I don't know where my heart is anymore because I had an operation on my, uh, breast removed. And I had a hernia operation since I'm down here. I feel as if I'm ready to go. . . . I know it's coming to me . . . the way I feel. So I don't want to live too long.

As the interview winds down, it is evident that Vandenberg has settled her affairs with life. Hers seems at times to be a stoic wait for death, ironically riven with casual, almost lighthearted commentaries about life in the nursing home. Yet, as before, she worries—for her son and over the possibility that she will become incapacitated and helpless. The quality of care and life in the nursing home are incidental to these primary concerns. Toward the end of the interview, asked what her philosophy of life is, Vandenberg sharply juxtaposes worry and an activity of daily living:

> One would be not to worry too much. I'd try to, to overcome that. And to eat. I love to eat. One time I was pretty heavy.

REBECCA BOURDEAU

Rebecca Bourdeau, a resident of Florida Manor, is discouraged and, as she reports, "worries about everything." A seventy-six-year-old widowed white female, Bourdeau had a stroke a few years ago and recently suffered a hairline fracture of the pelvis that left her in a great deal of pain. What seemed strange to her about the fracture was that she hadn't fallen. The fracture happened suddenly one night while she was in bed. The unexpected occurrence worried her terribly because it happened despite the care she took to prevent such accidents. She now worried over everything because her expectations about returning home had been dampened repeatedly and unexpectedly, first by a long period of rehabilitation following the stroke and more recently by the pelvic fracture. An overriding worry was that another setback would make a return impossible, causing her profound disappointment.

Bourdeau's worry was different from Vandenberg's. Bourdeau's was focused on the possibility that she might never be able to return home to her thoughtful and caring family. The possibility caused her to even feel she was losing her religious faith. Faith was incapable of stemming the disappointment she was experiencing. Fate, it seemed, was arbitrary and not working in her favor, which did little for her faith. In contrast, more at home in her nursing facility, Vandenberg's worries were for her son's health and the reflection of a possible future self she saw daily in other incapacitated residents. As in Vandenberg's account, the main linkages of Bourdeau's narrative hardly touched on Florida Manor's quality of care.

Bourdeau had been a resident of the Manor for two and a half years when interviewed. Speaking of life for her was an enduring narrative of past, present, and future domesticity. As with Vandenberg, I began by asking her to tell me about her life.

> *Rebecca:* Well, I've had five children. I wasn't married too young. I was twenty-seven when I got married. [Weeps]
>
> *Jay:* That's okay. It's alright. [Pause] Let's stop a while. [Pause]
>
> *Rebecca:* I had a good life actually, because I had a wonderful man and he was a thoughtful family man. He took care of his family and never was without work. It was warm and wonderful. He was a good provider. I never went without anything. [Weeps]
>
> We gave our children the best education we could. Most of them went to college at least, you know, part of the time even though they did drop out. But they all have good positions today. So I'm happy about that. I didn't have a very exciting life, but satisfying.

Bourdeau goes on to describe her husband's multiple myeloma, which led to his death four years earlier. She speaks of the fine man he was.

> He was a remarkable man anyway. Not great or anything like that. Never looked for any praise or anything like that, but he was the handiest man you could ever think of. He could do anything. He could, you know, he could do woodwork and he could do plumbing. We had a house that he completely made over. We bought a normal house in Albany, New York, and he completely made it over. Worked all the time. He was what you'd call a "workaholic." Never gave up. Sometimes I feel sorry that he didn't enjoy life more, but that was his life. He had to keep going.

She talks at length of her home, winters in upstate New York, her happiness, and the hardships she and her husband endured. It is a glowing nostalgia. The conversation turns to her move to Florida and her sons' lives, of which she hopes again to be a part.

> Well I still lived there [New York] by myself after he [her husband] died a few years, until this happened to me, until I had a stroke. I was living by myself and I guess it wasn't the best thing in the world. But that was meant to be, too. Now this house that we had built [in Florida], my oldest son and we were shareholders. He had it built for us, but he said, "Now you can live there the rest of your life. It won't make any difference to me." He says that and it's supposed to be his house you know.
>
> But it's not gonna happen that way at all because now my youngest son wants . . . has bought the house. The deal hasn't gone through yet, but he wants to buy the house and have me go back there and live with him, which

I think is great, but I don't know if I'm gonna make it. I'm so awfully disappointed. I just don't feel as though I'm gonna make it because here I had this one setback. [Weeps] Maybe that isn't meant to be either.

I ask her what she means and she explains:

I mean you don't know from one day to the next what's gonna happen. You think, well, this is all planned and everything, but things go wrong and then something else happens to make it different. My middle son, the one who lives in Fort Lauderdale, is supervising a courtroom. He has a good position. And the youngest son works for the telephone company on underground wiring and that. And the older son is in a business partnership with somebody else in the construction business. So he is very well fixed. He has a beautiful home. He has two sons, but he has been unlucky because his wife of thirty-nine years old passed away in March of cancer. So there he is by himself, too. That's what I say about life . . . it's a funny thing. You don't know what's around the corner. [Weeps]

I have two daughters and three sons. Yeah, I have a nice family. It wasn't planned that way, but it's a nice family. [Weeps] I cry a lot.

When she regained her composure, I asked her what made her feel the way she did, which we explained in relation to writing her life story.

Rebecca: I don't know. I get discouraged. That's the story of my life.
Jay: Really? What makes you discouraged, Mrs. B?
Rebecca: Well, I think the sickness that I've had, because I would like to get on with my life and go with one of the children and I can't seem to get it together. I guess otherwise my health is pretty good. I shouldn't worry about it so much.
Jay: Yeah. [Pause] Let me ask you this. If you could, like, write the story of your life, what would the first chapter be about?
Rebecca: I really don't know, except that it would be about my husband and I . . . how we met and what a good life we had and all that. I imagine that's what it would be about.
Jay: What would the second chapter be about?
Rebecca: To tell you the truth I don't know. I guess it would be about our life in New York and maybe moving to Rhode Island and living there a while and then moving to Florida. [Elaborates]
Jay: What about the last chapter? What would you say that'd be about?
Rebecca: As far as I'm concerned, there's no last chapter yet because I think I have more life to live.
Jay: Do you think about the future?
Rebecca: Well, how much future can there be when you're seventy-six years old? How can there be much future? I imagine you probably think the future would be my children—what they're going to think and what they're going to accomplish. [Weeps] Excuse me. I should hope that I would be living with my son somewhere, one of my

dear boys and that I could enjoy a little bit of life a little . . . probably a little more enjoyment with the family and grandchildren. In a
way it is promising, if I am ever able to go live with one of my boys.
It looks like it's promising because as far as I know my health is
good. I've had this setback, but other than that, it's been pretty
good. I seem to worry a lot these days . . . about everything you
might say.

Broaching the possibility that she might not be able to return home, I
asked Bourdeau if she felt she could make a home of the nursing facility,
reminding her that she had lived in the facility for about two and a half
years. I wondered whether, if she gave the place a chance, she might get
used to it, explaining that other residents felt it was not such a bad place
to live and had made it their home. Bourdeau responded:

> No. This does not feel like home. This will never be home. I know I have a
> lot of good feelings though, for some of the people that have taken care of
> me because they've been very nice to me. But it's not home. Home is where
> family and children are. That's what I want to get back to.

I asked her if there was anything that could be done to make it more
homelike. She doubted it, adding that no matter how good the quality of
care, the facility could never be home.

> I don't know what we could do to make it more like home. They try to do
> everything to make it . . . I mean they try to make it pleasing for everybody
> . . . the social part and all that. But right now I don't care anything about
> that. It doesn't matter when you don't feel good. It doesn't matter much
> what people are trying to do. I appreciate it, but it'll never be like home.

As we proceeded to discuss the meaning of home, the possibility of
making the Manor her home, and the Manor's quality of care, it was
clear that Bourdeau was set on a life on the outside with her family. The
idea of adjusting to life in the nursing home was out of the question. She
did not so much think of the last two and a half years as a period of
adjustment, but as one of rehabilitation. She repeated her appreciation
for the Manor's quality of care and, indeed, at one point when I asked
her if she considered the time she had spent at the Manor to be part of
her life or separate from it, her voice cracked:

> I imagine it's part of my life. How can I forget those years that I've been here
> and all the people and everything. I can't forget them. Oh gee.

In a way, the quality of care and life at the Manor were the farthest
thing from Bourdeau's mind, even while she felt positively about both.

Mainly, her mind and heart were in another place, led on by a different agenda. It was her role in a family life that preoccupied her, not the role of nursing home resident. The preoccupation, in her words, made her "worry about everything," including the loss of her religious faith, as the following exchange reveals.

> *Jay:* How would you describe yourself as a person?
> *Rebecca:* I don't know. Right now, I'm very discouraged and I'm not a bit upbeat. Maybe I should be. I really get upset about my life when I think of all the things that I could do and what happened to me and here I am. I keep saying that I'm not never gonna get better. You worry about not ever making it . . . dying, you know and not ever seeing your family again. [Weeps] My daughter thinks that's not true at all. She says that I'm gonna get better and not to worry about it. But I worry about a lot of things.
> *Jay:* You do?
> *Rebecca:* Oh yes. I'm a worry-wart. Isn't that awful? I worry about everything . . . worried to death.
> *Jay:* What's the meaning of life to you? Have you ever thought about that?
> *Rebecca:* I don't know. I'm supposed to be a religious person. But I think I'll lose my faith. I'll lose my faith very easily. I should, you know, cling to . . . how I've been brought up and that in a very religious background.
> *Jay:* What happened to change that, Mrs. B?
> *Rebecca:* I guess illness changed it all, because I used to be a very religious person. And of course, there's no religion in this place as far as that goes. I'm Catholic and you never have any services like usually you do, you know. I used to be a person who'd go to church every day and there was a little group of people I was friendly with. We went every day and met. That was a good feeling. When I came here, that all stopped and so I'm kind of lost when I think of religion. Now I've let it all slip by. There was nothing I could do about it. Sometimes I think if there was only a priest who would come in once in a while and all and keep spirits up. There are a few people—laypeople—who come in now and then, but it's not the same. I really think that those people should be commended because of the work that they do. They try to, you know, take the place of a priest or religious and they come and visit.

Still, there was hope for the future. The worry and disappointment that prevailed upon her were experienced in relation to an enduring sense of the possibility of going home. While she was as active as one could be in the nursing home, daily life for Bourdeau was mainly a matter of waiting and, admittedly, worrying. The mixture—being active, waiting, and worrying—was evident in the discussion of a typical day.

Jay: What would you say a typical day is like for you in this place?
Rebecca: Oh, it's awful. Ah, nothing, nothing much. Except that now I go to therapy and I've been going to therapy three times a week and, other than that, there isn't much. Once in a while there is something going on that I take part in. I belong to the sunshine group and we try to do things for others.
Jay: What is the sunshine group? It's a club of some kind, isn't it?
Rebecca: Oh, we try to make things for other people like . . . like that board out there, you know, the big board [a seasonal display]. It's not really much, but it's a little something to do to keep busy.
Jay: And what is the rest of your day like?
Rebecca: That's it. I get up in the morning and have breakfast and then you wait until there's something to do. With me, it's therapy a few times a week. I try to do some reading, but I can't concentrate on that. For a while there I was doing embroidery and that was taking up my time. I did quite a bit of that just before Christmas. But I haven't got anything planned now. God knows I wouldn't be able to do it anyway. So I wait and worry and wait.
Jay: Is time an important thing here? Time?
Rebecca: Time? Well, time is very important to me. Now I watch that clock like I was going somewhere all the time. But it drags. It drags. You know, when you don't have that much to do, it drags. You're sitting there sometimes waiting. Of course since my fracture I've been laying in bed and I never in my life have done that . . . lay in bed for days on end. I thought that was awful. It's funny. There was a day when I would be so happy to lay in bed and take it easy, when the children were small and I didn't have the time to do that. But now it means nothing.
Jay: What do you think your life'll be like a year from now?
Rebecca: I hope it's pretty much like it is now but living with a relative. You know, living with family. That's what I hope it'll be.

ROLAND SNYDER

Roland Snyder is also a resident of Florida Manor. He was interviewed twice by Carol Ronai, two weeks after admission and six months later. He died three months after the second interview. Snyder is a seventy-eight-year-old white male, widowed from his first wife, and divorced from his second. He has had two heart attacks, colon cancer, a colostomy, and is diabetic.

The narrative horizons of his first and second interviews are different. In the first interview, talk about life is linked with disillusionment and worry over death. His children did not see fit to care for him on their own. He had over the years been such a good provider and is gravely disappointed that he's had to be placed in a nursing home. Being in the

nursing home signifies the end of what he had believed to be a relationship of mutual care and responsibility, the end of life as he'd known it
and thought it would continue to be. Like Vandenberg and Bourdeau,
his feelings have little to do with the quality of his care. For Snyder,
being at the Manor means that life is over. Just about every mention of
earlier life and his family causes him despair. At several points in the
first interview he simply states that he wants to die.

The First Interview

The first interview, which is fairly brief overall, is taken up initially by
a lengthy description of farming in rural Florida during the depression
and World War II, a story of family life, hard work, success, and failure.
Every mention of his first wife and their seven children causes him to
sob uncontrollably. The account of his wife's cancer and eventual death
is especially disturbing. He describes his second marriage, one of conve-
nience, and his eventual divorce.

Later, he expresses his disappointment at having been first placed in a
nursing facility where he lived with no "menfolks" for two years before
moving to Florida Manor. Snyder tells of feeling that his children had
abandoned him.

> I don't know why I hated that place so bad. I had no one. I was by myself.
> There was no menfolks in there to . . . there was one other man that you
> could get on a conversation with. There wasn't but three of us in there.
> There was a bunch of women just like these here, some of 'em in wheel-
> chairs, some of 'em couldn't even get out of bed. I feel like that my kids . . .
> now I didn't, I don't want to stay with any of 'em now. But I feel like they
> kinda let me down. I tell you . . . we was a pretty close family. And it was
> hard on me. [Weeps]

The feeling of disappointment has Snyder thinking of death and occasionally suicide.

> I have wanted to die ever since I went in that home in Summerville. I have
> thought of takin' my life. Yeah, I told the girls [his daughters] . . . and I'm
> still not saying that I won't. I don't want to be in the shape that I see these
> people [residents at Florida Manor] yet. [My life] is nothin' no more. Just
> nothin'. [Weeps] I just wish I could die today.

For a time, the discussion centers on suicide.

At the end of the interview, there is an exchange about growing old.
What it means for Snyder in the context of disappointment is death.

> *Roland:*   I didn't realize that I was as old as I am until about two years ago
> when I went in that home.

Carol:	What does it mean to be old?
Roland:	I don't know. You're just here and that's all. Ain't nothin' to life. That's the way I look at it.
Carol:	Is there anything you like about being your age?
Roland:	No ma'am. I hate to get older. As long as I'm livin' I know I'm gonna be gettin' older.
Carol:	Do you think about the future?
Roland:	Yes, I do. I know that there's nowhere for me to go. There's here or in another place like it . . .
Carol:	Do you have any plans?
Roland:	No ma'am. I'm nothing now. It's just like I say, I just wished I could go. [Weeps]

Six Months Later

Six months later, Snyder is still disappointed, but not because his children have abandoned him. Talk of life is not as much related to death, as to what he has to put up with. He is not as much profoundly disappointed by life as a whole as he is by what fate has chosen that he forebear. His narrative horizon is daily living in the nursing home. He is angry and annoyed with the quality of care and the quality of his life in general. Complaints about other residents, especially his roommate, consume him. Except for a "nice looking" nurse he's taken a shine to, daily life leaves much to be desired.

The start of the six-month interview is much like the first, a long story of farming, hard work, close family ties, his first wife's cancer, opportunities, and failures. This time he says more about the bad market for yellow squash and zucchini in the years he farmed, among other trials of making it farming. He later speaks of his daughters' visits and, especially, recently seeing a woman friend with whom he once lived intimately. Prompted by interviewer Carol Ronai's question about how he would put his life together in the form of book chapters, he talks about a young Florida Manor nurse who, according to him, lavishes attention on him and gives him at least something to look forward to.

Carol:	It's about six months ago when I interviewed you the first time. Remember you weren't feeling so well then. You were pretty disappointed and discouraged I believe. So now, let me ask you this. Um, let's say we were gonna write a book about your life. Let's just pretend we were gonna do that. I was curious . . . what kind of chapters . . . what would the names of the chapters in your book be? Like what would you call the first chapter?
Roland:	I don't know cause I don't know nothing about writing a book.
Carol:	Oh, that's okay. You can still make up a chapter. Make up chapters. What would it be on? What would you write it on?
Roland:	Well, if it was my life history, it'd be before I ever got married.

Carol:	Okay. And then, the second chapter?
Roland:	Would be after I married.
Carol:	How about the third chapter?
Roland:	Well I expect it'd be three or four chapters of me and my first wife, 'cause we lived together forty-something years. I've forgotten now just how long. My memory is not very good now.
Carol:	What would the last chapter be on, the last chapter of the book about you? What would that be on?
Roland:	You'd be surprised.
Carol:	Would I? Okay, what'd it be about?
Roland:	A girl that works here.
Carol:	A girl that works here. It'd be about her? Tell me about that.
Roland:	Well, I don't know much about her, but she just made like she fell head over heels in love with me. And she's not but thirty-two years old. She's a nice looking girl and, uh, she um . . . in other words she waited on me. When I first met her, I was over yonder on the other side [of the nursing home]. Hell, she couldn't wait on me two weeks ago this weekend. She works on the weekends. And, uh . . . but she's going to college, going to nurse's school, trying to get a degree in nursing where she can make more money. She's got three or four kids. I don't know. She told me the other day she didn't have but three. I thought she had five. She brought five to see me. And, uh, I knew one of them wasn't hers—a girl, a little girl. Course, she said that was . . . she was keeping her, but it was her husband's child. And somebody told me that fella she married was just as damn sorry as he can be. Course they not living together now. He's married again. I don't know much more about her.
Carol:	So the last chapter would be about her?
Roland:	Yeah. But, now I didn't care much about that girl to start with. But she kept on till I got to where I thought a lot of her. And then she done me just like that woman that live with me for six years. She just quit coming to see me. But I think I know why. Cause the other weekend when she waited on me, she says, "Why in the hell did you let them put you in this room with George?" That's the guy who's in the room with me. I says, "Well I didn't know he's like the way he is." So they's good and they's bad, too. At least I looked forward to seeing her.

Underscoring both the good and the bad in life, the conversation develops into a tale of interpersonal attraction disrupted by what life in the nursing home has come to be.

Ronai interrupts to ask Snyder what his roommate is like.

Roland:	Oh, goddamn, he's a damn nasty. And he don't care what he says.
Carol:	You mean he's mean?
Roland:	. . . or who he says it to.

Carol: He's mean?
Roland: And they would bring him in here and put him in bed. Well they got
           to clean him up. And, uh, I suspect you seen him coming down
           here, out there in the hall walking. He walks on his toes, kind of on
           one foot.
Carol: Mmm.
Roland: And, uh, anyway. Yeah, this girl, she asked me the other week
           when she waited on me. I haven't seen her since. Now she said
           she'd see me this weekend, but she didn't. She worked. They all tell
           me that she worked. But I didn't see her. I don't know where she
           worked at. Some of them said that she was at Station 1. I don't
           know. But not this one. This here is 2 and that's 1 down there.
Carol: But you think she doesn't like to be in here because of George?
Roland: Yeah. And I've been trying to get out of this room ever since. I got
           the supervisor to come into my room, Monday a week ago. That was
           the day after she left on me.

The rest of the conversation is decidedly nursing home oriented.
Snyder's "typical day" contrasts with Vandenberg's and Bourdeau's. His
is less a matter of waking up, eating, waiting, sleeping, and passing time
than it is a battle with daily living. Describing his remaining wherewithal, Snyder remarks:

> When I was younger, I'll say I done anything I wanted to do. In other
> words, I was man enough to do it. I'm not bragging. But as far as fighting, I
> never did do much of that. Like this here roommate I got, I'm all done
> cussing him out and threatening to beat the hell out of him. They all say he
> don't know nothing, but he does. He knows, thank God, that I'll get him.
> Or he thinks I will. I wouldn't, but he thinks I will.
>   I slapped this woman this morning on the arm when I was going to lunch.
> She was a nitwit and she just run up the side of me [in her wheelchair]. I
> didn't know she was coming around me. I didn't even know she was back
> there. And she came around me and just run into me and my hand on that
> side. She caught it between the wheel of her chair and wheel of mine. And it
> did hurt. I cussed her before I could think and I reached over and slapped
> the hell out of her.

Snyder no longer despairs of death, which seemingly is kept at bay by
his attempt to bear up in the face of daily intrusions on his life by the
"worst ones," referring to the most incapacitated residents.

> I don't look forward to dying, but I don't dread it. Of course, if I live with
> him [roommate George] much longer, I might live to dread it. They got all
> the worst ones from here to that desk up there. The worst ones is from here
> up to there. They moved two here, down here, that was up there some-
> where since I been here. And they just holler. I don't know why one of 'em

ain't hollering now. One of 'em is bad about coming in my room. She won't pay you no mind. I go to cussing her and tell her not to come in and she won't pay you no mind. She'll come in and go to the bathroom . . . well I won't get into that. No, I'm not scared of death. I may go to hell if I die, but I'm not afraid like some people. I'm too busy fightin' with 'em to think about it much anyhow.

Still, as Ronai probes at the end of this interview, there is a broader horizon—the context of his life as a whole—one that can never be displaced by the current situation, even while he seems to have "adjusted."

Carol: I was curious. You've been in this place six months now. Do you think you've adjusted to it? You got used to it? You're not used to it?
Roland: Never will.
Carol: Never will. Why?
Roland: It's just too much different . . . what I was used to . . . my life. But I reckon I've adjusted.

* * * * *

All three of the residents in this chapter worried to death or were otherwise gravely disappointed about particular aspects of their lives. The three might seem to present in terms of the public image of the typical nursing home resident—abandoned, depressed, and ill. While, to be sure, all three residents share some of these characteristics, their stories convey complex narrative linkages, few of which connect directly with the quality of care in their facilities. Indeed, even as Roland Snyder becomes engrossed by the quality of his immediate care, particularly his resented placement with roommate George, Snyder ends by telling Ronai that he will never get used to the nursing home under any circumstances because it is too different from his life, linking adjustment to something much broader than daily living in the facility, namely, his life as a whole.

CHAPTER

3

Making a New Home

An idyllic image of domesticity communicates carefree childhoods, loving homes, parents who are good providers, happy marriages, long healthy lives, and intergenerational charity. The positive qualities are enticing sources of identity and the whole is a widely shared model for family formation. The qualities and model provide background explanations for why some nursing home residents "worry to death" about their current separation from loved ones or are disappointed that family relations are no longer what they were.

Another domestic image stands in contrast. As scholars of family life are discovering, in reality domestic life conveys both positive and negative qualities (see Skolnick 1983, chap. 4). In this context, we need to recognize that what some residents bring with them to the nursing home are domestic lives ridden with strife—difficult childhoods, poverty, loneliness, marital infidelity, sickness, and death. When these residents look back on life to tell their stories, the present contrasts less negatively with the past. Secure homes and nurturing familylike relations may not be matters so much lost, as possibly gained for the first time in a facility. Such is the domestic horizon of Martha Gilbert's story, a resident who has made a new home for herself at Oakmont, where she now lives. Yet, even for Gilbert, the idyllic image crops up from time to time as she talks about her sons and how they might have treated her, their mother.

New homes are made, too, by those who count wherever they have caring friends and whatever they've gotten used to as home, notwithstanding the family relations they once had or that continue in other locations. To some extent, getting used to something is a matter of relatively short- versus long-term stays. A patient who expects to be hospitalized for a few days is not likely to consider the matter as something that needs getting used to, let alone the possibility that the hospital may become home. Likewise, the nursing home resident who is a short-stayer, spending a few weeks in a facility undergoing physical therapy or convalescing after a period of hospitalization, looks ahead to discharge and a return to his or her former way of life. Long-stayers, however, face the possibility that the nursing facility may be their last home. For some of them, like residents Jane Nesbit and Ruby Coplin, who have faithfully attuned to "making the best of it" most of their lives, with or without the support of religious convictions, a long stay in the nursing facility suggests making a home and life of it.

MARTHA GILBERT

Martha Gilbert has lived at Oakmont for five years when I interview her. She is a seventy-six-year-old widowed white female with congestive heart failure and emphysema. As Gilbert first mentions when I walk slowly with her to the resident lounge near her room, exertion makes her short of breath. I soon learn that illness and exertion are constant narrative linkages in her life story, from her childhood in rural New York State through her move to the South. Hers is a hard and unhappy life from the start, far worse than what her life has become in the nursing home.

Without tears or remorse, Gilbert begins her story by describing childhood:

> I've had a rough life. I had to go to work when I was young. I've been on my own practically since I've been eleven years old. At that age, I was cleaning or . . . I mean I used to go from house to house and do house cleaning. Then when I was big enough where I could really be on my own, I got to be a waitress and I stayed that way even after I married. I did waitress work.
>
> I had two sons. The closest one is in North City [forty miles north of Oakmont] and the other one is in South Carolina and that's about all I can tell you. I mean, I don't have a very interesting life because I had to work all my life. It was a hard life, not a pretty picture. I didn't have girlfriends or went out to parties or anything else because I always had to work.
>
> My parents were very poor. So as soon as I was big enough where I could go out, Mother made me go out to work. I used to go to work after school, work until about nine at night, then come home and do my homework. I got real tired and I think that's one of the reasons I ran my system down. I wasn't able to fight anything, any colds or anything, because every time I got a cold, it would really hit me hard . . . because I was in no condition to fight it. I've had pneumonia three times and that didn't help my lungs any.
>
> The first time that I had pneumonia, I was about eleven years old. I had double pneumonia. I had it real bad. It crippled my system and everything else from the fever. And then I had pneumonia twice after that. I had two boys and they were both caesarean.

I asked about her husband and her life raising the boys. Again, it was the narrative of a rough life and being on her own, made worse by both her husband's and sons' long absences from home because of work.

Well, I'll put it this way. Ever since '72 . . . I lost my husband in '73 . . . I was on my own again. I had to work. And I just, well, the only time that my son, my youngest son would take care of me was when I wasn't able to help myself. Other than that, I was on my own. My son and his wife both worked, so they couldn't take care of me. The reason that I'm in here is because I need twenty-four-hour care and I couldn't get it. I had to come into a nursing home. It was a rough life I had. I've been here about five years now. Before that, I worked when I could. When I couldn't, my son would take care of me until I got better and I'd be on my own again. But, as I said, he and his wife both worked, so they couldn't take care of me. So, I had to paddle the boat by myself.

I was married and lost my husband in '73. I was married to him for twenty years before he died. And both of the boys are on their own. Like I said, one is in North City and the other is in South Carolina. So I don't see much of the children. They both drive trucks—those big trailers, you know. Convoys. And when they go out on the road, they don't come home for a week or ten days. They always go out of the state. They drive anywheres from here to California. Long distance. My husband drove a truck too. After I lost my husband, I was all by myself and didn't have nobody. I never had nothin', really.

Then when I got so sick where they told me I had to have twenty-four-hour care, I lived with my son. It was rough. My daughter-in-law figured that I had to do things for her. Well, you know if you're not well, you have a hard time doing things. I had a hard time just trying to breathe and navigate by myself, let alone work. She just figured that I had to clean house and cook and what have you and I couldn't do everything. I just couldn't. It was too much for me. So I had a chance to talk to my son in private and I told him that I just couldn't take it. The only other solution I had was to go in a nursing home. It was his idea. I think at the time I didn't think too much of it because I was too sick to think. I really had it rough.

I asked Gilbert what the word *home* meant to her, which returned her to childhood and married life.

Not much, because I always had to work. I didn't have much of a home life. It means zip. Even when I had children and they were young, I still had to go out and work. When the boys were little, we had a farm. I'd have to get up at four in the morning to help my husband milk cows and do chores before I would make breakfast. Then I'd have to go ahead and get the children off to school.

Whatever the circumstance—whether Gilbert's childhood, her married life, her life alone following her husband's death, or living with her son—it was rough and unhappy. Whether or not one would judge her responsibilities as particularly onerous for her circumstances, Gilbert's is nonetheless a narrative of hardship, which she eventually contrasts with her life at Oakmont. But the transition to a nursing home life wasn't easy, as the following exchange reveals.

Martha: Anything was better than to put up with it.

Jay: Put up with what? I'm not sure I understand.

Martha: With the life that I was leading.

Jay: Oh, you mean in your son's house?

Martha: Yeah. So when I had a chance to make the move, I just told my son that they had better put me in a nursing home. I couldn't take it.

Jay: Did you have any idea what it would be like before you came to a nursing home?

Martha: No. No, I didn't. I cried. I was in bad shape because I couldn't take it. I just never thought that I would wind up in a nursing home. After I got here and I was here for a while, I found out that it was best for me. But at the beginning I couldn't get it through my head that I had to be in a nursing home.

Jay: What was it like at the beginning, Mrs. G? How did you feel?

Martha: Lonesome. The environment is altogether different, you know. When I came in here, I didn't know a soul. I had to make friends all over again and I didn't feel good and everything. Every little thing that happened just bothered me too much because I was sick and I couldn't take it. Now I'm used to it, I'm well, and it doesn't bother me. But I do have a hard time breathing.

Gilbert's reference to being sick and not being able to take it reflects two important distinctions, made by many residents. One is the difference between being sick and being chronically ill or disabled. When residents say they are sick, they typically refer to acute conditions like having the flu, a bad cold, or being in pain. When they are not sick, they are mainly in "pretty good health," "having a good day," "well," or "feeling okay," even while they may otherwise suffer from chronic conditions like congestive heart failure and cerebral palsy (see Charmaz 1991). In this regard, Gilbert was more sick in her son's home than she is in the nursing home at the time of the interview. Her daughter-in-law made matters worse by expecting Gilbert to do household chores while she was sick, which Gilbert reportedly couldn't take.

The other distinction, not evident in Gilbert's preceding remarks but implied in comments both she and others make about one's quality of life in a nursing home, refers to how being sick as opposed to the quality of care affects the quality of life. Time and again, residents state that it is being sick, sometimes very sick, that makes being in a nursing home "rough" or depressing, not the quality of care as such, even while particular matters of caregiving, such as employee attitudes and the food served, can be sources of considerable irritation.

As long as Gilbert wasn't sick and though she had a hard time breathing, Oakmont was a pretty good life, was now home—and family. We talked about friendship, which in time lapsed into a discussion of domesticity.

Jay:	Would you say you had friends here?
Martha:	I have a roommate and we've been together five years. So we sort of understand each other and we get along pretty good. But other than that I don't associate too much. I'm more or less on my own, privately. I don't like to . . . I don't like big groups.
Jay:	I think I understand. I'm like that myself. What's your roommate's name, Mrs. G?
Martha:	She's Sara Sanders. She's been here as long as . . . maybe a couple of months longer than I am, but we've always been together, since we joined up. Even when they moved us from room to room—you know, changing rooms—they always managed to keep the both of us together. They didn't try to separate us. So that makes it nice. They know that we get along very good, so they don't. But other than that, I guess it's just the way I make it. You either try to get along well or you don't and I'm a person who tries to get along. I don't have too many enemies, I don't think.
Jay:	Now that you've been here five years, does it feel like home?
Martha:	Well so far it does. Five years is a long time. I've readjusted myself. So I think that, God willing and I don't get sick and much worse than I already am, I think I can make it. I know most everybody now. I don't associate too much with them, but I know them. The only thing, the only problem I have, I can't join everything that they have because I can't breathe. I have a hard time breathing and I mean I can't have too much activity because I'm short of breath. So I don't join the crowd too much because I can't breathe.
Jay:	When did you start feeling . . . I believe you said earlier that you didn't feel that this was home at first? When did you start feeling it was more like home?
Martha:	Well, after I'd been here about six months and they all tried and I know they did—the nurses and the aides. They tried to make me comfortable and they know I have a problem breathing. They understand me now better than they did at the beginning, but until . . . I guess I had to have the feel of it myself. I had a hard time trying to understand because they have their work cut out for them, but I couldn't join everything that they had because of my breathing.

I guess once I began to understand, it started to feel like home. At first, I couldn't get it through my head that I had to put up with it. When I found out that I couldn't be with my son, I couldn't be in his home and I got it through my head that I had to make the best of it, that's when I began to feel a little different. It wasn't all that great there anyway. That's when I began to feel that I really would have to make up my mind that this was my home. But it takes a while. I mean you have to fight and when you get to be my age, it's sort of hard to accept things. Now I guess I learned my lesson and I found out that I either accept it or you don't have anything. You don't have no friends. And the sooner I did that, the better I was and, since then, I've had no problem.

Explaining how Oakmont was now her home, Gilbert compared what she now had or had come to accept with the family life she never had before.

It's part of my life now. It's home. I know I can't depend on my sons. I haven't seen my son from South Carolina in ten years. Not much of a son, huh? He's not one to visit, and Jimmy, my youngest one, he drives those big convoys and he's out on the road. When he comes home, he has one day off and it's sort of hard for him to go ahead and just come home and to visit Mother because there are things that he has to do at home. I couldn't accept that at the beginning either. I figured that, well, he's got a day off, he should come to see me, his mother. But that isn't the way it got to be. I mean I had to accept that he couldn't do it. They, neither one, was ever too homey anyway, I guess. So here I am. It's hard, but after you accept the things you know you can't have, things begin to run a little bit smoother.

But when you look back, I've never had a family life. I always had to work. It was bad, real bad. Even when the kids were small, I had to work. Sara's my family now, my roommate. She's been pretty nice and she's got a daughter that comes in here . . . I mean if I need something, I can't depend on my son to get it for me because if I would say to him that I needed something, he'd probably be six months getting it. Where if I tell Dotty [Sara's daughter] that I need something, I mean she takes my order today and in a week's time when she comes to visit Sara, she brings my stuff that I need.

I encourage Gilbert to tell me about Sara, their relationship, and what that means to Gilbert. As before, she contrastingly links her current "easy living" with the sad points of her earlier life.

Sara's ten years older than I am. She's okay now, but back a while she had a slight stroke and things were a little rough because I couldn't communicate with her. That was about three years ago. But she seems to get better every day and that makes me feel better. Things are easier.

I've never had anything easy happen to me. Now, well, I don't feel very old because I had it so hard when I was younger. Now that I'm older, I think I've got things a little bit easy. If I didn't have such a hard time breathing, I'd be okay. I've never had a very interesting life. I've always had to work so hard and now that I'm seventy-six, I've got it easier now then I've ever had in my life. A lot of people don't think I'm seventy-six because I don't have gray hair. I don't use no dye. [Elaborates]

But like I said, it's easy living now as long as I'm not sick. Everybody says that they can't understand why Sara and I been together for five years and never had words or we haven't changed roommates because it seems like they have a problem with other residents here. They don't get along. They have to change the room or change the resident. I think Sara would do anything for me and one of the things I appreciate is, because I really have a problem with my health and when she knows that I don't feel good, she tries to help me. She's like a nurse. I don't have to depend on the aides or the nurses here because Sara takes care of me more or less. Even though she's older, she's more active than I am because she's never been sick as much as I have.

I didn't always have it as easy. I had a rough married life. You can't try to get along if you're separated like with my husband on the road for a week or ten days. There's no way you can get along like that. You can't tell me that if he's out truckin' away from home that long and he's gonna be by himself, he's not gonna look for companionship. I'd find things in his dirty laundry. So you just have to make the best of it. I loved him but that's not saying he returned the love, because I know that he had other things that occupied him more than me.

My whole life was like that. I've never had a happy life. I mean I couldn't go to this girlfriend and tell her what a good time I had. I couldn't go to another one and say what a beautiful party it was because I've never been to any of them. I could never go anywheres because I didn't have no way of going. [Elaborates] When Easter would come, the other kids used to dye eggs. My mother, she would go ahead and cook onion peels and dye eggs with onion peels and they were all brown. That's the only color we knew. I can't say I had a wonderful time because I didn't have it.

Well, after the rough life that I've lived all my life and then you come along and live in here and you don't have your problems, I means that's easy. If I didn't have such a hard time breathing sometimes, I think I'd be on Easy Street. I have to be careful not to catch a cold because if I do, it hits me much harder than anybody else because my lungs are so bad. Other than that, I'm living on Easy Street, like I said, and this is home.

JANE NESBIT

Jane Nesbit's story is one of lifelong satisfactions, filled with the usual tragedies certainly, but she is still accepting of what God has destined for her, as she remarks. It is not as much a narrative of contrasts, as is Martha Gilbert's portrayal of life before and life on Easy Street. Rather, it is a story of always making the best of what God offers. Nesbit's place in the life of the nursing home reflects her placement in life as a whole. As Nesbit has always done, she continues to make the best of it. At the same time, while hers is a life lived by God's grace, it is not one immersed in "lovin' the Lord," which is the narrative horizon of Chapter 5's residents.

Nesbit is a ninety-two-year-old widowed white female with arteriosclerotic heart disease. She suffers from hypertension, has occasional minor strokes that leave her temporarily dizzy and confused, and is partially blind. She has spent all her life in the South, having moved from Alabama to Florida in 1917. Nesbit also lives at Oakmont, being resident there three and a half years when interviewed.

Nesbit begins her story by briefly describing her childhood and the 1917 move. She then tells of her husband's tragic death, her widowhood, and her final placement at Oakmont.

> I was born in Alabama. Montgomery was the capital and my daddy was a mail carrier. I used to remember going with him. [Elaborates] He died when I was a child and that left me to take care of my mother. She finally died and that left me. [Elaborates] I wished a thousand times that I went on to school then but, back then, you know, I never would go back to school. So I married and had my family and come down from Alabama around in '17 I believe it was, the third day in March. Everything was covered in snow up there and we got down here and everybody is in short sleeves, aplanting. They had cucumbers growing. I got to pick cucumbers that year. I tell you, I've had to do it, though, since I was born. Everything just turned over for me to do because my two sisters married and I was left to do things. But life has been a pleasure to me. Most of my life's been in Florida.
>
> My husband got killed at Dailey's Foundry down here. He and another man were welders and they told them that the gas tanks were all clean. They rolled them out to do and, as soon as they touched the thing with a torch, it went off and killed both of them. Exploded. They said they heard the noise clear up here. And that left me at home with four children. He was killed in '41 and I had to try to get the kids through school, and I did.
>
> My son went in the navy. They talked him into going and told him that would be best for him to go in the navy to where he could help me out. So if it hadn't been for that, I don't know what I'd have done. The girls finished school and I'm thankful for all that.
>
> And then, after all of 'em got married, they didn't want me living by myself, so I lived in the house with my baby daughter. I lived there for about ten years until two of my grandsons graduated. Then we moved to Judson's Lake; stayed down there until I got to where I had to come out here. My daughter fell and fractured her back and she wasn't able to take care of me. So they just put me in here.

As we continue to talk, Nesbit recounts the events surrounding her husband's death at the foundry in 1941. While it is retrospectively conveyed as the tragedy it was for her and the children at the time, there is an aura of destiny about it, filled as it is with signs that his death was imminent. As we will see, a similar aura—of enduring equanimity with self and one's circumstances—conveys the meaning of the present as well. Recalling the death, Nesbit explains:

> When he was killed, that was the most shocking thing that I think that I ever witnessed. We got up and had breakfast. He was a coffee drinker all right, but he hardly ever drank over two cups. That morning he drank coffee and drank coffee. He got up to leave to go to work and one of my girls . . . she was always a tiny little thing . . . we called her "Teeny." He says, "Got to get some sugar off my little woman here." He was chasing that little girl around the table to get sugar off'n her before he went to work. She darted under the table and he couldn't get her. He made like he was going to get her though and havin' fun. [Pause] So he says, "Well I got to go." And he looked at me, turned around and come back and said, "Just another swig of coffee" and said "I got to go." And then he left.
>
> Well, this one that worked with him, his wife says that he said the same thing, like it was meant to be. His wife says he said, "I've got to have another sip of coffee and I've got to go." The same thing.
>
> And when that thing went off, it shook our house. I thought the whole thing was going to fall in. We lived close to the foundry. I knew good and well that somebody was killed or I had an idea that there would be. . . . Blew one of his legs off. They said that his lungs must have been crushed. That was bad, but I guess it was meant to be.

As we talk about destiny and the meaning of life, Nesbit's equanimity, her acceptance of fate, and herself come forth.

Jay: What does your life look like from where you're at now?

Jane: Well, it looks like I'm just ready to go any time. That's the way I feel and I hope it is.

Jay: Uh huh. Can you explain what you mean by that, Mrs. N?

Jane: Well, I've just asked God if there's anything that He's holding me here for. If it's to do something or to say something or whatever it is, I'm willing to do it. If it's to pass on and to go with Him, that's fine too. So I said, "Well, dear Lord, You know what it's about." So I'm willing to try anything. And I'm willing to just give up and say that it's gone.

Jay: Did you ever think back and ask yourself what's, you know . . . how did I come to be what I am?

Jane: Yes, I sure have. And I reckon it just wasn't meant for me to be a big highfalutin person and know-it-all. I'm proud of me like I am. I'm no big talker, nor no highfalutin person, just what God made me and I'm proud of it.

We turn to the present, especially her life in the facility. It is a narrative of participation, home, and family living. Indeed, Oakmont has come to be the home and family she needs to *return* to even when visiting her daughters. While she loves the daughters, Nesbit admits that the time she spends with them can be boring. Still, Oakmont is no bed of roses. Like most things, it too has its good and its bad sides, as she points out.

Some of the days here is pretty good and some of 'em isn't. Some days we have good days and some days we have bad days. Now today we haven't got help and there's a lot of days that we don't have enough help. Some days we get a good meal and the next day, or three or four days, we won't get nothing hardly. But this is something you have to be satisfied with. That's the ways it is anywhere. I said I thank God that I've got a place that I can come to, to where I'll be taken care of, and not have to depend on my children to do it.

I'm into the Sunshine Club. There's different days that we do things, but on Thursday is the Sunshine Club. We make birthday cards and welcome cards for the new visitors, to give the new peoples they've admitted. We carry 'em a welcome card, introduce ourself, and tell them who we are and what to expect. We want to welcome them here and see that they get good care and to get out and mix and mingle with people to where everybody'll learn you. There's wonderful things that you can do here that you'd be surprised. We make all kinds of stuff. We made pillows and we made quilts. And we've made change purses. We made baskets. I made seven baskets.

Now I'm partially blind. I can't see to do the needlework like I used to. But I glue, put glue on stuff to paste boxes and different things that we fix. So . . .

My daughters, they'll say, "Well, Mama, why don't you lay down and rest? You look like you can't hold your head up." I say, "Well, let me sit up as long as I can." So they know if Mama ever lays down there's something wrong.

At this point, the domestic meaning of visiting her daughters and returning to Oakmont is revealed.

Jane: Visiting my girls means a lot to me. I love to go home down there and I can stay down there for a little while, but then I'm ready to come back up here.

Jay: Home down there is where?

Jane: In [one daughter's nearby town].

Jay: That's near here, isn't it? Yeah. I think I know where that is.

Jane: Or in [another nearby town where a different daughter lives]. Some of my folks are down there. Anywhere that I go, it feels like home. So I'm ready to come back up here.

Jay: Oh, is that right? Why is that?

Jane: I don't know. Just ready to come back. There's a lot of friends here and we get along good. I can only stay a day or two and everybody [at Oakmont] says, "Why do you stay off so long? We missed you so bad."

Jay: The people here say that?

Jane: Uh huh. "Come back." "Oh, there goes Jane." "She's back." "Why did you stay so long?" I don't know.

Jay: How does that make you feel?

Jane: It makes me feel so good to know that they're thinking about me. And Lola . . .

Jay: Who's that, Mrs. N?

Jane: Lola Dryden [another resident]. She is around at my door every morning and comes every night. She'll come see how I am. It just kills her for me to be sick. She wants me right with her. I told her, I says, "Old mare ain't what she used to be. I can't get around like I used to no more." Lola thinks that she's old. I said, "Well, honey, you're just starting." I says, "I don't feel like I'm old." And she says, "Oh, you're kidding." And I says, "No." I says, "I don't feel a day older than I did six years ago." In a way I don't.

Jay: Isn't Lola down the hall from here? She's been here a while too, hasn't she? I don't recall exactly. And you've been here for, let's see, since '87 is it? It's been a while.

Jane: It just seems like home now.

Jay: How's that?

Jane: I reckon it's because I know I'm going to have to stay here. I say that when I go down to my daughters I'm always ready to come back. I get to thinking about coming back before I'm there too long.

Jay: Is that right? I wonder why.

Jane: I don't know, but it's just sit there and watch TV or something and nothing to do, kinda bored. Here I'm going back and forth doing things, talking with different people. So it's just different.

As homelike as Oakmont now is for Nesbit, the transition from life on the outside to making a home of the facility was not automatic. As for most, there was a period of adjustment. For some like Nesbit, it eventually proved to be a transition to a new home. As we talk about it, I ask about others' experiences. Nesbit contrasts herself with two residents whose minds she believes to be weaker than hers and who can't seem to accept things as they are.

Jay: When you first moved into Oakmont, Mrs. N, did you feel it to be like home, as it does now?

Jane: No.

Jay: No? What was it like when you first moved in?

Jane: I don't know. It was kind of dreary, dreary-feeling. Just that I just didn't know how to take it or something. Didn't know why I was put here, why I couldn't be somewhere's else. I don't remember all that much about it. After about a month or two months, the longer I stayed, the more I realized why I was here. Because my daughter couldn't lift me anymore. Dr. Dunne [her personal physician] told her that she's going to have to either put me in here or get somebody to go over to the

house and keep me and lift me. He says that he'd rather I be here in the
home where, if anything happens, that somebody'll be there to look
after me. So that's why I'm here I guess.

    As I said, about a month after that, I began to go around and meet
different people and one or the other. Things just began to fall in place.
It didn't take too long at all. It just, I don't know . . . well, you know
you're gonna be here and why worry about it, like anything else in life.
Take everything as it comes and that's what I looked forward to. It was
the Lord give me strength and courage to go on. That He's done. So
here I am and this here is my life now.

Jay: Do others feel the same way, do you know?

Jane: I believe some do. I hear talk about it. Not everyone. Now Adele and
Sally round here on the same hall that I'm on? Both of them, well . . . I
think that my mind is a little stronger than theirs because they do and
say things that really don't cross my mind. Like about being here, you
know, [they ask] why are they here? They can't understand why
they've been put here and who's taking charge of the bill. "Who's
paying my bill here?" They ask all kinds of questions. You don't know
what to tell them. The government is taking care of us and we draw
our checks and our checks go in on this and such. I tried to tell them
that, but you can't explain to them in a way.

Jay: Why is that, I wonder?

Jane: I don't know. Their mind is just different or something, weaker. They
can't see it like we do or something. Or maybe we see it wrong and
they see it right. I don't know.

The interview turns to social relationships. Elaborating upon her rela-
tions with those she feels to be familylike brings us back to resident
Martha Gilbert, whom we met earlier and who is another member of the
Sunshine Club.

> Adele and Sally both hang around and talk whenever they feel like talking,
> you know. [Elaborates] And there are the ladies that work in the Sunshine
> group. I can't remember all their names. Let's see. One of 'em's Katherine.
> She's close. Not all of 'em are in the Sunshine group. [Elaborates] Oh, I
> forgot Martha Gilbert and Sara Sanders. They were in the group. They've
> quit. Sara went to the hospital and she hasn't been feeling good. And
> Martha, she won't go nowhere unless Sara is along.
>
> But we're all like a bunch of sisters in there, we are. And I have to say that
> I'm very much at home here. We're close.

RUBY COPLIN

The circumstances surrounding Ruby Coplin's admission to Fairhaven, the nursing facility in which she makes a new home, differ from

Martha Gilbert's and Jane Nesbit's. An eighty-six-year-old white female, Coplin has an enlarged heart, suffers from hypertension, and is blind from glaucoma. According to Coplin, she sought admission to care for her husband, who was already a resident and afflicted by Alzheimer's disease, even while she required extended care herself following hospitalization for a heart attack. Coplin couldn't bear to feel that her husband was grieving for her alone in a nursing home. Her husband died about a year after she was admitted. Coplin was widowed for approximately one and a half years when interviewed.

Coplin's new home is not just a source of rest, shelter, and sustenance. It is something more than a network of friends and social support. Coplin orients to Fairhaven's residents the way she's oriented to the less fortunate all of her life. If Fairhaven is a nursing facility and is home for Coplin, it also is a place for charity, somewhere to offer kindness and be helpful to those less fortunate: the suffering, the destitute, and the lonely. Having defined her role in life as that of the carer, Coplin is not just another old woman sitting in her room or receiving help. She chooses to continue playing the carer role in the nursing home, even though she herself has grown frail and become totally blind.

Just as Coplin makes a pet project of being the carer, she makes a veritable career of telling her life story. Starting from her childhood in Miami, she offers more detail and speaks at greater length about her life than any other resident in the study. For well over an hour, she describes growing up in South Florida, her early career in retail sales, meeting the future husband who had seen action in World War I, the 1924 economic boom, the depression, and raising two sons, among other life experiences.

We begin at the end of her story, with her admission to Fairhaven. The role of carer is centrally linked to what follows. She calls her husband "Daddy," a name she grew accustomed to using in speaking of him with her sons.

> Dr. Marsh [her personal physician] told Jack and Gordon [her sons], he said, "Now your mother cannot go home. She must go to a convalescent home." Well, it was good for Daddy. He was grieving so that he called me everyday. He didn't know where he was. If I told him, it wouldn't have done him any good anyway; it wouldn't register. He kept wondering why I wouldn't come. See his mind would come and go. [Elaborates] I guess Jack talked to the doctor and Jack says to me, "Mother, I don't want you getting upset but you are going to Daddy's nursing home, but you will only be there until March 10th. I want a room for both of you together."
>
> Well, I took care of Daddy. I felt bad because he grieved so. They [the staff] did very, very little for him. The only time they did anything extra was to put him on Ativan to calm him down because he kept wanting his moth-

er. This all goes with it, you know. [Elaborates] It's a good thing Daddy went first 'cause he could have never lived without me. Never. He would have never made it. [Elaborates] So, anyway, the nurses and all complimented me and commended me for the way I took care of him.

[The night he died], I got up at 12:30 and I knew he was sound asleep and I bathed his feet and put his socks on. And so he was well covered and all. [Elaborates] So I got back in bed. As I said, it was kind of chilly. So I covered up good and dozed off. And when I woke up, Jack's [son] arms were around me and I knew that was it. The curtain was pulled and he had expired just, you know, while I was asleep. I think I fell asleep just before he died. He had a very bad heart. So he had a peaceful death. He went to sleep and what else could I ask for? You know, in that respect, the ending of a beautiful marriage?

If Coplin thought of herself as a carer, she was quick to point out that she was not "doting." Her aim was to care, not to interfere. Her relations with her sons and their families are described accordingly:

We had a good time. We made [laughs] milkshakes! I was over [at Gordon's home] last Sunday for dinner, for three or four hours. Gordon is semiretired now. I've taken care of them and their little ones. But I'm not the interfering kind. I don't dote on people. Never have.

Turning to life at Fairhaven, the theme of caring reemerges. Describing how she helps out, it is evident that she enjoys the role.

I just take each day at a time and do the best I can with it. I love everybody and I try to help those here. I'm being charitable, you might say. I wheel them around. You know, like I have the legs and they have the eyes. This one lady in particular, I kind of look after her. She's very bad with Alzheimer's and I . . . she sits with me now. So I kind of look after her at the table here in the dining room.

When I first came here, I did quite a bit. Like, oh, I did a lot of little things that I could help Susan with in the activity room. Anything they wanted me to do that I was able to do, I'd do, because I didn't lose the sight of this good eye until a year ago last July. The surgery was a failure because I had so much scar tissue.

But I've enjoyed being here. I love it here. It's home to me. And, you know, when you get older, it's kind of nice not having to wash dishes, make beds, or anything like that . . . 'cause I've worked all my life. But I've enjoyed it, you know.

Coplin's role as carer is not as active as it was before her recent total blindness. But she figures ways to be helpful despite the handicap. To her, even the act of attentively listening to others is a form of help. Describing a typical day in her life at Fairhaven, she notes:

Well, I'll tell you, I wake up quite early and get ready for breakfast in the dining room. We come in our robes and nighties and have a nice breakfast. And then if it's not bath day, we go back to our room. And my roommate is precious . . . we have the radio going and we get all of the news of the day. Then we'd usually dress and get ready to go back to the dining room for lunch. In between, you never know what might be going on. But there's not really too much going on in the morning.

There's not much I can do now like doing baskets, you know, crafts and things like that. I can't do much of that now. So, you know . . . but I can listen! [Laughs] We have a lot, well, of different churches come in with children and we will have a songfest. We listen to them and that. And I listen to those that need to share their misery and that's how I help.

When I ask her what she expects daily life to look like a year from now, Coplin keeps her temporal horizons close to the present, as many residents do. In the process, she explains that caring also means not complaining. Coplin's care extends even to the facilities' professional caregivers, helping the helpers, as she puts it.

I don't look that far ahead. I just take each day at a time. I'm hoping I can live to see that great-grandson of mine and have him remember me. He's seventeen months old now and he's doing the polka and trying to say "Nanna," but he gets it mixed up with banana. [Laughs]

I hope to go to heaven, if that's what you mean. [Laughs] I'm not morbid or bitter or nothing. I just take each day at a time and try to enjoy it to the hilt, if you know what I mean. And I try never to complain. I try to be . . . think of who helps to take care of us [the staff], you know. They're human. Some of these people [residents] don't understand. They give them a hard time, you know. I just try to think of others and just take each day at a time and enjoy whatever there is around and try to help those that help us.

Coplin compares residents in her circle of friends, those who are more able than she now is and those who are more helpless. It's a long and detailed narrative of mutual care and support. At one point, Coplin mentions those special to her and recalls having received a surprising compliment from a "nice gentleman" for helping his mother. It seems to cap a life of giving to others in return for what she herself has been blessed.

. . . a very close friend. She's Madeline. Her husband has Alzheimer's and we've become very close friends. Now, well . . . she wasn't bad when I first came in and I am very close to her. I feel that God has put her in my path, you know, to kind of look after. And then there was Mrs. Edison here. She was special. When Ray [Coplin's husband] was alive, we'd wheel her to and from the dining room. He enjoyed that. If she was cold, we'd go get her sweaters. And then she died. When she left, she had a lot of nice things, which I was surprised at. [After she died], I walked in [her room] one day and I didn't know who was there. I could see a bit then. This nice gentleman comes up and says to me, "I want to shake your hand." He said, "Mrs. Coplin, you're the most wonderful person I've ever known!" And I said, "Well, that's a nice compliment. What's this all about?" He said, "The way you were with my mother." She was two doors down from me and I felt like she was my grandmother and I kind of adopted her as my family. I guess it's that I feel I'm so blessed that I want to do for others.

* * * * *

Making a new home presents a narrative horizon that casts the quality of life and the quality of care positively. When home signifies nurturance, friendship, security, and shelter, what could be a more satisfying life than life at home? In this context, Martha Gilbert's earlier "home" experiences are a marked contrast with her current one. For Gilbert, the nursing home links together the domestic life she never had. Jane Nesbit and Ruby Coplin are now at home for other reasons, equally compelling domestically. What is more, as Nesbit suggests, if there is both good and bad in the facility, such is the fate of things anywhere. For Nesbit and Coplin, the nursing home's quality of life is a narrative extension of what life has always been like.

CHAPTER

4

It's Come to This

There are narratives that convey an overriding concern with fate. Some are sad tales of puzzlement over how, after one has lived by the rules or in good stewardship, it is possible that life has come to this: the uselessness of a sedentary existence with no discernible purpose. Residents like Myrtle Johnson look back on their lives—filled with hard work, enjoyment, and kindness toward others—and grimly wonder how God could have planned this for them. Theirs are not so much stories of profound disappointment over physical or mental deterioration or worry for their own or others' well-being, as they are narratives of quandary over the meaning of life in the face of circumstances.

Not all are completely sad. Resident Alice Stern, for one, tells of being placed in a nursing home because her soon-to-be-remarried daughter can't foresee caring for her mother with a new husband around. Stern jokes that her daughter is afraid the mother will sweep the husband off his feet and take him away. At the same time, she wonders how it's come to this: how it is possible that a daughter could ever place her mother in a nursing home. Stern can't fathom how any relative could abandon another one, which to her violates a foundation of family life.

The stories' horizons extend well beyond the local and interpersonal. If it is understood that there are things a nursing home cannot offer, this is overridden by the broader question of life's meaning. If there are complaints about, or an appreciation of, staff members' efforts, these pale against the issue of what people have come to be. In this narrative context, the quality of care, while a concern, hardly bears on the quality of life.

MYRTLE JOHNSON

Myrtle Johnson is a ninety-four-year-old widowed African American woman who has lived at the Westside Nursing Center for a year. She suffers from Parkinson's disease and has difficulty maintaining her balance. According to Johnson, falls have been the bane of her later years, the main reason she was placed in a nursing home. She also is in some pain from arthritis.

Johnson's story links together themes of independence and being helpful to others, which enigmatically contrast with a felt uselessness. Her story begins with the family's move to Jesse James territory near the Fox River in the state of Missouri.

> I was born in Brice County, Illinois, and I lived there until I was eight years old. Then I moved to Missouri. I lived thirty miles from the Fox River. You've heard of the Fox River Outpost? Well, I lived thirty miles from there.
>
> Jesse James was plying up and down that river, you know, at that time. Jesse James just bothered the banks and the trains. He never bothered . . . he would take money from them and he'd, like, pay the widowed woman who needed it. He was shot in St. Joseph, Missouri. He was in his home and he'd gone to straighten a picture—his mother's picture—which was hung up on a wall. They say that Johnny Howard sneaked up and shot him in the back. I've been in the home and I've seen that picture with a bullet hole in it. My brothers live near St. Joe now and they have for years. But Jesse James looked out for the poor people he could help. It was the railroads and the banks he robbed.
>
> The story was . . . and I don't know if it's true or not, but I imagine it was . . . that his mother and his sisters lived over at the edge of Illinois. There was a bunch of confederate reserves from the army who was traveling that way and they raped his sister. That evidently turned Jesse James into . . . he wanted to get back at somebody or something. So he started to rob trains. Really, the people around there never saw any harm in Jesse James because he helped so many people. I don't know. That's about all I can tell you about that.
>
> I was a country girl, always lived in the country. I grew up there. My folks was poor and I began teaching when I was sixteen years old. You could teach if you could get a certificate back then.

Explaining how she came to live in Florida, Johnson compares an earlier useful life with a life now hardly worth living.

> There was one thing my son disliked. There was snow in Missouri. You know how it would snow and we'd brave the snowdrifts. So my son took off for Florida. When my husband's health got pretty bad, my son had us move down here so's he could look after him. We moved into my son's house. My husband passed away and I lived there until I got so's every time I got on my feet I'd fall over. [Pauses and groans from leg ache] So I couldn't stay by myself any longer. My son and his wife worked and, of course, they couldn't be there all the time. So that's my story.
>
> But I worked hard all my life. And I enjoyed life. I'll say that what I enjoyed the most was when I lived on a farm in Missouri. Now that's where I enjoyed myself the most because I was able to get out and do things, you

know, help others. If there's one thing I don't like, it's just sittin'. That's what I have to do now. But then I try to make the best of it. But I would say that when I was able to be up and around and work is when I enjoyed myself the most.

My husband was sick for a number of years, but I took care of him. When I took him to the hospital, I stayed with him night and day. I never left his side. He's been dead now for eleven years. I made the best of what I could do and I'm not dissatisfied with it.

Of course I'm not happy sitting here this way. But then it's part of life and you've got to . . . I will say I've often thought about it, just since I've been passing between the chair and the bed. What use is it?

You know, I can realize why some people commit suicide. They don't have faith. People that have faith in God don't commit suicide. But I can see why when people are in my position and don't have faith in the Lord, they commit suicide. I've thought about that so much. You know, you often say, "Well, why did so-and-so do so-and-so?" Well, if you sit down and study about it, you can figure that out . . . there's nothing . . . But as long as you have faith in the Lord, you are going to go ahead and take what he sends you. But there's times you really wonder.

If in the context of her faith she cannot contemplate suicide for herself in the face of being useless, she still is perplexed that God has let her life come to this. As we discuss fate and destiny, I ask her what her life looks like from where she is now. She ties her answer to a doctor's explanation for her mother's fated death.

Well, life looks to me like a big blob! That's just what it looks like exactly, because what good am I? I've often wondered why the Lord lets me live on, because what good am I to anybody? I'm a burden, you see. Now, my son and his wife, regardless of how busy they are, they come over here once a week and they find me. I can call them anytime, you see. I'm a burden in a way. You see I'm a burden.

I wondered sometimes . . . I reckon it was a doctor who told me one time . . . He had a farm out close to where we lived and people lived on his farm, friends of mine. When my mother passed, I said, "Well, doctor, if I would have had more time, maybe we could have saved her." And he said, "Myrtle, I want to tell you something." He said, "I had stood by the bedside of people that there was no unearthly reason why they should go, but they did. I've seen other people who were literally pulled out of the grave and they lived on." So he said, "You can't tell." He said, "We're put here for a purpose. When our purpose is served, we're taken." So I often think of that and I wonder what purpose a person who sits around like this can be anyway. I think about it all the time. Maybe the Lord knows what it is. So that's what I know to tell you.

Destiny and luck reemerge as we talk about the meaning of home. Furniture evokes home, as do the rhythms of being around a household

and one's "things," as Johnson calls her personal possessions. The Westside existence that is a puzzle because it seems pointless is underscored
by the absence of these concrete reminders of a purpose in life. Describing her furniture as old-fashioned, she nonetheless cherishes it because
of its linkage with a meaningful existence and its related bearing on her
identity. Westside is not so much a home in this respect as a place to
receive care, a place she claims is entirely separate from her life, seemingly adding to the quandary.

Jay: Now that you've been here for a year, do you feel it is home?
Myrtle: No! This will never be home to me. Nothing like this will ever be a
home to me. To me it's a place where I get care and I have to stay. In
that regard, it's fine.
Jay: What would it have to be like to be more like home?
Myrtle: Well, I just don't know what it would have to be like. I guess if I had
my things, my furniture and stuff, around me. That would be more
like home. Then if I could get up and get around, do things, it would
be more like home. You know my furniture? You see, I had it from
the time I was married. It was old, but I loved it. Before I had to
come here, I lived in my son's house, next door to him. And he has
just been cleaning out that house, taking the furniture out of it now.
But I lived with that furniture all these years. It was old, but it was
dear to me. There wasn't any of it modern.
Jay: Why was it dear to you, Mrs. Johnson?
Myrtle: Well, because I lived with it all that time. It just became a part of me,
you know. I never was into fancy things. I'm just a common, ordi-
nary person. I never . . . I wasn't like a lot of people, you know.
When they were young, a lot of girls dressed so fancy and they
worried about being in style, but that never worried me. People
began to use face . . . makeup, you know, when I was young. Boy, I
never did that, but it was quite a thing at that time. But it never
appealed to me. [Jokes about being made up]
Jay: That's funny. [We both laugh] And what about this place? You were
talking before about your furniture and all and that it couldn't really
feel like home. Do you feel that this place is part of your life or
separate from it?
Myrtle: Oh, it's separate. I don't feel that I'm part of this place at all. My life
is entirely separate from this. I look on this as just a place where I've
been unlucky enough to have to come. It's just like going into a
doctor's office or anything else, you know. I don't feel that I'm a part
of it or anything.
Jay: Why is that, I wonder?
Myrtle: Well, I don't know. I'm just that way. I just . . . it's just not my way
of living and I just . . . I don't know why. I guess I'm peculiar.

Johnson is reminded of her upbringing and compares that with what
children and young people are like nowadays. She contrasts her child-

hood, adulthood, and family relations, among other social indicators of a different period and place—her time and place. Her past gave meaning to life, when in her "common and ordinary" way she understood the purpose of existence. As we again take up the present, Johnson returns to a predominant narrative linkage: the perplexity of "coming to this." As she speaks clearly and unemotionally of the present, she suggests that just continuing to live as she does is a burden.

> I'm a bump on a log. I'm absolutely useless. I'm just sitting here, a menace, just, you might say, worthless. Just sitting here and I have to be cared for. I'm not able to contribute to anything. [Groans from the ache in her legs]
> I hope I don't live the rest of the year out because there's no point in it. There would just be more worry and more trouble on my son and his wife. They never miss [visiting her]. They're just as faithful . . . they come every week no matter how busy they are. If I need them, I can call them and they'll come more often. But things like that are a burden to other people. They have to look after me. Of course, many people are left with their folks never bothering about them. But that's one thing, our family has always been close, what little there is of it. We've always been close.

Elaborating on the meaning of her felt burden to others, she asks rhetorically that no one feel sorrow for her. By and large, she's fine now as far as daily needs and cares are concerned. She is reluctant to bother anyone about such matters, least of all her son and daughter-in-law. If there is sorrow in her life, it soberly relates to the unfulfilled larger project of there being a point to it all. In the following extract, Johnson notes that as concretely minor a matter as getting around in a walker to tend a garden might seem, it can signal purpose and meaning.

> Life don't mean anything now. There's nothing to look forward to. All you've got is your memories to look back on. But as long as you are able to get around and do things, life means you can always find something to do worthwhile, if you want to, if you're able. But when you're not able, of course, it means very little to me.
> Like having to be here. Well, if I was able to get up and around, I'd be in my own home and doing things, you know. After I got so I had to use my walker, why I still got out and around and raised a garden. I could use that walker and put it where I can get a hold of it, you know. And I always was active. But when I fell over backwards, I broke so many bones and, finally, I just had to give it up.
> [When you were able to be up and around], you felt like you were still a human being, you see. But when you're like this, you know that you're . . . it's impossible for you to do anything for anybody. You're just trouble, that's all. You know you are. But when you're at home and able to do for yourself, why there's always . . . that's a different feeling. That makes you feel good.
> It's not being able to get up and do things. I realize I have to get old. I know that. But to me, just sitting down and seeing this or that you'd like to

do and you can't do anything, you know how that is. [Elaborates] This thing about being waited on, I don't like that. I can't say that I dislike it. I just put up with it. That's all I can do.

I don't have any future. I'm just here till the Lord calls me home. I think about it for other people. I think for my son. I often wonder what the future holds for him. I think about that a lot.

ALICE STERN

Alice Stern's narrative has the marks of the lifelong curmudgeon. She not only doesn't understand how it's come to this, but wryly jokes about it and speaks her mind of it as a bane on her existence. As it does for Myrtle Johnson, the existential context of Stern's rootless living preoccupies and puzzles her. This is about the quality of an abandoned and "drifting" life, not the quality of her care.

Stern is an eighty-year-old white widowed female who lives at the Greenfield Nursing Home. She was a heavy smoker and now suffers from emphysema. She can't "hold her water" and, like Myrtle Johnson, falls easily. Before moving into Greenfield, Stern lived in another nursing facility for a few weeks, and prior to that in a board-and-care home for women for a number of years.

Stern is interviewed three times over the course of a year. In the first interview, following her admission to Greenfield, she sounds like the newcomer who nonetheless has lived in congregate care for some time. The second interview, six months later, finds her a bit more settled but still in a quandary over the fate of life. By the third interview, Stern has noticeably declined. She is confused and has difficulty focusing on what is being discussed. But her existential puzzlement holds.

The First Interview

Stern's past centers on three marriages. Early in the interview, she dwells on the death of her first husband from a freak mechanical accident. She speaks of it with some sorrow, but is quick to add that there were two other marriages following that one.

> I married when I was seventeen and my husband had two children, a boy and a girl. He was working on a car and I don't know what year. The car exploded and killed him. [Elaborates] He died during the night. That was very sad. So I married a school friend, I mean a young person we had known. I married him and it didn't last long, for four or five years, and from then on I was just alone. But, the second one, he walked out. He didn't want to be married any longer and he just walked out. [Laughs] So that was the end of that. And I just wandered on. I had a family, my mother and

father. I lived with them in Maryland, just outside DC, you know. I just
went back home in other words and I worked a little bit as a waitress for
some. I never had any real experience. So I dabbled in waitress work here
and there. Then I married Stern, Frank Stern, and we got along fine until
one morning he was dead. He just up and died during the night sometime.

Continuing her story, Stern half-jokingly "wanders" and "drifts"
through life. In time, the words signal a concern for how it's come to
this, in particular how it is that her only living child, a soon-to-be-
remarried daughter, could have thrown her mother out and placed her
in a nursing home. It is all wrong somehow, especially as it seems to
have been prompted by her daughter's forthcoming marriage to a man
who, like the daughter, doesn't want anyone "tied around their neck."
Yet Stern acknowledges the daughter's concern for her mother's well-
being and, in that respect, feels that the daughter is good to her. It is the
life situation her daughter has forced upon her that puzzles Stern, especially as it suggests filial irresponsibility and the resulting loss of a familial anchor.

I lived with my daughter for a while when she decided, well . . . [snidely]
she met this gentleman who was going to marry again. She decided I guess
there wasn't room for Mother. So from then on I got thrown out, lived here
and there, in homes like this, you know, drifted and wandered around. She
just felt, I guess, felt like with a new husband, they didn't want something
tied around their neck. In other words, she wanted me to move. So that's
what happened and I don't think it's right.

I have been in these, one or two of these homes and I am satisfied with
that. I mean most of the ones that's here is in the same boat as I am. So I
can't say too much wrong with it.

That other place [previous nursing home], I didn't live there very long.
When I was there, a woman in a bed next to mine, she had some kind of
hysterical fit. She screamed and my daughter said, "I don't think you're
going to like it here." I would have been in the bed next to this lady that was
throwing the fit. Something happened that day and they moved her out or
something. I was there for a while, but my daughter still didn't feel like I
should stay there. So she got this place for me and she said, "Mom, I am
going to move you over to another place that is better." So this is the place
I've been in. She takes care of things for me like that. So that's good.

But, like I said, I've been driftin'. You wonder how this could happen. You
really do.

Stern recalls the board-and-care home, "Miss Beulah's" it was called,
but returns to the enigma of abandonment.

I did live at this other place called Miss Beulah's. That was the lady's [own-
er's] name. She was a little bit like a mean schoolteacher. She had her rules

and if you stepped your toe over the rules, you were in trouble. It was a home that took in elderly women and I didn't get along . . . my big mouth. These poor old women she had, I think they were dying up there. She had them and they were scared to death of her. I talked back to her and she didn't like that at all. If I saw something that I didn't think was exactly right, I would say something about it, like I always done. I had never been in a place like that, where I had to bow down and hold my mouth shut. So it didn't work out too good there. I just felt like I had as much right as anybody else to talk. I did not get along too good there. The other poor women, they just backed around like they was scared to death of her. I didn't get along too good.

My daughter eventually found this place. She thought I would like it. There wasn't quite as many here or something. She was pretty good to kind of look around for me. [Laughs] I am like a drifting leaf or something. I don't know where the next place will be. But I am satisfied here as far as that goes.

I can't say it's a happy life. Been abandoned, you might say. I have always been in with the family, but now I get the feeling that they do not want to be bothered—excess baggage or something. I don't want to push myself in on them. So they feel like they don't need any extra and I just stay away from them and I am satisfied here. I have no reason not to be, but it is not a home atmosphere at all.

My daughter tells me, "Mama, get out and walk around the yard." Well, I don't feel like it. My legs are not in that good a shape. I had trouble with my legs before I got here, sorta like rheumatism or something. My daughter cannot understand. She says, "Get out and walk around." When I was at another place here, I would go and sit on the porch and I could see the street and the traffic going by. But here I haven't even looked for what the porch looks like. I am satisfied here. I have a TV and I figure, well, I will do that. It is not that I am not satisfied. It's just not much else. It's more or less an old ladies home here for ones that don't have a family and I have to go along with that, you know, like wander on. But I do have a family. I just don't know.

Thinking back on her life, Stern talks about her two sisters, one now dead. The past is linked with the present as she tells of feeling mixed up by a world that's lost its meaning, which for Stern is tied to a life with family. Unable to explain her fate, she wonders why she's being punished.

Now I have one sister left. There was only three girls and this one that's still living is awful good to me. If she thought I needed a dollar or something, she would have it in the mail to me. She is working, making pretty good. She told me that if I needed anything, to let her know. The one I was living with, she passed away. It is a mixed up . . . a mixed up life, you might say. I wonder sometimes why I am being punished. It seems like the good Lord is punishing me for something. Why? I don't know.

I ask Stern how she explains what has happened to her and she continues to be perplexed. She feels she has been shortchanged on what she thought she had bargained for—fair and honest living—conveying to her the incredible injustice of fate.

> I can't explain it. I really can't. Because I honestly . . . I am no angel, but I honestly don't know of a trick or a bad deal that I have ever done to anybody. It would be on my conscience. I couldn't sleep at night if I had done somebody a dirty trick like turning me in for something they had done or done anything against. I couldn't sleep at night. It would keep me awake. I don't know. I can't understand it . . . why I been cheated like this.

This conjures up a litany of enigmas: her feeling of being unwanted, her overly long life, and the untimely death of her younger sister. The death is especially puzzling to her, reflecting what many residents say in this connection, that time of death should accord with birth order.

> I'll tell you, life looks pretty empty. I feel really unwanted. I am trying to overcome that now. For some reason, the good Lord leaves me here. I have almost died from my breath. I have an awful lot of emphysema. I guess a lot of it is from smoking. It almost seems like I have died a couple of times, but I am still left here for some reason. I don't know why, at this age. It is strange, they say, if you are left. I don't know why the younger sister passed. I'm the older one. It would have been better for me to go and for her to stay. It seems like she enjoyed life more than me anyway.
>
> She [the younger sister] liked to go away, liked to visit. She always took a chance. I asked her not too long before she died, "Were you ever up in an airplane?" and she said, "Yes." Me, I'm too chicken. You can't get me in an airplane, but her . . . she is a rascal. She took a plane trip back to see her son, by herself. She went out and got on the plane. I wouldn't do that for nothing. I am chicken all the way. But she tickled me. She passed away. Lord, that was a big surprise when she passed away. Wasn't right.

As Stern shares feelings about the unfairness of a life that's come to this, I ask her what she might have done differently if she could have lived her life over again. She remarks:

> I can't imagine what I would do. I have never thought of it that way. I really don't know. I don't know how I could live it different because I got along. I have lost three men and I am still here. My children's daddy was working on a car and it exploded on him. I had told him, "Take that car to the garage." He was putting his hand over the carburetor, making the suction, and it exploded on him. He died that night from the burns. He inhaled the smoke, he said. I really don't know why I am left. What good am I? A shell. An old empty shell sitting around. Just can't explain it.

Stern's sense of fate's just and unjust doings is communicated in the prayers she recalls saying as a child. The prayer reflects the precariousness of parental lives in her generation's childhood.

I come from a big family. When my mother and daddy lived, my prayer instead of "Now I lay me down to sleep" was "Dear Lord, spare Mother and Daddy till we are grown." There was lots of dying then. The thought of a bunch of children being left . . . five, six, seven, whatever . . . to me, that was a horrible thing. That was the worst thing that could happen to anyone. So that was my prayer, that the good Lord spare them until we got grown. And He did. We were all grown, married, and more or less had our own homes when they passed away. That part was alright. I mean it wasn't alright. We hated to give them up. I mean we did have our roost kind of set in. We had homes, most of us were married, and more or less settled. [Laughs] Of course, it was nice to run home if you had a little argument or something. [Laughs]

At the end of the interview, we have a lengthy conversation about aging, illness, and death, which is again punctuated by the puzzlement evident from the start, particularly the question of why she had to leave her daughter's home.

Jay: How would you say you feel about growing old?
Alice: Well, I tell you, I don't feel good about it. If I had something more to hold onto or a little bit of a steadier place. It is just that I am kind of drifting. Will it get worse or better? And why this? How'd it come to this?
Jay: Will that get worse or better, Mrs. Stern?
Alice: My living? Will I have a harder time to find a place that I enjoy or like? I don't know. It seems to be that it is a kind of worry to me. Like if I have to leave here, what's going to be the next place? I am kind of hurt at my family. I don't mean to be bragging about myself and my dispo-sition or anything, but it seems like I never butted in. In fact, I don't know why my daughter wanted me out. I was there, I had a room there, and I kept my own room. I didn't cause her any extra work and I helped if she was going out or if she was going to be out. [Scoffs] And all because this man come along that she met at this singles dance.
Jay: At the singles dance?
Alice: Yes and she is going with him, steady. I out and said to him, "Why did you put me out? I wasn't going to interfere with you and her." He just nodded. He didn't want to say nothing back. He was afraid I guess I'd say more. But I never did find out anything. I don't know.
          Now if my health breaks, what's going to happen to me? You know, if I was bedridden? Who knows what's gonna happen. No, I really don't know. My future's as blank as a side of a wall. I really don't . . . I can't picture anything. I really cannot. It's kind of a worry. Where do you go from here? I tell you, the government, I think, is paying for this. That is kind of a relief if it is. I hope it is. I am on Medicare and this last one, Medicaid, that's sort of like the medicine that wherever you live is taken care of. So that's good if it's true. And the daughter's

taking care of this. I mean she got the place and brought me over here and all. I guess if there is any paying to be done, she would tell me about it. But anyway, she is kind of taking care of that, till I die I guess.

Jay: Do you think about death, Mrs. S?

Alice: Yes, I do. I would like to die in my sleep. I think most everybody would. There is many a night when I lay my head on the pillow and say, "Oh, if I could just die tonight, never waking up." I don't know what is ahead of me, but I mean I feel that way.

Jay: Why is that, I wonder?

Alice: Well, I don't have nothing to hold to. I am like . . . I am just drifting, you know, hoping it turns out all right. That isn't any way to live. It isn't fair, you know. It's a kind of shaky setup. How did I get into all this? [Pause] You have to have something to look forward to, some kind of a future to hold onto or something. I don't have nothing . . . [jokingly] an extra change of clothes is about all and they ain't too good.

I don't know. I have to depend on my daughter I guess and she'd rather go to a garage sale than stop by and see her mother. She knows what a dull existence I have here.

Jay: Dull?

Alice: Dull! *Dull* is what I said. I don't expect them to entertain me or anything, but it is just kind of dull. I don't know. It seems to me that if my daughter was in a place like this, that I would drop by or call her or keep in touch with her more. I would want her to know that I know that she is there and if I could do anything. Families just do like that.

Stern is both appreciative and jokingly critical of Greenfield's quality of care, which she extends to institutions in general.

Still, this place is holding me together and it don't seem too bad. I mean I am as well off as these others and they aren't complaining. In fact, I might be a little better off because they don't seem to have much more company than I do or as much.

[Points to her roommate's bed] And that one there, she is not one of these that mixes. She's colored but that doesn't make a difference to me. I mean I am just the same with that. But her family comes and on weeknights they keep me awake for that matter. But I don't say anything about it. I only have one good ear, so I can lay on my good ear and go on to sleep if I want to. Anyway, her company don't bother me except they block the bathroom. I hate to ask them to move. About two of them will be sitting there by the [bathroom] door. If I want to go to the bathroom before I go to bed, I have to move around two of them. They should know that they don't have to be right up against there. [Elaborates]

They [the nurses' aides] know I can be as nice as I am going to be and I can be the other way too. This one comes in here in the middle of the night and turns the light on and asks, "Let me see. Do you want anything?" She is supposed to be looking after you. [Scoffingly] So she comes in and wakes you up! Like the son-in-law once said about the hospital (he was in the army), he says that they come in and wake him up from his sleep to give him a sleeping pill! [Laughs] He would fuss to my daughter. [Elaborates] Bless his heart, he is gone now. I swear there are a lot of things like that. You can laugh about some of them. You can get mad about some of them. This one come in and woke me up and I said, "Can't you find something else to do in the middle of the night?" I don't think that she has bothered me since then.

I can be grouchy or be the other way. I am a little bit like that. If I get wide awake in the middle of the night, it is a little bit hard to get back to sleep and I don't appreciate it. I told one [aide], "Can't you find something else to do instead of waking me up?" I was fussing and she said, "Oh, I didn't know you were like that." But I didn't want the argument to go on. I felt like saying, "Well, you know it now! Remember!" I didn't say it.

Six Months Later

Six months later, Stern has had a birthday and is eighty-one years old. Her health and mental status remain just about what they were before. This time she is interviewed by Carol Ronai.

Stern again recalls her life, having married three husbands, all of whom died. She jokes about sounding, in her own words, "like I'm killing them off." She continues to mull over how it's come to this. When Ronai asks about the last chapter of her life story, Stern admits to thinking about suicide because no one wants her. Stern feels that her whole family is avoiding her, especially the daughter.

I think there's been times in the past year that I've thought of suicide. It seems the whole family is afraid that I'll want to come and live with them. They just don't know what to do. They're ducking me like I was a plague. And I know I don't butt into their business. My daughter, she couldn't be sweeter now for anything however she tried. But she absolutely asked me to leave. She said she . . . this man come into her life . . . and she decided, you know, that she likes him. Gonna get serious. I don't know what they're waiting for to get married. Don't look like he got much intention. [Laughs] Maybe she's afraid he'll fall for me and I'll steal him away!

But, anyway, before he comes into the picture, she told me . . . at first she said, "Well, Mom, you can live here. I've got a three-bedroom house." It was just her. Her husband was passed away and I thought that, well, this is home, you know. Then out of the clear blue sky, "Mom, you'll have to move." And that was because he was coming in. Well, I wasn't going to bother with him and her. I don't know why. She just wanted me out. She didn't give me too much of a notice. I said, "Can't we wait till next week?" She said, "No, I want you to go tonight 'cause I'll change my mind if we wait."

So now she's doing everything, seems like. Comes by almost everyday and brings me something. It seems to me like she's thought it over and she

. . . but she's never asked me to come back or anything. I don't think I'd go if she did. But she seems to be very attentive, you know, giving me attention, bringing me something. She's bringing me things to eat—strawberries were the last—and she brings me all kinds of little things: Mickey Mouse and the little doll and the little dogs. She knows I like things like that sitting around. I never got over my childhood, I guess. I think they're so cute but . . .

I don't know. Ask me more questions, baby. I done run out of wind.

Ronai continues and they talk about Stern's past. Ronai asks her whether Greenfield could be home, to which Stern responds no. Stern nonetheless comments on Greenfield's good care compared to other places she's known, the point at which we return to the interview.

I tell ya, I seem kinda different. I talk too much or something. But people seem to like me and I think they're glad to have me here. I don't know, it seems like I've gone and spruced up the ones that wasn't talking and I seem to be well known. I guess when I first came in here, they said, "Have you met so-and-so, Alice?" It seems like, you know, they welcome me. I don't know what more you could do.

But I tell you what I like about it. In this other place—Miss Beulah's—she was kinda strict. If she snapped her fingers, she wanted you to jump, you know. She wanted her rules right to do. Like she wanted you in the bedroom at eight o'clock and she didn't want you back out. And the other place was a bit like that, too. Here, it's a little looser. I do notice the colored girls come in here. There, they were supposed to come in before you went to sleep, you know, and see if everything was all right. Never once came in. Here, a lot of the colored girls come in and ask, "Did you want anything before you go to sleep?" or something like that. That's okay, but not in the middle of the night. So I think that's pretty good. I'm satisfied here, as far as that goes. Can't say much against it.

They talk about Stern's placement at Greenfield, something that Stern again mentions she cannot understand. The quality of Stern's life is informed by linkages to the meaning of family, not by the particular cares of the nursing home. It isn't so much what Stern imagined the quality of care in a nursing home would be before she entered one that gives Stern "chills," as it is the puzzle of how it could have come to this.

Carol: Let me ask you this, Mrs. S. Before you went into a nursing home, what did you think it would be like?

Alice: Well, the thoughts of it would just give me chills, that this could happen.

Carol: What kinds of thoughts did you have about it?

Alice: I felt like it was strangers. The idea of that made me shiver. I felt like they'd look at you like, you know, "Who is that coming in?" I just didn't want to go. It broke my heart. To think my own family, you know, some of my own—my sister and my daughter—would let me go to face strangers. I remember my daughter after she told me I had to go. She had arranged all this, too. She had arranged . . . her and her daughter . . . what time to pick me up. Her daughter was there, my granddaughter, and my granddaughter kept saying, "Grandma, I told her I'd be there by eight." They had done set it all up. They hadn't talked to me at all. I asked Susan [her daughter] when she was standing there . . . I had a plastic bag of clothes or something, a satchel, maybe a suitcase, and I said, "Susan, couldn't we talk this over next week?" "No, no. I want you to go tonight," she said. And my granddaughter spoke up and said, "Grandma, we better go. I told her I'd have you there by eight o'clock." And I thought, "Well, they've already set it up." That kind of hurt.

Carol: I see what you mean.

Alice: It hurt, 'cause I said . . . I said I would have never sent *my* mother out. I would have got down on my knees and scrubbed floors if I had to, to make a dollar and keep her. I wouldn't never tell her to get out. So that's the difference.

But now Susan just seems like she can't, like she can't do enough for me. I think it's kind of coming back at her, how she didn't . . . And I hope her conscience hurts her a little bit. [Laughs] I got to be nasty, dear Lord.

But I trust in the Lord, I'd say. I'm not too religious. Some of them, I think, take it too far. But I believe I know there is a God in heaven. There's got to be. Things are too unnatural to not be a God in heaven. Oh, I don't know. I can't express myself like if I could.

The conversation returns to Stern's early life. Describing what she was like as a girl, Stern contrasts that with the present, laughs about it, and even remembers the first interview. She half-jokingly recalls her youthful love of clothes as the most important thing in her life at the time. But the persistent quandary of life is paramount.

I was just sorta like a country girl. I never dressed fancy or anything. And I was never fresh around the dances, you know. I didn't go to a dance unless it was more or less a church outing or something. I never run around to dances along the way. I was quiet, I think.

Now I'm just a plain country woman growing old. That's all I know. [Laughs] One man sit in here and asked me questions about me getting old and we got to talkin'. We laughed and cut up. [Jokingly] He said, "Well, how do you feel about your men?" I said, "Well, I ain't chasing no man, or looking for one either." [Laughs] And things like that, you know. But there was some of the same type of questions.

But, I tell ya, it used to be clothes. [Chuckles] I used to love clothes. And now I don't seem to care about anything. Clothes don't matter. That's nothing to me now.

I tell ya, it just looks like, for me, it looks like a struggle. I absolutely . . . I always was a person that liked to know what's coming tomorrow. Ahead, you know. I don't know. Many a night, I laid in my bed and I think what . . . what'll happen to me? I'd rather have, you know, know a little about it. I sure don't. I can't figure what all's happened to my life. That there is the thing.

The Third Interview

A year after the first interview, Stern's recollections are lengthy and detailed, but it is difficult for her to sort her thoughts and express them coherently. She laments her memory loss. She is now on oxygen. The sound of the pump and being "hooked up" crimp the style of an ebullient woman. Yet her curmudgeonly self comes through, as does the narrative puzzle of her life.

Mainly, life's dull, just dull. I just sit there and think and wonder how it all come to this. It's kinda quiet and she [roommate] generally goes back and then I come back over here . . . unless I'm looking for company or something. [Pause] I'm tryin' to remember . . . I come over here and lay down and I may go off to sleep. If I slept a little, in the evening I wouldn't be sleepy. So I might get a dress out or something and, uh, sew a little seam up the side or something like that, or something else. [Labored breathing] Oh, this thing! [The pump] And if there's anything on that TV . . . now there was one program I missed, doggone it, that I especially wanted to watch. I done forgot what it is. If I look back over the program, I'd remember. But I forgot it. What I have to do is write it down. [Chuckles] I got my pad here.

I don't mind it too bad now. They're good to us. But I still don't know what's coming next. [Turns to look at dozing roommate] That poor soul don't do a thing, but she's there and I've got to think about her every time I do anything. I think she's in ga ga land. To tell you the truth, sometimes I don't know myself if I'm still here. You know what I mean? How'd this happen to me? Bein' in this place and all. God only knows.

* * * * *

Myrtle Johnson and Alice Stern both have complaints about daily life in their nursing homes, from the dissatisfaction of "just sittin'" to the thoughtlessness of aides who barge into the room in the middle of the night. The women nonetheless appreciate the fact that they are being cared for. Still, to them, these are matters separate and distinct from the overall meaning of life, which is an enduring issue. It is this larger horizon—the question of why "it's come to this"—that preoccupies them and provides the primary narrative linkages for the quality of their lives. In Johnson's case, it relates to her love of God and in Stern's it bears on her relation to loved ones. As with other similar residents, puzzled as the women are by fate and the overall meaning of life, the quality of their care is a comparatively minor concern.

CHAPTER

5

Lovin' the Lord

Horizons of meaning for residents arise from many directions, not the least of which is otherworldly. Whatever the features or qualities of earthly life, they can take on meaning in connection with the life beyond, where as one resident who loves her Lord put it, "They ain't no rushin' and no pushin', just bein'."

According to these residents, longings for the earthly past, wants for the present, and wishes for the future are small favors to relinquish in comparison with what the life beyond will bring. While the cleanliness of one's premises is important, what does it matter that a bed is temporarily soiled when one is confident that "God will provide"? If a nurse's aide has a bad attitude or a roommate incessantly complains about her family, does either have much significance compared with heavenly bliss? Can the pain of bodily ills and the heartaches of personal loss be as important as God's bounty?

The stark contrasts in such questions tell of residents who live in this world but orient to another one. Certainly, in relation to matters of this world, cleanliness, kindness, and daily life satisfaction in the nursing home are desirable. But their place in this world is temporary and hardly matters in the final analysis. In relation to what is said to be important in the end, the negative qualities of care are just irritations, the positive qualities mere comforts. At stake in the end is something grander than daily living, the source of everlasting life—God's kingdom. For these residents, this is the ultimate context for speaking of life, a horizon that makes all matters meaningful, great and small.

To love or serve the Lord is not to ignore the ills and discomforts of daily life, only to think about them as less important in a larger scheme of things. For these residents, their roles in life are, while in this world, shaped by and for the beyond. Those who love the Lord hold to a different world and in that context speak and evaluate life and its immediate conditions.

The interviews conducted with such residents could be boldly framed by otherworldly concerns. At times, no matter how insistently I probed

69

for views of the quality of care, responses were linked with otherworldly meanings, the residents insisting on the relevance of another reality. At these times, residents mainly spoke past my inquiries, with life everlasting or "churchified" being the preferred narrative context.

JULIA McCALL

The first of the two residents discussed in this chapter, Julia McCall, brought me into her narrative more than any other respondent in the study. She not only highlighted her life "working for the Lord," but engaged me in affirming it, taking for granted that I too worked for Him. Time and again, McCall turned responses into questions, rhetorically asking me whether I didn't think or feel the same way, and following that, blessing me for what I said. McCall also was the resident who had lived the longest in her nursing home, being at Westside Care Center for twelve years.

McCall is a ninety-year-old widowed white woman who has gone completely blind in the last few years and suffers from congestive heart failure. No longer able to read the Bible, she is an avid radio listener, spending hours tuned into religious talk shows or services. When I met her, she was holding a radio to her ear, engrossed in the word of God. As we settled down to talking, a long-standing involvement in church life came forth.

Jay:	Ms. McCall? Why don't you tell me a little about your life?
Julia:	About my life?
Jay:	Yeah. Tell me about it.
Julia:	Well, you done asked, bless your heart. I was raised in a little place in Georgia called Damen and my granddaddy, my mother's daddy, was from England. Well, them days my granddaddy, he did get killed in a war. He was only twenty-eight years old and he was buried there, I believe in the Arlington Cemetery. My other granddaddy, his name was Joe O'Donald and he owned half of Georgia. He sure did. He had a gold mine. [Elaborates] I bet you heard of that, ain't you? It's close to Clinton, Georgia, and he had a cotton gin. [Elaborates] It took somebody pretty rich to have a cotton gin, didn't it?
Jay:	Um hm.
Julia:	When he first got his cotton gin, he was 49 and he was in Clinton. I had a pretty good life. My granddaddy liked me. I went to school and lived in a house. He gave my mother a home close to the school. [Elaborates] There's a Methodist, a Baptist church there . . . Clinton Baptist Church. Have you heard of it?
Jay:	No, I haven't.

Julia: The school was named Clinton High School in Clinton and I went to school with the preacher Taylor. Gus Taylor was the teacher. He preached at the Baptist church and I went to church there. I was a member of the church there. I was christened when I was a baby. I joined that there church when I was twenty-three. I went to school and that was the only place I went to school. He taught school. [Elaborates] I graduated from high school at fourteen. That was . . . wouldn't you say that was kind of smart?

Jay: That was.

Julia: And I went to singing school in Clinton at the church and I could sing and took music. I could sing ballads. Don't you think that was kind of smart too?

Jay: That certainly was, I'd say.

Julia: Bless your heart. Well, I got married kind of young. I was just sixteen. My husband was a good bit older than me and we lived on a farm. My granddaddy give us the farm, about fifty acres of land and we lived there. But some people got back from that war and couldn't do much of anything after that war.

Jay: This is which war, Ms. McCall?

Julia: President Wilson was president. My brother was in that war. Oh . . . that's right . . . I had three sisters and one brother. They're all dead, been dead a long time. I just kind of lasted.

Jay: You sure did.

Julia: You know I guess it's because I actually had a pretty good life. [Pause] I don't act like I'm grouchy, do I?

Jay: No.

Julia: Bless your heart. I think I've had a pretty good life. I think the Lord's been good to me. I been in church all my life. [Elaborates] I've been in this place for twelve years. That's a long time. I was seventy-nine when I come in here. I didn't think I'd live to see ninety. I've been in pretty good health too. I've just about had every sickness, but I was tough. I got over it, ya know. I've had a lot of pains and sicknesses, but I was pretty tough. I'm still livin', ain't I? The Lord provides, bless Him.

I was raised to be a nice person. I was raised to go to church. Don't you think that's right? Huh?

Jay: Yes, I do.

Julia: I was raised to go to church. Sure was. And I went all the time. Yesterday was Sunday, wasn't it?

Jay: Yes.

Julia: I got my radio that I could get a preacher on. He's a Baptist at the First Baptist Church. Do you go to church?

Jay: I don't go to that one.

Julia: Are you a Baptist?

Jay: No, I'm not.

Julia: What are you?

Jay: I was Congregationalist once.
Julia: That's kind of like Catholic, ain't it?
Jay: Well, no, not exactly.
Julia: Well, you know, there ain't much difference in none of them. All working for the Lord, ain't ya?

This last statement—"All working for the Lord, ain't ya?"—highlights the subjective meaning flowing through McCall's narrative. As she returns to her childhood growing up in rural Georgia, she reminds me that, regardless of the religious differences in town, all were working for the Lord. When she describes the many people, good and bad, she has met over the years, she downplays the differences because, in the end, all are God's children and work for the Lord. As she repeatedly draws me into her story, asking me about my life, family, and beliefs, differences once more are erased because we both are working for the Lord.

In the context of working for the Lord, the troubles and troublemakers of life evaporate because they are mere veneers over what, to McCall, are actually good intentions and "sweet" people. For example, while the quality of her care at Westside at times leaves something to be desired, McCall says that she knows in her heart that she's well cared for, especially as the Lord keeps watch over her. The horizon of lovin' the Lord makes everyone her friend—staff, those residents she knows well, and those she doesn't. All are equally valuable in the sight of God, as McCall points out.

> You know, I got a lot of friends. A lot of friends in here I don't know, but I think I have. There's a lot of friends in this place. You see, I can't see. I can hear them mostly. I can tell who it is. I got a lot of people in here that, well, some's can be nasty, but they're still good people. I like my nurses. I like my nurses really good. If it weren't for them, I don't know what I'd do. They're my favorites. They sure are good to me. They're better to me than anybody, even better to me than even my children. But, really, they're all sweet, God bless 'em all. God loves all his children no matter.

As we talk about all her friends, McCall explains that she not only has "sweet" nurses but believes the nurses consider her a favorite resident, which leads to a story about Ann, a nurse who no longer works at Westside but still visits McCall and, according to McCall, will undoubtedly join McCall in heaven.

> I got some sweet nurses . . . I can't remember all of them, but I got about three nurses now. I got two that come at night and I think they're my favorites. I bet I'm their favorite patient. I think the way they act, they like me. If it weren't for them, I'd be, well . . . But I can dress myself. I can do a lot of things by myself.

I think I'm going to heaven from here. The Bible says that heaven's full, don't it? Well, I think He's got a place up there for me, don't you? [I nod]

I have a little friend. She was with me when I first come in here. I wasn't blind then. I done a lot of things, ya know. Her husband was a flyer and she learned to sew and she was doing a lot of things for me. She was working in here. Ann still comes to see me. She belongs to the Grandmothers' Club, kind of, you know. I went to the Grandmothers' Club a long time, as long as I could see. That was a long time, and then I went blind. Ann comes to see me.

So, as I was going to say, just before Christmas, she'd come and she'd sit in the room. Then I told her, I said, "Ann, the Bible says heaven's full up there." But I said, "I think God's got a place for me." I says, "He has," and I says, "I believe I'm going to be up there." And she says, "You know what?" I says, "What?" And she says, "I'm gonna be right up there with you." God bless her. She's got a mother living and a mother-in-law. The mother-in-law is in a nursing home. She's about the same age as me and Ann don't like her. I thought maybe people that Ann sees would be real sweet people, you know. She really likes me.

I ask McCall the question about living over again and doing things differently, which leads to a series of exchanges dotted with comments and questions about hell, heaven, believers, nonbelievers, and everlasting life.

Julia: I don't know. I think I would just live it. I don't think I've had too bad of a life. Do you think if people still hold on to God, do you think they're too bad a person?

Jay: No.

Julia: I don't feel like . . . I don't feel like I'm old. I don't want to go to hell, do you?

Jay: No.

Julia: I wouldn't want to live it over. It might be worse, don't you think so?

Jay: Well, it might be. I guess I never thought of it quite like that.

Julia: I have never had anything that I have really hated. I ain't never really hated nobody, have you? I don't hate people, do you? I'm sorry for them sometimes, aren't you? Like some's—some nurses and old ladies here—got bad attitudes. I'm sorry for them when they don't believe such a thing as God. Have you ever talked to people like that? I've talked to some of them once and I don't think they've got good sense. I don't think they've ever read the Bible. But they all God's children.

You know, as long as I could see, I've been going to church on Sunday. I went a lot since I've been here. I had Spanish people do church. They come in and we was having a little church.

Well, now, I don't have me anything much to look forward to here, but I told you about Ann coming to visit. But as I says, I'm looking to going to heaven and being up there. What are you looking forward to?

Jay: Oh, I don't know. I guess I'm not sure, really.

Julia:	Are you looking forward to going to heaven?
Jay:	I would think so.
Julia:	Bless your heart. I think that's the best thing we can do for us.

I try to turn the conversation to more mundane matters like daily life in the nursing home and McCall's view of the quality of care. She responds, but the matters seem to be the farthest things from her mind. Her remarks are made as if mundane affairs were fleeting concerns, which McCall attributes at one point to forgetfulness.

Jay:	Does it feel like home to you here?
Julia:	Sure, since I been in here. I have to sleep here. I don't get to go nowhere much anymore. I go all around here. Once in a while . . . I got one daughter . . . she's sick and goes to the hospital and she comes visit sometimes to take me down there [in the sunshine]. And I got the nurses take me down there in the sunshine and all. And we have a nice, sweet time.
Jay:	Ms. McCall, do you feel that this place is part of your life?
Julia:	Well, I sure do. I been in here a long time. I think this is one of the best nursing homes. I think over all the world, I don't think you'd find a better nursing home like this. Now what do you think about that? I think the Lord blessed me to be in here, don't you?
Jay:	Uh huh.
Julia:	Do you think this is a pretty nice nursing home? It's a big one. Did you know that the man that gave all this property is from Georgia? Did you know he was from Georgia?
Jay:	No, I didn't.
Julia:	He sure was. That's where I'm from, like I said. And like I said, they're very sweet to me. I'm going to heaven. Like Ann says, she's going to be up there with me. I think that's kind of sweet of her, don't you?
Jay:	Yes, I do.
Julia:	She's pretty, too. She's in her forties, like you. Didn't you say that's your age?
Jay:	Yes, I believe I did.
Julia:	She's got three children. In here I got a lot of other friends, too. God bless 'em. They're all God's children. [Pause] Sometimes I'm getting kind of forgetful, you know. But don't you think I do pretty good for my age?
Jay:	[Affectionately] Very good, Ms. McCall, very good.
Julia:	[Chiding me] Do you know somebody else that's better than me?
Jay:	Oh, I don't know. You're pretty good, I'd say.
Julia:	[Laughing] I know you're a sweet person. I know that. I'm gonna tell my daughters about you. I'm gonna tell 'em what a sweet person you is. Bless your heart.
	I try to be a nice person. I try to be a good Christian and I think . . . the Lord has been real sweet to me or I wouldn't feel that way. I have

had a lot of sad things happen to me, but I think the Lord . . . I think we got to look up to Him.

Jay: Tell me about the sad things, won't you?

Julia: Well, losing my husband and my only son and all that was sad. My mother and dad was pretty old when they died, but I think when you lose them when they're young, I think it's kind of . . . it's, you know, you don't ever get over missing them. I try not to be sad. I don't know. Some people just want to be sad. Some do in their beds. I don't like to see the sick people being so sad.

I look to heaven, to go to heaven and be up there with the Lord. The Bible says if we do right, we'll rejoice. Don't you think we'll be happy up there?

Jay: We probably will. [Pause] But what about this place? Tell me about life in this place. How is the care here?

Julia: Well, it's not too bad. There's some pretty nice people in here. I think some don't know much, but they can't help it. I think the nurses and doctors is the most smartest people there is, most of 'em anyhow. I got a sweet doctor. I've had him for over thirteen years.

I was real sick once, real sick. They had put a tube in my hand. I couldn't take it through my mouth. It was poison to take in my mouth. He sat by the bed and held my hand so I wouldn't take it out. I said, "Well, why don't you just let me die?" He said, "I ain't gonna let you die 'cause you're too sweet to die." He'd take care of me during the daytime and the nurse would take care of me at night. I told him I wasn't afraid to die. And he said, "I'm glad to hear that because I don't hardly ever hear it."

No, I'm not afraid to die because I'm going to the right place. I think I'm going to meet my Savior. I tell you, if we don't read the Bible . . . I was trained to read the Bible from the time I started to read. You know, I've read it three times and every time I've found something different. I sure have. I read it right through and I didn't know my name was in the Bible. Did you know my name was in the Bible?

Jay: Is that right?

Julia: Yeah. Julia. J-U-L-I-A. That's what my name is. I didn't know it was in there. I read it through three times. It's in the last chapter of Romans. If you'll look, you'll find it.

And so it went. As McCall recounted her past, it was a life serving the Lord. As she spoke of the present, I prompted her to detail what she felt to be good and bad about it. She returned repeatedly to everlasting life. Needless to say, the future was a time of life closest to her destiny, when she would be in heaven, as she reminded me again and again.

I was hardly a bystander in her narrative. According to McCall, I was to be right up there in heaven with her, as sweet a person as she re-marked I was. As she drew me into her narrative with questions of her own, her love of the Lord took control of the interview as much as it conferred a lesser status to the mundane matters of concern to me. The interview became a resource for her own project, which served to remind me that there was more at stake in life than the qualities of earthly living.

MARY CARTER

Mary Carter also loves the Lord. Her brand of love is to serve Him by going to church, cooking, and singing in the choir. From the start, hers is a life, if not actually spent in church, then lived in relation to church activities. Childhood centers on church affairs, adulthood embellishes the connection, and now old age affirms what she always has been, as she puts it, "churchified" through and through.

Carter is an eighty-five-year-old widowed African American woman. She suffers from pulmonary vascular disease, and hypertension, has ulcers on her legs, and is wheelchair-bound. Her husband died in 1962 and she never had children. Her closest relative is a nephew, who visits her regularly at Fairhaven, the nursing home where she lives.

Carter was one of the few respondents in the project to be interviewed four times. The first interview took place a few days after admission. She was discharged three months later and interviewed the second time in her apartment. Six months after the first interview found her returned to Fairhaven, where she was interviewed the third time. A fourth interview was completed in the nursing home a year after the first one.

Not all residents who come to reside in a nursing home, even long-stayers, stay there continuously for the rest of their lives. Some, like Carter, enter and depart several times before they stay put. While Carter's first interview was conducted a few days after admission, she had had a six-month stay at Fairhaven the year before. Carter was well acquainted with the nursing home when we first met.

The First Interview

Following introductions and some small talk, I began the first interview by asking Carter to tell me about her life. As Carter preferred, I called her "Miss Mary."

> *Jay:*   Miss Mary, why don't you tell me about your life.
> *Mary:*   Well, I have ulcers on both of my knees. I had an operation about four years ago on my leg and it formed kind of an infection on the heel. [Elaborates] So that's why I'm out here. They try to keep me off my feet most of all, you know, until I get strong, you know what I mean.
>   My life seems to be very happy. I had a good husband. He's dead now. Been dead since 1962. My life has been good.

When I was real young, startin' in '19 I was a cook. I cleaned house and all like that. I enjoyed it very much. I used to wash the clothes for the lady that I was working for in Jacksonville [Florida], and clean the house and take care of her mother. [Elaborates] Yeah, it was a pretty good life.

Jay: If you were to write the story of your life . . . you know put it into chapters . . . what would the first chapter be about?

Mary: Well, I'd have a chapter of religion. I love church. That's most of my chapter. I get up in the morning and lay down at night. The Lord is my shepherd. I shall not want. I lean on the Lord. For one thing, I thank Him for everything 'cause, I tell you, not many people don't live long as I live, I'm telling you. Eighty-five years old is hittin' toward a hundred.

Jay: What would the next chapter of your life be about, Miss Mary?

Mary: Well, I used to sing in the choir, too, at my church and then at Bethel out on Tenth Avenue. I enjoy singing and also, you know, so many different things. I enjoy it 'cause . . . when I get so I can get around, I'm going in the room [in the nursing home] where they have a church on Sunday. I love to sing. And the lady that plays the piano, she love to hear me sing. Sure does. And I sung the song one time, [singing] "Meet me at the river . . . " [sings several verses].

Jay: Oh, that's wonderful! You used to sing that often?

Mary: Yes, I'd sing that here, out in the wheelchair. Uh huh. They love to hear me sing.

I loved the choir in my church and I love the good singing and everything. I love my church. That's the reason why I say, when I get better, I'm gonna connect myself right back to the Main Street Baptist Church.

The goal of getting better leads her to talk about her eating habits, which then prompts her to recall her work as a cook and housekeeper. Mundane as these activities are, she thinks of them as service to the Lord. Carter's is not a life easily divided into otherworldly and earthly affairs. As she speaks of these and other activities, her religion is fully present. Even the matter of arranging her husband's funeral serves the Lord.

Mary: I'll tell you, since I had ulcers, they don't want me to pull too much grease. I mostly cook with butter when I'm home, cook with margarine and things like that. That grease is bad on ulcers, you know what I mean. I used to cook.

Jay: You were a cook?

Mary: I used to cook roast and baked pies and sweet potatoes and cook cracklin' cornbread and pearly rice. Oh, I just cooked a lot of things. I remember the lady that I worked for. She had about seven people coming and I had to fix something right there. I potted a big ol' roast.

Then I put it in the stove and let it bake. And honey, they went for that, honey, I'm telling you. And you'd make gravy, you know, stir a little mix in, you know what I mean. Oh yeah. She enjoyed the cooking. I served the Lord all my life.

I enjoyed all the parts of my life, when I was married and then, since I got single, I enjoyed myself very good. I don't seem to worry about nothing. I have a lot to be thankful for. If it wasn't for the Lord, I don't know what we'd do.

I used to cook for a doctor once out in Jacksonville and wash clothes and clean house and take care of two children and everything. I've had a right good life. That was a pretty happy time. They was good people to me. See, I didn't have to work but Monday through Friday. I didn't have to work Saturday and Sunday and that was beautiful. When I wanted to go to church, I could always go.

I always believe in doin' good by the Lord. When my husband passed, I did him right. We went to the funeral home . . . I wouldn't tell you no story [no lie] . . . Covington Brothers had his body. So we looked at the caskets and the first casket was $200. I said, "I don't want that." The next one was $300 and the next one was $400. I said, "I don't want that." But the $500 one, I got that. I done the best I could. I had my husband put away decent, doin' good by the Lord. And you know, people in church didn't know me and him were married?

Jay: They didn't?

Mary: No, we was separatin' for so long. They had the church decorated so beautiful. I was real happy. And I asked the preacher to please make it short 'cause I got a brother-in-law who has heart trouble. So he didn't preach no longer than forty-five minutes.

But I was closest to my daddy and my mama. They're about the closest. I mean, Jesus is ahead of that and then they behind. But I loved my husband. I tried to stay with him. I sure did.

All I have left is a nephew. He lives on Fourth Street. His name is Robert Brown. He's kind of sickly. He has bad asthma. He come in to see me every week.

We talk about daily life in the nursing home. She compliments the staff and especially the administrator, whom she calls "the manager," for the concern he shows for the residents. She describes at length how the staff serve the Lord in their own right, which, she repeats, she herself has done all her life.

I'm very happy because the manager sees us being taken care of. I'm telling you can tell that. He checks in on you, whether you had your meetin's in the morning and asks did we enjoy our food. We have plenty to eat. And then, when they serve dinner, he walks to the dining room and goes to the kitchen and sees if the people are fed good. I think that's good. And we have a nice colored man at night that helps these girls, the kind that do lifting. Last night, that girl got on her knees and he says, "No, no. I'll lift this side up." So I thought that was very nice. I really did. He say he is used to taking care of old people. They all be servin' Him right.

We all servin' the Lord, really. When I was up on my feet, I was stood there right in the choir. Sometimes when we had to raise money for tour . . . our choirs . . . I would buy vegetables and go down to the dining room and cook them and bake chicken and bake biscuits and all like that. I give service when I was a young woman, I'm telling you, from about twenty-five years old, I give good service. I sure did.

But I think it'll be a good life now. It's pretty good through all my sickness. What I like about all the nurses is that they are good to me, the white and the colored and all. They are really nice to me. They treat me so good. I have a lot to be thankful for.

In sharing thoughts about the nursing facility, the meaning of home for Carter takes a twist that it doesn't have for many others, tied as it is to her long residence in the local black community and especially her active participation in church. Even though Carter is newly admitted to Fairhaven at the time of the interview, her presence is a homecoming because several old church friends who now reside in the nursing home and the new friends she made when she was at Fairhaven the first time around welcome her back into their lives. Also welcoming her are kin who work in the facility as housekeepers. Returning to Fairhaven, Carter brings some of home with her into the facility. Still, at the end of the interview, after several residents and staff members "peep" in on her, a more enduring sense of home prevails—coming home to the Lord.

Mary: [After a brief interruption] You see how they peep in on me when . . . they be doing that all day.
Jay: Is that right?
Mary: Yes, Lord. Now they even . . . a lot of 'em know me, like I told you.
Jay: So coming back here is like . . .
Mary: That's right . . . like comin' home. Comin' home to the Lord. I like to be churchified. That's my life. That's chapter and verse.

In Her Apartment, Four Months Later

Four months after Carter's first interview at Fairhaven, she is back in her apartment, discharged from the nursing home one month earlier. Carol Ronai conducts this and the next two interviews. The second interview is adapted to reflect Carter's new circumstances and I focus here on Carter's comments about home, the nursing facility, aging, and death. Well into the interview, asked to compare living in the apartment, which is subsidized for the elderly, and living at Fairhaven, Carter remarks:

Well, I tell you, I'd rather be on this side. Out there's [Fairhaven] nice, but it is . . . you see, I got my things here. See all these here is mine. I've been here . . . pretty soon it'll be ten years. I come in here when it opened up. And the rents are not bad. It ain't but $112 a month. This is for senior citizens. They built a lot of these.

Mostly, I love church and I love music and that's my hobby. Most I like church cause sometimes I can even sing by myself. We had good church out there [Fairhaven] too.

When I was a little girl, my daddy built us a little kind of pulpit like a preacher, you know, preachin'? And we'd get out there in the playhouse, then we'd . . . the children would come up for preaching and when we'd get through preaching, why, we'd sing. We'd have out our little songbooks, you know, and my daddy said, "Look at my children." Mama . . . with long dresses she didn't care nothing about, put them on us like they was robes, you know. We had a good time, I'm telling you.

I won't recount the details of her life that Carter repeats in the second interview: The years cooking and working as a housekeeper, her marriage and long separation from her husband, her husband's funeral, her church activities. She emphasizes that she hadn't wished to remarry because, according to her, all the men left were dope addicts, noting in the process that dope traffic now makes her wary of the neighborhood. She worries for her nephew, who continues to visit her and who could get mugged anytime.

As Carter speaks of daily life, Ronai takes the opportunity to ask questions about life in general, causing Carter to recall fondly Christmas festivities at Fairhaven.

Carol: If you could live your life over, would you do anything differently?
Mary: Well, honey, I don't really believe I would. I'm very thankful and very fortunate because I know I can't live it over again. See, I'm getting older, honey. I'm not getting younger. You see, I already lived three scores in my life. I'm starting on the fourth score. I'm eighty-five and my nerves ain't bad and I have a lot to be thankful for and my speech ain't bad and I thank the Lord.
Carol: How do you explain what's happened over your life?
Mary: Well, I haven't had no bad life to live. My life is very pleasant and I learned to get along with people, like all of them people out there [Fairhaven]. We all be servin' the Lord.

We had . . . what you call a parade contest of the halls, you know, for Christmas. So Helen [social worker], out at the nursing home . . . she fixed us for her hall. She didn't fix us until, you know . . . Christmas come on, I think, a Monday. So we had a parade, you know, on Friday, on which one had the best hall. So that Friday, she come in there and asked me which dress did I want to wear. I told her I'd wear white. So I had me a new wig on and she cut some paste board and made some wings, you know, and then put that silver thinglike down there on it and tied that to the back of my chair, you know, where it comes down here.

Carol: So you had wings on the back of your chair?

Mary: Uh huh.

Carol: That's fun.

Mary: They called me the engine and then Helen, she put some little dolls on the side of my, you know, dress. Oh, she dressed me up real pretty. She didn't show off her group until they started, you know, the parade of halls. So when it got ready to go down there to see which had the best hall, they had three prizes. We won the first prize! Lord, it was funny to see me with them wings on the back of my chair and I had some gold earrings and they was showing up, you know. I was in the parade before I left to come home. It's like I was in the parade that Friday and next Monday I came home. Lord, that was fun.

At the end of the interview, Ronai and Carter talk briefly about aging, health, and death. Despite her bodily aches and pains, Carter finishes by relishing her Lord, appreciating what her apartment window reveals of His bounty.

Carol: How would you say you feel about growing old?

Mary: Well, I know I'm growing old, honey. I can tell it in my legs. I'm not as strong as I used to be.

Carol: Do you like anything about being your age?

Mary: Yes, I have to be thankful because the Lord gives life to me. He let me live all this many years.

Carol: Do you think about death at all?

Mary: I know I got to die, honey. So there's no use worrying about that. All I just want to be ready when the Lord calls me. 'Cause you know He don't notify you. It's something you got to be ready when He comes. You can't say, "Well, God, I ain't ready yet. I ain't." You can't do that. He give you all these many years to get ready.

I look out this window and look at the vision way over yonder and I say, "Lord, we got a good God. He's good to us. He give us the birds that sing and the trees for the wind and everything. He's good to us."

The Third Interview

Six months after Carter's first interview, she is interviewed a third time, once again at Fairhaven. She has given up the apartment where she lived for a decade, not able to keep up rent payments while in the nursing home. A relative is storing her furniture.

This interview, conducted by Carol Ronai, starts with a discussion of how Fairhaven compares with apartment living. Carter resists the idea that Fairhaven could be home. But as the discussion unfolds and particulars of daily life are considered, Fairhaven is cast in homelike terms and living there, as elsewhere, viewed as part of where her life ultimately "really be"—at home with the Lord.

Carol: You've been here now, off and on, for many months. How is it being here?

Mary: Oh, honey, it's nice. People are so nice to me.

Carol: That's good to hear. Do you like it out here?

Mary: Yes, I like it fine, but I like home the best.

Carol: Why do you like home the best?

Mary: Because that's where I live.

Carol: Uh huh. But could this place ever be home to you?

Mary: It'd be hard for it to be for me, to tell you the truth. I just like the old place . . . 'cause I been there nine, ten years and I haven't missed a week's rent since I been there. I'm more used to bein' in that place. Course, out here is nice too.

Carol: But you don't think it could ever be home?

Mary: Oh no. See, yonder's [her old neighborhood] where my things is at, over yonder.

Carol: If your things were here with you, would it be more like home?

Mary: I don't think so for a while. Maybe I would get used to it, but it would be hard for me. I tell you, when you get used to a place like I did before, honey, been there about goin' on pretty near ten years . . . why you, you miss the place where you at.

But I got a friend that's got a cousin works out here [Fairhaven] and she's very nice. I got quite a few friends works out here and some cousins in housekeepin'. And I got my nephew; he's forty-three. That's my sister's baby. She's dead now. He comes by every other day. When he come, he don't come with no empty hands neither. He bring in somethin' to eat and he go to the drugstore and get my medicine and things for me. [Elaborates] He does nice things for me, but he's not too well hisself. Whenever he get ready to go, he always kisses Auntie and say, "Auntie, I'm goin'. I'll be back tomorrow." He's so sweet.

Carol: Tell me about a typical day in your life now.

Mary: Well, honey, I'm happy. That's the most of it. I'm lovin' the Lord, like always. I'm not layin' up here worried. I'm really glad to get to see every day. I gets up in the morning and puts this old wheelchair over this side and I go in the bathroom. And I go down the hall to Coffee Club and then I go play bingo.

Carol: You enjoy all that, do you?

Mary: Yes, I sure do, honey. And then I sing. I go down there when they be singin' and playin' the piano. It's a lot of things I like to do.

Carol: Your days here, are they different from your days at home?

Mary: No, they seem to be the same. Not too much different, you know. Well, I know I be growing older 'cause if I live to see the tenth of June,

I'll be eighty-six. So I know I'll be getting old. I'm beatin' on four score and almost six. [Elaborates at length]

Carol: I see what you mean. Let me ask you this, Mary. Is it hard for you to go home and come back in a nursing home and go home again and come back? Is that hard on you?

Mary: No. I done got used to things like that. I've been out here the second and third time already. I'm glad I'm like that, honey.

Carol: How's that, Mary?

Mary: I don't get myself all upset by it. I don't. I can only live one day at a time. That's all. So I'm home now, honey.

Carol: What does home mean to you?

Mary: It mean my whole life. That's what home mean. I done gotten used to bein' here. It's part of my life.

Carol: Some people talk about it as being separate and they get all depressed.

Mary: It ain't separate to me. No way, honey. You know, some people gets old and everything worries 'em. Some people, like a lady over here in that last bed, she's talking about how her children do and they won't come out here and see about her. I say, "Honey, don't worry 'bout them children." The oldest one, he come see her regular, but the other son don't come see her. She be complainin' about that. She just sit up and worry about that. I say, "You gonna stop that worryin'." I say, "You gonna have heart trouble." I say, "You can't live but one day at a time." That's what I told her. That's good advice, ain't it?

Carol: Uh huh.

Mary: Sure do. My life, just like I told you, is singing and prayin' and reading the Bible, you know, and all like that. I like that, servin' the Lord. In the morning, when I get up, I say my prayers, you know, thank the Lord for bein' livin', each and every day of my life. And that's a great release.

Carol: A release?

Mary: It's just, like in the morning you get up with a bad feelin' and you can maybe sing a song or say your prayers and everything else then just goes on. You know our God, He's almighty God. He loves all his children. He don't love one and hate the other. That's where my life really be, always bein', no matter where you is, honey, here or yonder.

Ronai and Carter cover old ground. They discuss Carter's former neighborhood, crime in the vicinity, the quality of care in the nursing home, other residents, daily activities, Carter's past, and her future. For better or worse, the quality of care, the neighborhood, and their differences pale against a horizon of otherworldly concerns. The linkages of serving the Lord overshadow everything. At one point well into the interview, when Ronai asks if Carter had the opportunity to write her life story what the various chapters would be about, Carter explains:

Most any in the Bible is great, I would say. They's my story, honey. I say all
the scriptures in the Bible is good. Now I like that Psalm, say "Fret not
thyself." Happiness is singin' and prayin' and thankin' the Lord for the
good things He is to me, no matter what it's like here, honey, and it ain't
bad. I thank God for livin' to eighty-five. They say you can't plan ahead
'cause, you know, sometimes the Lord cuts you off. That's what I heard old
folks say. So it ain't good to plan too much, honey.

The Fourth Interview

The fourth and last interview is completed a year after the first one.
Carter's daily life at Fairhaven continues to be one of acceptance and
happiness. Her life story and its chapters have no meaning separate
from biblical chapters and verses, as the following brief exchange illustrates:

Carol: Let's say you were going to write a story about your life, sorta like we
did before. What kind of chapters would you have in your book,
about your life? Like what would the first chapter be about?

Mary: The first chapter would be, "The Lord is my shepherd, I shall not
want." And the other one is, "Jesus wept." Just all of them kind of
verses, you know, is in the Bible.

Carol: Those would be in the story of your life?

Mary: Yes, it sure would. I love church. My church is Main Street Baptist
Church.

Carol: What would the last chapter in the book about Mary Carter be?

Mary: Well, I used to sing in the choir. [Hums] Never was too quiet. But after
I got like this, you know, I couldn't go over there much. Used to sing
in them two choirs. We had three choirs. Number 1 and number 2 and
number 3. Number 3 is the little children and they could sing, too.

As they discuss daily life, Carter speaks of God's kingdom, something
beyond earthly possessions and desires. If she is working toward anything in this life, it is, as she puts it, that "building up there," which
gives significance to the "down here." Nothing else matters.

The Lord let me come to this earth buck naked. But long they suffers for
clothes and things. When they face the heavenly Savior, all He sees is you.
Our whole body go in the earth and only our soul will go on up to heaven,
you know. Nothing else matters. That's right. That's the truth.

    Yes, honey, I want to go to heaven when I die. I want nothing down here
to keep me out of heaven. They say it's a sweet place. You don't have to eat
no more. You just drink honey. You eat honey and drink milk. You don't
have to eat this food what we eat down here. And the Lord say they done
with devils. They [devils] come to the gate and He'll push 'em back. And
them that served Him, He'll let them in. So, Lord, I hope I'll be one of the

ones, honey. I'm trying to work for that building up there. I go to bed praying and wake up praying, honey. The Lord, I know, has been good to me, as ill as I have been. He's been so wonderful.

* * * * *

In this secular day and age, it may be hard to imagine how the quality of life can be distanced from daily living, other than perhaps among those we label unrealistic or eccentric. Yet there are people, like Julia McCall and Mary Carter, for whom the significances of each day are suffused with meanings separated from earthly affairs. The horizon for their judgments about matters such as the quality of care and the quality of life in a nursing home is outlined in spiritual terms, for which the good and the bad in the final analysis are "all God's children" and the most trivial activity can "serve God's purpose." Such are the narrative linkages of quality for those "lovin' the Lord."

CHAPTER

6

The Vigilant

Not all residents are stoic about or orient otherworldly to the conditions of everyday life in the nursing home. Some are enduringly vigilant for infringements on their personal space by other residents or staff members. For the vigilant, it matters that people keep their places and mind their manners. Their narratives attest to "taking no lip," especially from the disrespectful.

Residents who are believed to know better but who persist in bothering others, are verbally abusive, or otherwise inconsiderate to a roommate should be physically removed from the premises. The resident who knowingly wanders into someone else's room, disturbs belongings, or pilfers cannot be tolerated. Those who don't know better should be kept under tight rein. Public spaces such as hallways, lounges, and the dining room are to be used with due regard for others' privileges and a wariness for hazards. While hallways, for example, are generally wide enough for the passage of wheelchairs in both directions, wheelchairs can be unwieldy. This is understandable and minor accidents can be rectified with an apology. But residents who carelessly careen into others and staff members who overlook the incidents are contemptible.

To the vigilant, nurses and aides should do their jobs with the utmost concern for those served, being kind and considerate in the process. The staff should promptly attend to bodily cares, see to personal needs, quickly respond to requests, and generally keep the premises clean and odor-free. The aide who openly and perfunctorily cleans a resident following a bout of incontinence, ignoring the resident's right to privacy, should not be working with frail, elderly people. Vigilant residents don't expect to be treated royally by staff members, even while some are alleged to desire that, but they clearly and forcefully do demand decency. At times, such residents wonder why they are thought to be demanding.

Vigilance is a narrative horizon girded by lifelong independence and linked to an ethic of distributive justice. A firm standard of fair treatment narratively prevails. Vigilant residents apply it to themselves, and can be excruciatingly circumspect about their own conduct, lest they carelessly overstep its bounds. From these residents, we hear mention of how they scrupulously keep to themselves, how they would never do thus and so to someone else, and what they would not say under any circumstance.

Vigilance and ethic combine to highlight the quality of care. At times, quality of care is so narratively foregrounded that the overall quality of life for these residents centers on matters such as uncooperative roommates, administrative indifference, impertinent aides, even plastic bedsheets. For some, like resident Bea Lindstrom, this is directed outward and angrily or sarcastically conveyed. For others, like resident Betty Randolph, it also is aimed inwardly and is a source of agitation.

BEA LINDSTROM

While there is a sense in which all vigilant residents "take no lip," Bea Lindstrom expresses it vigorously as she informs me and Carol Ronai of how she responds to rude and unfair treatment. Lindstrom is interviewed twice at Bayside Nursing Center, the first time five weeks after her admission and the second time six months later. She is aware of, and is frustrated by, a mild dementia, but still manages to tell it as she sees it.

The First Interview

At the first interview, Lindstrom is a soon-to-be ninety-year-old. A widowed white woman who has had a hip fracture, she spends much of her time in bed. She is a lifelong heavy drinker and smoker, which is an alleged source of her dementia.

As she tells her story, she becomes angry with her forgetfulness, the first hint of her sense of distributive justice, but, in a rare instance, turned on herself. She describes her early years in the Florida panhandle and outlines the rest of her life in terms of her husband's career. Having recently moved into the nursing home from her apartment, she expresses hope of soon returning to the apartment.

> I was born in Pensacola. I just had a normal life. Went to school. That's about it. Of course, I didn't finish school because I met my husband and we got married. But I was never sorry for anything I did.
>
> I tried to teach my children the right thing, you know. I always told them that I wouldn't spank 'em if they told me the truth. But if I caught 'em in a lie, I would . . . they'd have to pay for it. Taught them respect. I never had any trouble with my children. I had two, a boy and a girl. Yeah, my daughter lives in California. My son's in town. She has six children.

Right after we got married, my husband got a job with Pan American Airways, started flying for them. He was almost ready to quit when they were, you know, when we . . . not tables . . . [frustrated]. See how I get? A person shouldn't do that to herself! Ain't right! [Pause] Trouble. That's it. He would always keep from having trouble because he was a captain from almost the time he was hired.

He retired but he's one person that couldn't sit still after flying, you know. So he got into business, mostly making pizzas. And he did do good. He did real good. He was a man that he couldn't ask you to do it unless he did it. So he always tested his pizzas to see how they were. If they'd taste alright to him, he'd put 'em on the market. If not, he didn't. Start again.

So we went to California for a while, started a business, and did wonderful. He did that till we went back to Pensacola. Not Pensacola. Where? [Pause] Damn it! Stop it girl! What is it I want to say? [Pause] Oh . . . it was the northern part of Florida somewhere. So we stayed there until he got . . . He never smoked or drank or done nothing, but he died of cancer of the pancreas. He was fifty-two. I missed him so much. But I guess the Lord has His ways. So I couldn't do much about it.

I had lots of friends. I sold my house, which was quite large, too big for me. So I sold my house and moved into this smaller apartment. And I sorta snapped into it then, you know. If anybody needed any help, like babysitting or anything, I'd do it. I wouldn't charge them. I mean I loved it. I like doing it, being with people. I love that apartment building. I'm going back there and it's not too soon! I'm on the fourth, no, sixth floor.

We discuss life in the apartment just before she entered the nursing facility. Lindstrom recalls the home accident that caused her to be hospitalized and eventually placed at Bayside. She's sarcastically animated as she describes the course of events.

Bea: They have an alarm in the place [her apartment] so that if you get into trouble or one thing or another, you pull a string and it rings this alarm. It comes in the bathroom and in the kitchen. [Pause] No, not in the kitchen, but in the bedroom. But it doesn't come in the kitchen and doesn't come in the dining room. [Frustrated] No, there's no dining room because the dining room and the kitchen are the same.

Jay: Oh, I see, so you can eat in the kitchen.

Bea: Yeah, but that alarm system doesn't work there. It misses you in that space. Well, what happened was that I was going to cook some lunch . . .

Jay: Did you fall in the kitchen?

Bea: Did I fall? Oh did I fall! I broke two bones in my wrist and I broke two in my . . . I call it my belly. In other words, I have been broken up for about two months now. It's gettin' old. I don't like it. I don't like it at all!

Jay: Where did they take you after the fall?

Bea: Well, they took me to Crescent General Hospital first. They x-rayed me and tied me up, bundled me up and everything. After that, they said that I couldn't be left alone. They wanted to know how much beer and whiskey I drank. I said [sarcastically], "What? Can't afford it!" And I said, "Oh, Christmas I might have two or three, maybe more. That's it!"

Jay: Yeah.

Bea: But that's not going to kill anybody. It takes . . . how long does it take 'em to drink it? It don't take me long! Now my husband never did drink. He didn't smoke, but he still died of cancer. So what the hell!

As Lindstrom turns to the nursing home, her temper and vigilance loom forth to eventually present a view of the world's moral order as dog-eat-dog. According to Lindstrom, in this kind of world, fair and equitable treatment is fleeting. Yet she's not about to take it, no matter how difficult, especially not from the so-called colored people who "have a little bit too much to say." Her racism is riven with the desire to maintain personal dignity and interpersonal respect.

Jay: After you were discharged from Crescent General, what happened?

Bea: They sent me here, [whispers] with all the colored people.

Jay: I'm sorry, I can't hear you.

Bea: [Referring to the nursing staff] These colored people, you know . . . I think they have a little too much to say.

Jay: Oh?

Bea: But they don't do to me 'cause I talk back to 'em.

Jay: You do?

Bea: Yeah, I talk back to 'em. You can hear them screaming at these poor people [residents] that are halfway there and halfway gone and it's pitiful! I usually try to stay out of it. I do pretty good. One of them colored aides I had the other day and she started in on me. Yeah, she started in on me. I told her I wasn't gonna take no lip from anyone. I told her I was gonna leave. And she said, "Who would have you? Blah, blah, blah." I said, "You'd be surprised who would have me." So I told her off! And I told some of the people around me that I knew about it, you know. And they must have told her because she put her foul mouth to a close right away.

Jay: She did?

Bea: And she hasn't spoken to me now for two days. I don't care. I have a temper. I have a horrible temper when it comes to things like that. You have to in this world. It's dog eat dog. People will bite your head off if you don't watch it. You got to watch out for number one.

Jay: Uh huh.

Bea: I don't use it often, but don't knock me around. I don't mess with them and they don't mess with me. Just don't fool with me because I'll stick up for myself. Always been like that; always will be.

As Lindstrom talks of other matters, both in and out of the nursing home, she reminds me of her vigilance, the need to guard her personal

space, dignity, but, equally important, her aim of not imposing on others. Referring to the many characters, called "cards," who were resident
in her apartment building, she comments on how much she "loved"
living there. At the same time, she never went too far with them, which
she likewise expected in return. If the staff members and residents at
Bayside are not characters and don't provide the enjoyment the cards
did, the former are nonetheless held to the same moral standard. Referring to the nursing staff, Lindstrom explains:

> Yeah, this place is hell. Hell! 'Course, they got their ways. Like I guess they
> feel like that they're supposed to do what they're doing, but I think that it's
> a little bit rough, about orders, you know. They don't have to be that strict.
> 'Course they don't bother me. I mean they don't really, honestly and truly. I
> just keep quiet mostly and mind my own business. There's nothing else to
> do. If you got into it, you'd have to fight them too. As long as they let me be,
> I go right along. They let me be; I let them be.

The seriously guarded quality of her life doesn't overshadow its funny
side. She uses a joking sarcasm to portray both her past and present,
even the "hell" she purportedly now withstands. In the current situation, residents and the nursing staff are fumbling characters on a stage,
rude and full of foibles. It is a narrative of "stupid" aides and "really out
of it" residents who, ridiculous as they might be, had best stay in their
place, if "they know what's good for 'em." Mainly, the nursing home
experience is a black comedy she tries to watch from a distance, not join.
Lindstrom jokes about how she maintains distance, engrossed in the
quality of care.

> I wasn't really happy about moving in here. To tell the truth, there are some
> really nice colored people in here that are very sweet. I tease them a lot.
> Some of them can take it; some of them can't. They're stupid. So it doesn't
> take me long to discard the ones that don't like it. I leave them alone. Never
> play ball and have the ball bounce twice.
> But the worst is how it starts out. Like this morning when I woke up, it
> was terrible. No bacon with my eggs, coffee was cold, and things like that.
> Don't know their ass from a hole [frustrated] somewhere. And then she
> [roommate] has the accident [fecal incontinence] and they come and start
> cleaning her up 'cause she's got everything messed up. Christ! While I'm
> eating. It's a joke.
> You have to wait for everything. I've watched them. [Elaborates] It's a real
> comedy. Then they make you sit, you know. Breakfast, they bring that to
> you. Then they give you a bath. You've had a bath already, but you take
> another one. Well, I says like where Clark Gable says, "Frankly, I don't give
> a damn." Stay clear. You know what I'm talking about? [I nod] But I want to
> be treated fair and square.
> I don't want to be too friendly with any of them, 'cause they can get right

under your feet, you know what I mean? I just can't help being sympathetic sometimes, but that's when you can get yourself into it. Some of them [residents] are pitiful. But, more or less, I stay to myself. If they got over-friendly, it wouldn't take me long to get rid of it. [Laughing] I play a kind of trick on 'em. I learn their goofy footsteps and things like that and when they come around, I pretend I'm sleeping [feigns snoring], like that. Then they don't bother you. I do the same with them dumb nurses.

Yeah, it's really a joke around here, like a carnival sometimes. You got people here that eat lunch and they got their food up here [points to her hair]. Some of them, you know, go around with their mouths [makes grunting noises]. They can't help it, but they are living here. You got one fellow whose got a pair of shoes and he'll take his chair and rag and a hankie, whatever he's got, and go around and wipe his shoes on it. You should see these clowns. And we got this woman . . . she goes around like she is going to cry and there's a fellow who picks on her. You have to watch him because he knocks her around.

It's a joke, really. You kinda watch it go on but I don't get involved. Best that way. It can be really funny. But, like I said, I don't let any of 'em mess with me, if they know what's good for 'em.

Six Months Later

Ronai reinterviews Lindstrom at Bayside six months later. Much of the discussion is again taken up with Lindstrom's life story—growing up in the Florida panhandle, the husband's career as a pilot, his death, and events in her son's and daughter's lives. The story is brought up to date when Ronai asks Lindstrom what life looks like from where she is at now and to describe a typical day.

Bea: Well, you wanna get it in plain English?
Carol: Plain English.
Bea: Like hell!
Carol: Why do you say that?
Bea: I don't like it here. I hate it. If I could get out tonight, I'd get out. I told one of the girls [aide], I said, "I'm tempted to just get out myself, get a taxi, and go home." She said, "Oh, I wouldn't do that." I said, "Why not?" She says, "They might call the cops for ya." So she scared me there. But that's it, honey. I'm tied down.
Carol: Let me ask you this, Bea. Describe for me a typical day in your life now.
Bea: I barely ever get out of this hole. I'd be so happy if I could. [Pause] I'll tell you how it is. They wake ya up. You run to the john. That's how it is. And then you get dressed and you go, you go for breakfast. It's not too bad, but it's the same thing every morning. No kidding, it is. Scrambled eggs. So you're not interested in that. But, anyway, there's coffee. And that's it. Ain't no home.

Living here is a rough one. Ya got so many bosses here. I don't like bein' bossed. And I don't have anything to be against the blacks, but some of them are a little bit tough. But I hold my own. I don't take it. Always did.

So that's my story. Like I said, this ain't home. It'd never make it. I don't know . . . too many bosses I guess, and the food, well, you know what I mean. They come in at night and want you to go to bed and you're not sleepy. I won't do it! I'm not going to sleep because they want me to. It's my life too! [Pause] I'm a hellcat!

Violations of her independence are as much the expressed cause of Lindstrom's negative feelings as her engrossment with shortcomings in the quality of care. Lindstrom calls Bayside a jail. She resents the condition of her room and shows Ronai how even the bedding is an imposition on her sensibilities. She informs Ronai that happiness is being independent, respecting others' rights as others respect one's own, bringing Lindstrom back to sentiments expressed six months earlier.

Bea: Well I certainly don't claim this here to be part of my life. I don't claim it at all.

Carol: Why do you say it's separate, that it's not part of your life?

Bea: Honey, I just don't like it. If I could do what I wanted to do and go and come when I wanted to. I don't like to be lost, like I can't handle things. Sure, I would do what my husband would ask me to do. And he would do what I asked him to do, but we didn't *tell* one another they *had* to do it. I think that's the way it should be. And, honey, it sure ain't that way here. Every Tom, Dick, and Harry's always interferin' in your stuff.

They brought me in on a slab in this place. If I had known what I know now, honey, they'd never got me one foot in. This doctor here, I don't think he knows his beans.

Like I say, I don't like this place. I want to get out and if I could get out, I'd go. I won't be happy here. I just like . . . I feel like I'm in jail.

Carol: I've heard other people say that.

Bea: Yeah, even the bed. [Strokes her bed] Run your hand over that.

Carol: [Feeling the bedding] Plastic-feeling, not too comfortable.

Bea: [Sarcastically] I'm not gonna pee in a bed!

Carol: I guess some of them do.

Bea: Well, honey, I ain't some of them! They don't remember that, honey. I asked them to take this thing [plastic sheet] out.

Carol: They won't do it?

Bea: They won't do it! And it makes me mad as a hellcat. They got no respect for no one. Ya have to keep an eye on 'em day and night. [Pause] Oh, hell, I'm just getting ugly and decapitated [sic].

Carol: Decapitated?

Bea: Oh, I don't know how to describe it. Like I say, I'm not happy here.

Never will be. You have to keep an eye on 'em all the time. The treatment stinks. I've seen it all. If I could get back down there where I lived, honey, you couldn't drive me out. See, they didn't ask me to come here. They took me from the hospital, see, and they put me on a slab and brought me.

Carol: So, Bea, what's important to you?

Bea: Oh, bein' happy. Doin' what you wanna do. Respect. I've got a mind of all the things I wanna do. That's what I wanna do and I don't like to be told how to do things and things.

A place like this, honey, ain't good for an old lady like me. We don't like no one mussin' with us. We keep to ourselves.

BETTY RANDOLPH

Betty Randolph, another vigilant resident, is a seventy-one-year-old white female who suffers from innumerable problems of aging. Among other things, she has cardiovascular blockage, osteoporosis, arthritis, and has had a hip replacement. Joint degeneration has caused her to have knee and shoulder fusions. She is interviewed twice by Ronai.

Randolph keeps watch for infringements on her dignity. In turn, she is careful not to impose on others, sometimes to a fault. Just as she would expect others to be angry with her if she showed little regard for them as persons, Randolph is not about to take lip from those who are disrespectful to her. Trying as Randolph does to make things right according to her acute sense of fair play, she does not let things get out of hand. All of this admittedly makes her nervous.

For Randolph, the quality of care is a mark of the effectiveness of her personal ethic: Mutual kindness and respect results in good care. She makes certain that she is kind and polite to others, especially staff members, in the hope that, assuming they are equally bound by the same ethic, they will be kind and polite in return. This is highlighted in Randolph's second interview, conducted after Randolph has been discharged from her nursing home and placed in a small board-and-care facility.

The First Interview

Randolph's first interview takes place five months after she is admitted to the Greenfield Home, a skilled-care facility. Before that, she resided for about a year in another nursing home. Randolph begins the interview with a description of her harsh life growing up with alcoholic parents, then spent briefly with a husband, but mainly on her own. As we will learn later in the interview, Randolph is, according to her, a lifelong loner.

My father drank, my mother drank, and I was always left home to take care of my stepsisters and that. Actually, I don't even know who my father was, because my mother had been married three times. So I just don't know.

But the best time in my life is when I got married. My husband was a fine man. I lost him too quick. We were married five years when he walked out and dropped dead. They said he had a coronary and there was nothing they could do for him. He was dead when they got to him.

But if I had the five years that I had with him . . . if I had to do it over, I'd be grateful for every minute of it. He was kind, he was understanding, and my whole life was his. Of course, then we were in Arizona. He wanted to come back, but we didn't want to come back to New York. That's where I was born and raised and he was. But we didn't want to and so we stayed in Orlando. He got a job in the hospital working as an orderly because he had come out of the service and he had been in the service quite a while and he just didn't want to . . . he wasn't the type that could stay home and do nothing. He had to work no matter what it was. So that's when he took the job. We came back [to Florida] in March, I mean, in January and he dropped dead March 12, 1956. It's like I said, he was the best man in the world.

After that, I had a nervous breakdown. Then I was on my own. I came up to the northern part of Florida and I lived there for seventeen years. I worked in a nursing home there and I stayed there, yeah, for seventeen years.

But I've had a hard life. When my mother drank . . . she got married to this man and they both . . . she never drank until she married the third one. Really, they really went at it. I used to have to go out at night in New York City when I was about twelve or thirteen and bring 'em home out of bar-rooms so they wouldn't get arrested. And then I had to be with my two half-sisters to take care of them all day and night. I was a hard life and I very seldom talk about it because it's like I said, a lot of times I think that I could've had a better life, but I didn't.

The conversation turns in various directions. At one point, Randolph angrily comments on the friends she believed she had in one of the places she lived. They were friends until they became unjustifiably cruel to her. As Randolph notes, "Friends can cut your throat." Paraphrasing a common cliche, she adds, "With such friends who needs enemies?" She speaks of the vigilance needed in life when no one, not even friends, can be trusted. Ronai asks Randolph what life looks like from where Randolph is now. Randolph takes the opportunity to describe herself, putting independence and sentiments of distributive justice at center stage.

It's like this. If a year ago anybody told me I'd be in this shape, I'd have said they're crazy. Of course, I'm an independent person. I'm used to doing things for myself. I don't want nobody to wait on me. And this is the way I am. But I can't make people understand that. When you take care of yourself since you've been fifteen years old . . . I've worked and I've never asked anybody for nothing. Even when my husband was living, he knew I was independent. That's the way he did what he had to do; he never told me what to do. [Elaborates] You put yourself in my place, that you're knocked down like this in this place. It's an awful hard way to go for someone like me. It's really hard. It's like I said, a year ago, if anybody told me this would have happened, I couldn't believe it and I wouldn't believe it.

These people here don't understand me. They think I'm throwing a tantrum. It isn't I'm throwin' a tantrum. I'm just taking care of myself and I'm doing it for myself. What's mine's mine and what's theirs is theirs. Fair's fair, I always say.

It was just this morning. I didn't know she was an RN. She was walking around in street clothes and sittin' behind the desk. I didn't know she was an RN and I just said I would not take any medicine from somebody I didn't know. Would I expect any different if I was in her shoes? No. I didn't know she was an RN till they told me. It's because I had that happen to me one time. I was given the wrong medicine one time. So you can see where I'm coming from. You have to be on the lookout all the time. You don't know if she's an RN or not. What she wore behind that desk could have been the secretary there. How did I know?

Linked with Randolph's guardedness is the view that interpersonal respect has "gone to hell in a handbasket." A lengthy exchange with Ronai conveys particulars, as well as Randolph's admitted racism. Randolph speaks of letting Josephine, a "colored" resident, "have it" because neither Josephine nor the "colored girls" on the nursing staff, who allow Josephine to wander about, show respect for others.

Carol: Before you came to live in a nursing home, what did you think it would be like?

Betty: I didn't think it'd be like this. I really didn't. I can't complain much about some of the people here. The dietician, Karen, and the other ones are good to me. The nurses are good to me. There's only, maybe one or two, like the one [resident] out there this morning . . . Boy, I let her have it. I've just had enough of her foolishness and I let her have it. I don't like doing it because it makes me nervous. But, sometimes, I don't know, maybe I'm thinking wrong, but the colored people come in and they take over things. Ya might say the world's gone to hell in a handbasket.

Carol: What do you mean, Mrs. R?

Betty: Well, I just seen that they think they're better than we are, some of them. It's just like that colored woman that I had the fight with this morning—Virginia. I was sitting out there. I got a $900 chair sitting over there [in the corner of Randolph's room] that's mine and she walks around and she's all wet. And she'll walk in here to go sit down in that chair and I don't want her in that chair. I have the right; it's mine. No, but with her I didn't have the right. She said I don't.

Look, I know she don't know any better, but when they see her going in and out of all these rooms, why don't they get up and go get her and take her back to where she belongs? But, no, those colored girls [staff] just sit there and let her do it. Like I went out to the doctor last Tuesday, I come home, and she was in my bed, all wet. Boy did I get the nurse to get her out. She was in my bed and I said to the nurse . . . went down and got the nurse and asked to please come and get her out of my bed. The nurse come up and I said, "I want some clean sheets on my bed. I'm not gonna sleep there." She said, "Oh that won't hurt you." I'm a particular person; that's my problem.

Carol: I guess I wouldn't want to sleep in a bed like that either.

Betty: Even with my clothes, if you go look at my closet over there, I keep all my slacks in one, my skirts in the next, and my jackets in the back. That's the way I've lived. Anybody knows me could tell you that they could walk in my house any time of the day or night and my house was . . . you could eat off the floors.

But this is what bothers me. This one here [Virginia], she roams all day. There's another one that roams that can't . . . he hit me the other day in my knee.

Carol: He hit you?

Betty: He backed his wheelchair up into me. They didn't say anything about it. And they know that was my bad leg that he had hit.

It's like I said. Some of these here, you could bend over backwards, honey, and you couldn't get along with some of these patients. I had one this morning—it really got to me—I was trying to turn my wheel-chair out to get to the table. She comes along and says to me, "Get out of my way!" I said, "Wait a minute." I said, "I'm just trying to get to the table." So she yells, "Well get out of my way!" And that's just how a lot of them are here and I'm not about to take that from no one. So I gave it right back to her. [Elaborates]

Randolph worries about having to openly contend with injustice. She initially attributes her feeling to growing old, but then ties it to her ethic of interpersonal respect. In the process, Greenfield's quality of care is cast in terms of the ethical view and its place in Randolph's life noted.

Betty: I guess it's getting old and getting . . . you get agitated about a lot of things maybe when I shouldn't.

Carol: What would be a little thing that you get agitated about that you think you shouldn't?

Betty: Well, I know I shouldn't get agitated about . . . like I said, these two that roam all day. But I told them [the staff] that it's got to be a halt brought to it. They [the two roamers] belong over on Station 2. That's where they should be kept, not roaming around. It makes me nervous to get involved in things like this, but like I said, too, it's only right.

Last year, I was down in [another] nursing home and that is a fabulous nursing home. There were patients there like these that roam, but they were kept over on the other side. They weren't allowed over where the patients could get around and that. They weren't allowed over there in the other patients' rooms. But here, there's no due restriction. They let them do what they want and it's not right.

Carol: And that makes you feel . . .

Betty: Worried. I worry knowing that I have to stay here and have to yell at them about it. That's part of the problem I guess. Not that it's all that bad. It's that I'm the kind of person that stays to herself and doesn't interfere. I'm a loner. A place like this . . . well, it makes a difference for someone like me. You start thinking about the treatment and all, like it's no good if I have to yell all the time.

Six Months Later

Six months later, Randolph has been discharged from Greenfield and lives in a small board-and-care home called Miss Palmer's. Randolph's fastidiousness and acute sense of interpersonal justice continue paramount and are linked with nervousness. At one point, it appears that no congregate living setting, neither a nursing nor a personal care home, could accommodate Randolph's view to life.

Carol: And they call this an adult congregate living facility, kind of board-and-care. How do you feel about being here?

Betty: Well, some ways it's alright and other ways it's not.

Carol: Oh?

Betty: This one down here, the one in the kitchen [Miss Palmer], it seems every time I say something I'm wrong. That I don't understand, because I never had this problem at Greenfield.

Carol: I'm not sure I know what you mean.

Betty: It seems that, you know . . . See I've had a problem with phlebitis over a year now and I don't have any family or anybody to take me anywhere. When I came out of the hospital, the doctor suggested that I should have my blood done every week because I'm on a strong drug, Coumadin, and it's dangerous, so she [Miss Palmer] should take me to the lab. Well she didn't take me yesterday like she said she would. Says she's got other things to do. If I had known she didn't want to take me, I would have called Medicoach and that. But she offered herself to take me. So that's what I expected her to do, or don't offer. Right? A promise is a promise.

It seems that all the time around here, no matter where I turn or something, I'm always wrong. I try not to bother anyone. That's how I am. I do something, I'm wrong. I get jumped on for something and that, and I'm getting a little tired of it now and it makes me nervous.

Carol: Would you rather be back at Greenfield or just out of here?

Betty: Well, I've tried, honey. I try to cope with it because, it's like I said, I don't have any family to stick up for me. So maybe the reason why they keep at me is because I don't have people to come in to see me.

Carol: Oh I see.

Betty: And they know I don't have anybody. So they figure they can pick at me and stuff. There's nobody I can tell.

Carol: That's sad. Have you talked to Miss Palmer about it?

Betty: Doesn't do any good. She won't listen to you. She just has her favorites. She has about four or five favorites and they can do no wrong. But everybody else is wrong.

Carol: You don't have anyone here you're close to?

Betty: No. I don't bother with none of them. I don't bother with none of them around here.

Carol: Okay.

Betty: And that one you see walking now [a resident]? She can go around and slap everybody and nothing's done about it. She threatened the other day to slap me and I said if she hit me, I'd knock her screw off. It just seems that it's always something that's wrong. It's not right. I try to be fair, really. I want 'em to be fair with me, too. When I said something to Miss Palmer this morning coming back from the lab, I said, "I'm sorry I caused you so much trouble." I said, "I didn't ask you to take me." She said, "Why don't you shut up and stop letting little things bother you."

I've worked all my life. I've taken care of myself. I never thought that I'd be in a position like this. If I had known it would come to this, I don't know what I'd a done. But when you got to live like this, it's not good. Maybe it's really not good nowhere.

Carol: What kinds of things would you want that you're not getting?

Betty: I like to go out. I like to go out even if I don't have the money to go shopping. I just like to go shopping. Here, I don't have anybody to take me to the stores.

I like a place where I have my own things, where I can do what I want to do and nobody's on me. I get up when I want to. I go to bed when I want to and that. I've done that ever since I was fifteen years old.

My parents died and I had nobody. I had to learn to do it. I had to learn to go to work. I can go back to the time that I lived in New York. I was born and raised there. When my mother died, I was living in Massachusetts. After she passed away, my father passed away. I was fifteen years old. What was I going to do? I had to think. So I got a furnished room, paid $14 every two weeks for it. I worked in a laundry putting sheets through the iron for $56 and I paid my room rent out of that, bought my clothes, I ate, and I been doing that ever since.

I can handle money. It's like when I used to live in the apartment, I used to buy my groceries. I knew how to handle it because I'd figure out that I buy my groceries for the month and you come to my house and the freezer would always be full. My icebox was never empty. Because I kept a system. I paid my bills first. I paid my rent first, my light bills first, my water bill, my telephone bill, and after my bills was paid, then I bought my groceries.

I always kept a nice home. Anybody would tell you that. They'd tell you I kept a clean house. I was always cleaning my apartment. Then when I got sick, it seemed everything fell apart. See, I have osteoporosis, which is a bone disease. I have ulcers. I have a bad heart, too. So, like I said, it isn't good for me to be living alone and that. I don't know how much more of this I can take.

I wouldn't live this kind of life if I could help it, nowhere. I'm a person . . . I don't talk much and I don't have much to say to nobody. I've always been a loner and that's the way I've been. And I've been that way since I had to live by myself all my life.

You can see the point where I'm coming from. If I say something, I'm jumped on right away. If I don't talk, I'm mad. If I say something, I'm looking for an argument. So which way do you go? There's no crossroads.

Carol: You're saying it's a no-win situation because of, well, who you are and what others are like.

Betty: Like I said, I've lived all my life as a loner because I've lived alone and I've done what I wanted and I had no bosses. There was nobody to tell me to go to bed at this time or nobody to tell me when I could get up or nobody to tell me what I've got to eat. If I don't want to eat, I'm not going to have someone say that you've got to eat.

People don't realize that when you've come up the hard way, it's really rough. You learn that you have to fight your way to get along in this world. This is about . . . seems about all I've done. I try to get along with people and all I hear is an attitude problem. I've got an attitude problem. If people would try to understand me, it would be different. I don't want to bother them and I don't want 'em on me either. But they don't try to understand me. And it's really hard when you try to make somebody understand you and try to explain, they think you're mad. [They'll say,] "Go sit down!" It's not fair.

* * * * *

For these residents, being independent combines with an ethic of distributive justice to make the quality of care an all-consuming matter. The quality of their lives virtually revolves around the quality of their care. Their narratives are filled with judgments about how staff members should behave but don't and how certain residents should act but rarely do. According to such residents, if the world were fundamentally different or had not "gone to hell," vigilance would not be necessary. As it is in a dog-eat-dog world, being vigilant is the only recourse, the only means of assuring a modicum of respect. Such are the narrative linkages of vigilance, interpersonally difficult at best and anxiety-provoking at worst.

PART

II

SPECIAL CIRCUMSTANCES

CHAPTER

7

Travelers

We turn now to residents whose special circumstances offer horizons of their own for subjective meaning. The two residents of this chapter—Jake Bellows and Peter Rinehart—were itinerant travelers, one in show business and the other in sales. To paraphrase one of them, they did a "lot of livin'" on the road and have stories to tell about it. For them, home was a place experienced as a break from life on the road. Home was time out from the usual and customary. These men *went home* for vacation; they didn't leave it.

Bellows and Rinehart accept the nursing home as a place offering care, security, and shelter for the weary, who might not otherwise be able to carry on. It isn't home, but under the circumstances the next best thing to it. Indeed, care apparatus and sickness aside, for traveling men like themselves, the nursing home is a kind of hotel, having both the best and worse features of such establishments. As they see it, residents more or less get fed, have a bed to sleep in, and get their cares attended, but understandably not to everyone's satisfaction.

For Bellows and Rinehart, destiny isn't so much puzzling or decried as it is something that, like life on the road, one follows. They refer to fate in phrases such as "c'est la vie," "things just happen," "goin' where the road takes you," "so be it," and "easy come, easy go." While the men describe the many paths their lives took, the so-called ups and downs of the years, and the good and poor choices they made at various turns, they recognize that such matters are part of the design of living. They don't lament fate; it's just there, the essential "road" ahead.

For them, life does come to an end. Ends being what they are, they are filled with bitter, if not sweet, moments. The men don't turn to religion for answers to why things come to this, nor do they pray to God to intervene on their behalf. They are not especially religious and speak with skepticism about those who are. They scoff at the thought that, if there were a God, He or She would deign to indulge the desire for divine intervention to prolong life or make substantial changes in it.

Yet they take pride in the quality of their lives and what they have accomplished, which are not defined by their present circumstances. While it wouldn't be correct to describe them as awed by fate, they appreciate what fate has brought, both the easy triumphs that have come by and the hard lessons they've learned along the way. As Bellows and Rinehart remind us, such is life.

JAKE BELLOWS

Jake Bellows is a seventy-six-year-old widowed white male who has lived six months at the Greenfield Nursing Home. For years, he has been afflicted by what he calls a "vascular condition," which has cost him his left leg. In the last few years he was in and out of the hospital for other health problems. Two sisters, a brother, and a son live some two hours away by car. They visit him regularly, about every month or so, which according to Bellows suits him fine.

Except for service in the army during World War II, Bellows has spent his adult life in show business. He has little formal education, but is proud of being self-taught and having parlayed good writing skills, incentive, and inventiveness into profitable "gigs." More than for any resident interviewed, Bellows's life is a collection of stories, in his case centered on the stage, the experiences of which he enthusiastically recounts. He begins with his education.

> I went to, uh . . . I have a three-year college, what do you call it? [Audibly sorts his thoughts] The equivalency of two years of college. I didn't go to college and I didn't go to high school. I had to stay home, but I taught myself. I learned correspondence courses, stuff like that at home. I learned myself. I taught myself how to become . . . I was a public speaker and writer. [Laughs] So I'm not a stupid bastard, you know. I learned a little bit while I was at it.
>
> Mainly I was into acting and music. I was a musician and master of ceremonies at night clubs and theaters and so forth. And writin' scripts and writin' plays. I've done it all. Everything. I wound up with a little bit of money and I retired and quit. It's all spent and gone now. I'm a veteran.

I ask Bellows about childhood, which turns out to be a version of the story of how he got into show business. The story begins, jokingly, in south Georgia.

> I was born in south Georgia. [Laughing] I couldn't help that. My daddy was a rather successful farmer. I was born on a farm in Nelling County, Georgia. Then we moved to Maple County and he went into public work there. I started school there. In 1924, we moved to Tampa, Florida. Daddy was in

the construction business there as a carpenter, a good one, and he did all right at that.

So I went to school till the fifth grade and quit 'cause there was . . . we had too many kids. I had five sisters and a brother. So I had to, you know . . . my daddy became sick, so I had to help support the kids. So I cut my formal education short and I taught myself. I guess that's how you say it—educated myself by reading books and other people's schoolwork, stuff like that.

To make a long story short, in time that got me into show business. I learned to play the guitar. After that, I remained in strict show business from then on and graduated up the scale to producer and so forth, right on up the scale. I had an act that I did in a night club that was seen all over the country, on the road most of the time. I worked in five pictures and a lot of production, lots of dramatics and stuff like that, all the way up and down. I think that about covers it.

When I ask him what it was like doing that kind of work, he lights up and relishes telling me about his accomplishments and his acquaintances. As he notes how much he once earned, he remarks "easy come, easy go," which is his first mention of a sense of destiny.

I wouldn't do anything else! If I had my life to live over, I'd do the same thing again. Well, I'd try to make it a little more fruitful, you know, moneywise. But I had fun. I loved it. I loved every minute of it and I met some nice people on the way up. It kept me on the way up like I was a star. I never was a real featured star. I was pretty well known, but not great big. I worked in five pictures. [Pauses] Oh, I told you that. So I got up there on a totem pole a little bit. I was pretty well known as an actor on the stage. As a movie actor, I was just mediocre, you know.

I played everywhere. Every city in the union besides Las Vegas. I never played Vegas, but everywhere else. I didn't play Alaska, but I did play Hawaii. I never went to Alaska but I wanted to so bad. The main thing was money. Alaska paid big, big money way back near the depression, I mean near the sixties. I had a chance to go and I coulda got a thousand a week like nothing flat. I was working for $500 up back then. That was big time considering the salaries of some of them was $200, $125, $150. My wife and I worked as an act for almost nine years and we were making upwards of, well, an average of a thousand a week, for about seven years of it traveling all over the United States, everywhere.

We spent as much as we made, of course, but we lived. We lived high on the hog. We spent high on the hog. We'd tell people, "What the hell, why not?" you know. Easy come, easy go.

That's about the size of my career. What else? [Pauses] Let's see. Of course I'm an artist. I paint and of course I'm a writer. I've sold a few things. I've got a lot of manuscripts to prove it . . . I mean rejection slips to prove it. I'm not a very successful writer, but you know how when you write something you know it's good or you wouldn't have written it? Some of the ones that I think are the very best pieces were rejected and didn't sell. Some of the little things I'd write and say to myself, "Oh well, I'll send it in anyway." They'd sell! I can never understand it. Nobody else can. Things just happen, I guess. Some of the greatest writers in the world have written the same thing I'm saying. They couldn't understand why the stuff they thought was so good came back with rejection slips and stuff they didn't think much of sold. C'est la vie.

Life was not all onward and upward for Bellows. He was especially annoyed by rude changes in entertainment. The night club acts in which he worked a good part of his adult life as producer, stand-up comic, or general entertainer, grew into striptease shows. As he looks back, he takes pride in what he accomplished despite the changes. A comedy act he developed is particularly noteworthy, a story in its own right, which turns into yet another story of appreciation for his work.

I was in show business until '72 and I quit. I just got so . . . the nightclub business had run down into striptease joints. That's what it amounted to. I just got sick of them. I wasn't around actors and show people. I was around scum of the earth, low class. I couldn't stand it, so I quit. I sat home and did writing and put in an occasional club date once in a while. But something like that, that's a different thing.

Mainly, I did solo work. I'm an artist. I paint pictures. My impression book isn't here; I wish I had it here to show you. You'd see all the things I've done without me having to talk about it. When I talk about it, it sounds like I'm bragging, but I'm not! I played a lot of gigs, big times. Like one time I did speed painting in oil on stage and talked comedy. Talk was all I was doin'. I could paint a picture in two minutes, two feet by three feet in two minutes. Used great big house painting brushes and the pictures turned out very nice in oil paintings. I just learned how to put the paint where it's supposed to go and make it look good, you know.

At the beginning of the act, I got all my stuff, my equipment and easel there on the stage. I talked to them [the audience] and cracked gags all the time, and the orchestra's sitting there in the background. I'd try to get funny there for a little while and talked to them all to get acquainted, you know. It was a comedy act—the buildup, the preparation to get into the act was comedy. I talked to them to keep 'em laughing. I said, "Now name a song that depicts a scene of some kind of springtime in the Rockies or the moon over Miami or whatever you can think of. Pick a scene of some kind." While the orchestra played the chorus of the song, I painted for them on this canvas. So, like, they named Blue Hawaii or something out there and I'd say, "Okay, boys, play it" and I'd start painting. By the time they played two chords of the song, the picture was done. So I'd turn around, hold it up this way and that way, and I'd get a hell of a hand because it turned out to be a damned good picture.

A lot of 'em seen it all over the country. We played up in Alberta, Canada, and right after that I went into a barber shop and got a haircut, see. This guy kept looking at me and looking at me and said, "I think I know you from someplace. You look so familiar." I said, "Well, I'm an actor. You probably seen me on stage." [He said], "Ah, that's what it is! I saw you working in Miami, Florida." We were conversing back and forth and he said, "I've got something to show you. I want you to come home to dinner with me tonight. Will you go? Are you too busy?" I said, "No, I'm not doing anything." So he called his wife and told her that he was going to bring a guest home, a little surprise. So I knew that he was going to tell his wife that he had Jake Bellows that he saw in Miami. I figured that was it. I walked through the door. I'm cutting the story down so I won't bore you. We walked in his house and there on the wall was one of my canvases I done in an act in Miami! I said, "That was one of my pictures out of the act." That was pretty nice.

Things like that happened to me all up and down the road. I wrote for a lot of people in show business and they've become big stuff, you know, through the years. Some of them have turned out to be drunks and everything else. A few of them made it big.

But it was up and down, goin' where the road takes you. One week here, two weeks there . . . What the hell am I trying to say? A few weeks out of the year, we'd sit there. I'd have three months of excellent work, play the highest-rated night clubs, theaters, or whatever. The rest of the time in plain toilets used for low class. Well, I had to work. I couldn't just quit and sit on my butt just because I didn't want to play that place. I had to play, had to make money, you know. So it's been up and down for me all my life in show business. Most every actor will tell you about the same thing. Such is life.

As we continue to talk about show business, Bellows describes his acquaintance with various celebrities. He takes special pride in having worked with George Burns and Gracie Allen's vaudeville act. But the happiest time of his life was his association with the Marcus show, a touring company. He beams as he recalls those years.

That was the happiest time of my life. It was a big company of sixty people. A.B. Marcus. Man, that was big time. They played all over the world, everywhere. I didn't go with them on all the tours. I didn't go overseas with them at all. I worked with them in the States. But, boy, that was a show! Some of the greatest actors in show business started out in the Marcus show. I didn't start out with them but I was with them for a while. That was the highlight of my show business . . . and, of course, the picture work I did later.

Just as the ups and downs of show business are accepted as part of life, the current situation marking the end of his life is taken as meant to be and accepted. Yet show business is still in his blood.

But it's finished. I don't have anything to look forward to in show business. I'd like to write about it, talk about it, remember a lot of the things about it, but there is nothing to go back to anymore. At my age, I can't. I could do a couple of pictures sitting in a chair. I can work in front of a camera, act, sit in a chair, sort of like seeing a cripple still be a performer that way. But as far as walking onto a stage again and being a comic like I used to be, I can't stand up.

It's the last chapter in the last story. The end of the road. I think that's the way to say it. C'est la vie. So be it. I don't know how else to express it. I'm on my last legs and know it and don't care. I'm an atheist. In other words, I got brains. I have no fear of death. I'm not religious at all. No superstition. I'm happy the way I'm going out. I like to entertain people. If I could find the right kind of situation or audience so I could work without having to walk on stage, I could still do a painting act.

A long and checkered career in show business, especially life on the road, colors Bellows's talk of home, casting his sense of the nursing home's quality of care in related terms. Being on the road nearly fifty weeks a year meant home was less a natural anchor than it was a place to forget show business for a while. Taking a vacation meant *going* home, not getting away from home, as the following extract indicates.

Jay: Let me ask you something a little different. We haven't talked very much about home. What would you say the word *home* means to you, Jake?

Jake: I tell ya, Jay . . . it used to mean, well, it meant I quit for the season. I took a two-week vacation and I went back home to Millsburg. That was home. Otherwise, leave the house locked up, let someone I knew very well take care of it for me, and then we'd hit the road.

Jay: You say *we'd* hit the road?

Jake: I was talking about my wife Rose. When we were doing our mind reading act, a mental act . . . we did a mind reading act together. You've seen those things I imagine?

Jay: Yeah, I've seen a bunch of those. They're funny. [Elaborates] So Rose went with you most of those places?

Jake: Oh yeah. She was one of the greatest acts, mental acts I've ever seen. But the wife turned out to be a drunk and it got worse. I couldn't depend on her. She'd louse up, get drunk and louse up the show. So I finally had to . . . well, she was absolutely finished by the time we tried to get some help. The doctor said she was finished, like a vegetable. Liquor got her, just deteriorated her brain. Then I heard she was dead. I didn't even go to the funeral. I was on the road.

Jay: How long were you married to her?

Jake: Twelve years. No kids by her. I was married five times. The first wife, Edith, was okay. She was the only *lady* I was ever married to. The rest of them were bitches. It's like any other show business.

Jay: So home life stayed pretty much the same over the years?

Jake: Home . . . yeah, it's been about the same. It's a place to go back to and forget show business, forget everything, just sit down and relax and enjoy the distance. Home's about the same now as it's always been.

We talk about the nursing home, which Bellows doesn't feel is quite home. It's not that he wishes to go home because the nursing home is so different as a source of shelter and comfort from the family home in Millsburg. Rather, compared with "home," Bellows feels Greenfield does not provide enough in the way of time to relax, gab, and enjoy the distance, as he had put it, what home did for him two weeks a year. Greenfield is more like a stop along the way. Bellows explains:

When I came here, the bottom dropped out because there are very few people in here besides the help that are intelligent. The rest of them have lost their minds through the years or didn't have it in the first place. Just one of those things, you know. The help here is all right. They are all intelligent people. You can gab with 'em and sorta relax that way. But you don't have much time with people who work. The nurses and the other help, they're busy. Got a hotel to run. They've got something else to do. [Points to another resident] There's old man Dewey. And up here's old man Smith and me. Usually in the daytime when you see one, you see all three of us sittin' there together, all around together, pretty close together, gabbing. These guys . . . just another place down the road, sittin' around and chewin' the fat.

At the end of the interview, Bellows speaks of the course of life in general. He comments on the virtues of smoking marijuana and offers a friendly diatribe against religion. He discloses how, after all is said and done, fate, not this or that decision or condition, made life what it was for him, "always has."

I have never taken a dishonest nickel in my life. I've never been a crook in any form. I've tried to live a good, clean life, which I didn't completely. I smoked pot, which I dearly enjoyed. I'd enjoy it now. If I had some, I'd smoke it now and I don't give a damn who knows it. I like it, I smoke it, and it didn't hurt me none. If I had some, I'd smoke it right here and now. Of course, music has been a big part of my life. Religion is an absolutely disgusting subject to me. I don't even like to discuss it.

Like life's got some purpose or something? Hell! Things just happen. Things that come up in your life happen that way. The way the card bounces. I mean the way the cards fall or whatever the word is. The way the cookie crumbles. Whatever the hell. No, life don't turn out any particular way. Like I'm in this here joint. Life is like unrolling a tape. You don't know what's there until you unroll it. Some people told me that life is already there and you just have to live what it is. As it unrolls, you just live it. As you think back over your life, you didn't exactly plan anything that you did. It just happens that it was convenient to do at the time and you did it. That's the way it was with me. All my life I'd . . . a lot of times I'd plan on doing something and I wanted to do it and that wouldn't turn out at all. I'd do something exactly backwards before I attended to something. Well, maybe not that bad, but relative to it, but not the same thing. So, you can't . . . you don't judge yourself. You just go where life takes you and life does take you. You don't take life anywhere. It takes you.

There's not much to think about. You live your life, do the best you can at the moment. Whatever you do at that particular time is what you have to do. At the moment, it happens you got to do that, not something else. I know that circumstances ruled my life, not exactly what I wanted, but circumstances. Surrounding circumstances forced me to do exactly what I did. Every bit of it. Sometimes I wish I could have done better and made a lot more money than I did. But it didn't work out that way.

PETER RINEHART

Peter Rinehart also spent much of his adult life on the road, mainly selling Oster products. He took his wife along with him, a house trailer hitched to the back of their van. Like Jake Bellows, home for Rinehart was not a home base but time out from the usual and customary.

Fate presents itself clearly in Rinehart's life. At one point in our conversation about his past and his present situation. Rinehart refers to himself as a fatalist, calling attention to the equanimity with which he has experienced life change. To Rinehart, his three-and-a-half years at Bayside Nursing Home wasn't much of a change from what he had gotten used to—a life on the road, occasionally taking a vacation at "home."

Rinehart is a seventy-seven-year-old white widower, paralyzed from the waist down, the result of a fall. The fall features prominently in his story, dividing it into before and after. It presents a further horizon for evaluating the quality of his life. He has chronic pain in his lower back and is completely incontinent. Yet, like other residents who suffer from chronic conditions, except for the lower back pain, he says that he's in good health.

Rinehart is less of a storyteller than Bellows. But, in several exchanges, life on the road is similarly foregrounded.

> Jay: Why don't we talk about your life a bit now? Tell me a bit about it, Pete.
>
> Peter: Well, Jay, I was born in Connecticut and lived there for twenty-one years. Then I went into sales later in life and I was in sales for about twenty-five, thirty years. My wife and I traveled all over the country, in a travel trailer that we . . .
>
> Jay: You had a travel trailer?

Peter: Um hm. And we hauled that with a Ford van . . . not a Ford van. It was a Dodge van. And I was in that until I fell. It was 1971, I think, that I fell but I'm not sure.

Jay: How did that happen?

Peter: We were living in Donner Springs. We had our place there and the reception is bad there for television. So I had a tower put up and I used to go up and adjust it whenever it needed it.

Jay: You had an antenna up in the tower?

Peter: Yup. On top of this tower. And I had been up there before and adjusted it many times. That morning I got up there and finished adjusting it and I threw my tools on the ground. I had a cigarette and was looking around. Then I went to come down and the first step I took down, my foot slipped and the safety belt broke. I came down fifty feet.

Jay: Oh boy, that's a long way.

Peter: I had a spinal injury and they've been fooling around with it ever since. Still haven't been able to get rid of the pain.

Jay: You have pain too?

Peter: Pain continually. And that brings us, probably be about up to date. I've had, I don't know, five or six operations, including a brain tap that didn't work. They don't want to fool around with that anymore 'cause they don't know what it would do now.

Jay: Yeah. So you have chronic pain, Pete? Where exactly? In your lower back?

Peter: In the worst place it could be: right where you sit. So I haven't been able to sit for any length of time at all.

We talk at length about the injury, how it affects him now, and related details of his medical history. Rinehart recalls his work years, which he shares convivially. Curious to see how the recollections would figure into the writing of a life story, I change gears.

Jay: Pete, if you had the chance to write your life story, what would the first chapter be about?

Peter: Oh, I guess after high school, I went into industry and I was there for a while before I went into sales.

Jay: Yeah?

Peter: And, as I said, I've been in sales till the time I fell.

Jay: So the first chapter would be about industry and sales and so on, if you divided up your life?

Peter: Yeah.

Jay: What about the next chapter? What would that be about?

Peter: After I fell?

Jay: After you fell?

Peter: Is that what you want?

Jay: Well, whatever that would be. You'd write about that?

Peter: That's what I'd be doing.

Jay: I see.

Peter: Just laying here. I was up in Jacksonville at a rehab center there for five months and they couldn't do anything. We went as far as we could go. Then I came down here and I've been between here and the hospital ever since.

Jay: What year was it you said you fell? Was it '71? I forgot.

Peter: I think it was 1971. I'm not sure, but I think it was '71.

Jay: So it's been about, almost twenty years?

Peter: Not quite. Let's say eighteen years, something like that I've been laid up here. My wife and I were ready to go on the road within a week after I fell. [Elaborates] Boy time flies, doesn't it? Such is life, I guess.

Jay: What would you say the last chapter of your story would be about?

Peter: The last chapter would be my being here as a patient. And the time I had to go over to the hospital for treatment.

We drift away from the distinct chapters of a story and talk about his two daughters. But this is cut short when he resumes commenting on sales work and life on the road. According to Rinehart, being on the road in the company of his wife was the happiest time of his life.

> The wife came along with me. I was married twice and I have two daughters by my first wife. They're far apart. One's in California and one's in Connecticut. No sons. So, as I said, the wife . . . the second wife . . . she come along with me traveling. Two daughters . . .
>
> My wife and I actually didn't need a home, but we had it. My sales work covered the entire United States and my wife traveled with me. Those were the happiest years of my life. We had to pull the travel trailer with us. I had a trailer behind the van. I didn't want a motor home. The type of work that I was in, I could just go in a place, drop off the trailer, and I'd have transportation and all the merchandise in the van. I sold all kinds of stuff . . . the last, I sold the Oster Commercial Blender and I sold that till I fell. Then I couldn't walk or move. And I can't drive. So here I am.
>
> The wife died in '85. She had cancer. She didn't know she had it until she went for a physical. They found a spot on her lung and they went in . . . they had to take her left lung out. Seemed to be doing well. Then she started getting pains in her stomach and they opened her up and found a cancer between the liver and the pancreas. She only lasted a couple of months after that. Thank God she didn't suffer very much. [Pause] I don't mean she didn't suffer. She didn't suffer too long.
>
> I fell before she knew she had cancer. She'd come over to see me here as often as she could. She was in no condition even then to take care of me. I'm so helpless as far as bowels and urinary tract. I have no control. But they treat me very good here, then and now.

Rinehart tells me that his daughters call him weekly, which pleases him. He talks about them some, endearingly. But it's his traveling years that preoccupy him and provide the central linkages of his narrative. I ask him if he had a chance to live his life over, what he'd do differently. He remarks:

> Go into sales from the start. I'm not patting myself on the back, but another fellow and I had the reputation of being the best in our line in the country. I've always thought since I got into sales that if I've got the ability to sell, I'm not going to work for somebody else. I'll be working for myself, which I was. My wife helped me, of course.
>
> God, the only state we weren't in was Alaska. It was just too cold. Actually, it's useless to go to Alaska anyway on sales. You have to fly all your merchandise in. I'd have to drive all the way to Alaska. It just wouldn't pay to go to Alaska the way things are now.
>
> But between the two of us [he and his wife] . . . the hospitalizations and expenses . . . I got wiped out. We got wiped out entirely. So that's what it is. Like they say, "Easy come, easy go."

A sense of acceptance was apparent. While Rinehart was proud of his accomplishments, looking back he was not remorseful. According to him, life had brought him a good living, happiness, and now took care of him in his later years as best as could be expected.

> I see people that are worse off than I am. I feel sorry for them, but I'm not looking back with remorse. It's something I can't help. It happened and I have to live with it. Life's been happy and pretty good to me otherwise. I made a good living. You take the good with the bad.
>
> When it [the fall] first happened, I hoped that I would be able to get back to normal. Then I hoped to get . . . they got me into a wheelchair. I hoped to be able to stay in a wheelchair, maybe graduate to crutches and that. It never happened that way though. But it didn't make me despondent.
>
> Gradually, I began to know that I would probably never walk again and I've been about the way I have been now for the last couple of years. They brought a specialist in from the University of Pittsburgh and he put a brain tap in the nerve center of my brain. But that didn't work.
>
> I'm hoping to clear up the pain in my back so I can, if nothing else, sit up. But I read a lot and that takes time and they treat me good here. The aides come in and I kid with them and that. The rest of the time is about the same as an average day when you aren't working. Only instead of working now, I read. It's a long weekend, you might say.

We talk about Bayside and Rinehart compares it with a hospital. He says that he understands the reasons why care in a nursing home is sometimes not as good as it might be in a hospital. At the same time, he describes Bayside as, in some ways, the "nearest thing" to home.

> *Jay:* Pete, before you came to live here, did you have any idea what it'd be like?

Peter: Vaguely. I had an idea. My wife and her sister found this one that they thought was the best in town. And that's why I got here. I guess it is the best. It isn't like a hospital.

Jay: Oh? What do you mean?

Peter: Well, in a hospital you just ring and you got service right away. Here, it's not a hospital. You ring for service and they're on a lean budget, so you may get them right away or you may have to wait half an hour. Depends on how busy the aides are. That's part of it and it affects the care we get.

It's not all the aides' fault either. Of course, aides are hard to keep. I see changeover in the help here all the while. Some have been here a long time, but others will come and go. And I imagine . . . I have no basis for saying this, but I think they're probably on a minimum wage. When they get something better, they leave here and go there. That's my opinion, but you can understand that.

Jay: But, otherwise, does it seem homelike to you?

Peter: Home to me was a place like we had planned to retire, where you could retire, do what we wished, do what we wanted, when we wanted, worked part-time if I wanted to, and just enjoy things. But, as I said, you get wiped out fast. Anyway, mostly I wasn't home. So what's the difference, huh?

Jay: I guess not much if you put it that way. What about here?

Peter: Here? Well, it's not home really. But it's the nearest thing to it, I think. As I said, they help here, well, they treat me as a family. You heard me before? The aide that was in here. I kid her quite a bit in the morning. She was doing something . . . I don't know what . . . and I say, "Hey birdbrain, cut that out," funnylike. That aide knew I was kidding. It didn't bother her at all. Yeah, and she can shovel it back to me too. You can do that with people you're close to and know your ways.

I focus on the meaning of home, particularly the question of whether a nursing facility can be home and if having had a life on the road makes a difference in this regard. At first, Rinehart compares life on the road with life "at home."

Like at home even before I fell and before my wife was sick, the travel trailer was like home even though we had another home. She did about the same things she'd do at home, if we were living at home.

It was eight foot wide and twenty-five feet long. Had everything in it that home would. You had your stove, refrigerator, toilet facilities, everything was in it. We did, many times, stay self-contained for over a week, with no electricity or anything else. But we had battery power. We had forty gallons of waste water. So it really wasn't . . . we was glad to be home again, but there wasn't too much difference. The best part of it is that we saw about every place that was worth seeing in the United States. I really enjoyed being on the road. I suppose you might say a life on wheels.

Rinehart explains that while a travel trailer is not exactly home, it makes the transition to a new environment that much easier. As we continue our discussion, it is evident that home to him means familiarity and having a modicum of personal control over daily life more than it means having a home base. In that regard, Bayside doesn't quite feel like home. Still, in the context of a life of travel, Bayside is one more place on the road. As the following extract shows, in that respect, the subjective meaning of being in the nursing home isn't "too much of a changeover."

Jay: I was wondering, Pete, what would it have to be like here for it to be more like home to you?

Peter: Well, at home if I needed something there'd be somebody there to take care of it right away. There'd be people there to . . . people there to cook my meals, to live a normal life. That's the difference between, I think, living home and living in a place like this. It's different. Here, you have a set menu for breakfast, lunch, and dinner. And of course at home you can get up and around, which you can't do the way I am now.

Jay: Yeah. Is it the place itself or the incapacity that makes the difference to you, in terms of your feelings about home? What I mean I guess is, is it the place you're in or is it the incapacity mainly?

Peter: I don't think either, Jay, because, as I said, we traveled all the while. We were only home about a couple a months a year. So actually, that way, it wasn't too much of a changeover coming here.

Jay: Do you think of this place as part of your life or separate from it?

Peter: I think it's part of my life. I've seen people that weren't as well off as I am and some that were very far from what I am. They're very despondent. Can't face it. Well I don't have that feeling. I can adjust very easily. I think part of that is the fact that we traveled so much. You got to meet different people every week. I think that's the main difference. Of course, when you're stationary at home, you had a home. If you want to stay in bed all morning, you stayed in bed all morning.

Yeah, it's part of my life all right. What would I do if this place weren't here? I'd be another place like it, probably not as good as this place. I've adapted myself for quite a while here. I did adapt all right. Like when the aide brought you in, it didn't bother me to have you come in, even though you were a stranger. Not that you're a stranger now. Somebody else might have cringed down a bit, you know, don't want to meet nobody.

In the end, what Rinehart's life has become is not to be lamented as much as accepted because it is part of one's fate. Rinehart explains as he describes himself.

Me, I'm realistic, down-to-earth. I get along with people. That's why I was a success in sales, I imagine. I guess I don't have much of a future now. Not really. But I've taken the attitude, more or less, that this has happened, I'm here, I can't control it. So be it. So why should I be here crying my eyes out, feeling sorry for myself? Right now, until I get able to use my body where I can sit down, I haven't even thought of any plans for the future. Then again, what will be, will be. Maybe I'll never be able to get out of this bed. Who knows?

They had me where I could sit up for about an hour, but I relapsed from that and got where I can't sit. It's a feeling like if you're sitting on a golf ball. That's the kind of pain it is, if you can imagine that, in the worse spot it could be.

I have a lot of free time thinking here sometimes. I told you what I thought about politics and that. I know even though I'm in bed I know that, physically, I'm probably better off than a lot of other people that have nothing wrong with them except old age and they don't accept it. It doesn't bother me, and even though I'm the way I am, I still have, I think, all my brains yet. And I'm not entirely dependent on somebody else. That's a funny thing to say because I can't move out of this bed without help, but otherwise, I think I'm in good health. I feed myself, which a lot of 'em here have to be fed. I can read, which I like to do. If I could sit up, I could write the way I always did, I believe. [Elaborates]

I don't think about death. I've always been a fatalist. I believe when it's time for you to go, you're gonna go. Everyone that saw me after I fell? I didn't know whether they were lying or whether they meant it, but they said I looked so well and behaved the way I did, even after I fell. I don't bother nobody. I try to get along with all of them. I don't think I'm hard to get along with. My philosophy of life . . . as I said, I'm a fatalist. What comes, comes. Like when I fell . . . I didn't want to of course, but it happened and that's that.

Mainly, I pass the time. Time doesn't bother me, really. You got a lot of time here. But, like I said, I like to read and I read mainly mysteries and spy thrillers. I was reading one by a British author, but don't much like those because the British describe too much. Takes 'em a whole page to describe one thing. [Elaborates] If I get tired of reading, I take a nap and if I feel like reading after I take a nap, I will or I might just lay there with my eyes closed, resting, you know, like in your hotel room. Sometimes they'll come in . . . the aide will come in the room or something and . . . it's funny . . . she thinks I'm asleep and I'm not. So that's life for me. Easy come, easy go.

Barring a change, Jay, I'll be just like I am. Hopefully, I'll get to the point where I can sit up. I'm seventy-seven years old. I've had a good life. Down the road, unless things change, I'll probably be about the same as I am now.

* * * * *

One mark of a nursing facility that would seem to affect the quality of life is the extent it is homelike. This typically means things such as an atmosphere of soft, noninstitutional lighting and colors on the walls and being surrounded by one's own furniture. For the residents of this chapter, special circumstances present a different horizon for signaling home. Home is a kind of vacation, as a hotel might accommodate or a long weekend might offer. For these residents, the quality of life is not figured chiefly in terms of care provision or homeyness, but in relation to another place along the road of life that fate has taken them.

CHAPTER

8

Sisters

Residents sometimes say that, besides the pain, suffering, and helplessness, one of the most difficult things about living in a nursing home is "it cuts you off," meaning that it separates you from the rest of life, from loved ones, or from home, often forever. The exceptions are those who make a new home in the facility or who bring loved ones with them, or those who never had much of a home or family life to begin with, and those who for one reason or another accept their fate with equanimity.

In this chapter, we meet African American twin sisters Lula Burton and Lily Robinson. Their special circumstance is that they hardly have ever been "cut off" from each other and now continue to live together in the same room at Florida Manor. At the time of their interviews, the sisters were seventy-four years old and had been in the nursing home for a year. Before that, for ten years, they shared a house of their own.

A benefit of having family members or significant others coresident in a nursing home is that a life once shared continues to be a source of meaning for daily living. Of course, there are familial coresidents, either or both of whom are demented or otherwise noncommunicative and, as such, can share little. Communicative family coresidents do not necessarily share good times or look back solely on positive moments from their pasts. But for coresident family members such as Burton and Robinson, narrative horizons that extend beyond the period of coresidency provide a ready-made, long-standing familiarity in a living environment normally said to be devoid of it. Equally important, talk and interaction are not limited in meaning to short-term exchanges and relevancies, the bare "how-do-you-do's" of daily living.

This is not to say that the twins or others whom we will meet in the next few chapters simply transport home with them into their facilities. Burton and Robinson, for example, know and speak of the difference between "real" home and the nursing home. They acknowledge the homelike quality of care, but they also recognize that the quality of their lives, as they understand it, is linked with sources and commonalities removed from the present. More important in their special circumstance, the sources and commonalities continue to present themselves as the twins share memories, thoughts, and sentiments, highlighted in their mutual use of the pronoun *we* to speak of what they share in life, both past and current.

The primary commonality in the twins' case is "service," what they believe to have been their purpose, not just their lot, in life. They are like Mary Carter of Chapter 5 in this regard. The sisters speak of serving those for whom they worked, mainly cooked for, as a mission beyond the job alone, one that was meant to be. This is no longer realized in the nursing home because of their incapacity, but it continues to be a desire. Its memories make them happy, shared as the "we" who fulfilled their purpose in life. Yet, Robinson especially is wary of the present, particularly the danger of crime, drug abuse, and their impact on the young, whom, were it not for Robinson's incapacity, she would continue serving for their own good.

LULA BURTON

Like her sister Lily and a few other residents interviewed for the study such as Julia McCall and Mary Carter, Lula Burton has spent much of her life in church and "in service." While Burton doesn't express her love of the Lord with the same fervor that McCall and Carter do, nor is she as otherworldly, her lifelong concern for others is suffused with religious meaning.

I interview Burton alone in a lounge located near her room where I wheeled her, as she is confined to a wheelchair. Burton suffers from hypertension and diabetes, which has caused her to have one leg amputated. Her brief life story has a humble beginning in a rural area of north Florida and develops into a narrative of work and devotion to others, much like her twin sister's story. Burton's is not a charmed life but it is filled with simple joys. Notice, at the end of the following extract, she uses the collective pronoun *we* to refer to herself, a repeated form of identity shared with her sister.

> I was raised from childhood with farmers. Then I married a farmer. That was a great deal of my life. I was a farm girl and I married a farmer, but we didn't have any children. And I like . . . Do you wanna know what I like? [I nod] I like fishing, going to school, always loved the school. I'm a good fisherman. Fishing . . . I like fishing. My hobby is fishing. I don't know nothing else, but working on the farm and fishing. I love that.
>
> My occupation was cooking. I like cooking. That's about the size of it. After I married, I adopted a son. He's twenty-nine now. I sent him to school, four years of college. I helped with my nieces and nephews, helped those

boys and girls go to school. That's the only thing I know, helping people. I helped my mother and father to make ends meet, like working on the farm. My father was a great farmer and my husband was a farmer. I'm just a farm girl. Then I started cooking. I cooked at a sorority house out there on sorority row. I cooked six years at one place and I cooked six years at another place. A-E House. I don't know what the initials meant, but it was a house where I cooked. I cooked for some boys right there, too, fraternity boys. That was another place. And I lived on the premises for five years with Mr. Caleb S. Porter. He worked out there at the university. His wife passed; so I had to leave there. I was chief bottle washer there. I did all the cooking and planned the meals. We got along fine until she passed. He thought he'd marry again. I wasn't with him when he married the next time. I didn't work for him anymore.

I was a church member. I sang in a choir. I was secretary for the church for fifteen years. That's the only thing I know that I really done, a lot of service. My childhood . . . I was going to church when I was eleven years old and I still belong to the same church. I just wanna say that I love church and singing in the choir. I was a choir member. I call myself a good member. We were real good members of the church. Our pastor always told that to us, me and Lily, every time he come to visit and he's been there over forty years.

Now what else do you want me to say?

I take the opportunity to present Burton with the idea of writing her life story and ask her what the chapters would be about. She recounts much of what she's already said, this time divided into chapters. Her last chapter is a summary of aspects of her life that continue to be important to her.

The last chapter would be cooking. I was a cook. My last chapter would be . . . I'm trying to think what year I last cooked in. I think about '70, '71, or '72 I spent my last year cooking. And that's all I can write about, cooking. That's my whole life story, cooking. I spent my life doing that. School started about September. So I'd break through the summer, about three months, and then start right back the next month and live as a cook, plan meals, and cook. I loved it. To me, it was more than a job, helpin' others and all.

I could write a chapter about my son. I adopted him and sent him to school. He went to school and he's out now. I adopted him when he was eighteen hours old and I adopted him in 1960. I picked him up in the hospital, the same day. I never met his mother till I got the baby. But she's a sweetheart. Very sweet child. She was a sweet woman. I think she gave him away not because she didn't want him, but because she wasn't able to support him. So my husband and I thought we'd adopt him. He's a dear heart, a very sweet heart. I love him to death I think. I know he loves me 'cause every time he calls, he says, "Mama, I love you." I tell him, "Well, I just want you to know I'm not your mother. I'm just your adopted mother."

He says, "Well, you're the only mother I know and you're still my mama." So we let it go like that. He's my son and I love him to death. He made pretty good in college, because he's the manager of this store now in Atlanta. So I know that's something he loves.

The rest of the chapters, like I says, is church work. That's all I know that I could say anything about that I really enjoyed and did well was working in church . . . service. And cooking, the only thing that I know that I would enjoy doing and I did that. When I had the operation on my leg, that's when I stopped working. That was in '72. I had my leg amputated. I had to stop because I couldn't get around.

We talk about the important people in her life: her mother and an older sister who became like a mother to her after the mother died. The important people are shared with sister Lily, which is repeated in Lily's interview.

My mother was the most important person in my life. I just loved her to death. She was a sweet person. I had some lovely brothers and I had a lovely sister. I had a sister who passed in '69. She was older. She was one of my important friends and dearest sister. I love Lily of course, but Althea [the older sister] was closer to me than Lily. Lily and I were twins. We was a twosome, onesome. And Althea was closer because Althea reared us up. She was our mother and father and brother and sister too. Most important person I had in my life was her. I had a husband, but she topped everything. Name was Althea Stevens.

I had four brothers. I had one brother was a sweet brother, sweeter than any other. His name was Paul Williams. He was living way down south of here. Every time Lily and I asked for something, he would always send it to us. He was very kind to us.

Now Lily and I are the only two in our family. All our family is dead. I mean brothers and sisters. So it's just Lily and I now. Lily and I are very close. We've been living together now about ten years, even before we came here. She and I lived in our home. Then we came out here. Lily is my closest. My son and I are very close.

The conversation turns to the meaning of home and to why Florida Manor is not home. According to Burton, the Manor is *like* home, but not home. Home is conveyed in the terms of her life story, applying the vocabulary she knows best: Home is where one plans meals and cooks according to good taste. To that extent, the Manor is not home. While food preparation and the taste of food is important to many residents, for the sisters it resonates with a central linkage of their narratives, adding to its significance and spilling over into the other life connections of service. As we will learn later, to that extent the Manor is a horizon that can never include home.

Jay: What does the word *home* mean to you, Ms. B?
Lula: It means a house that you can enjoy yourself in. That's what home is. That's what I call home.
Jay: Now that you've been here for a year, does this feel like home to you?
Lula: It feels like home. The people are nice and I enjoy being here. It's like being home and friends and relatives and things. It's beautiful to be here.
Jay: So it's home.
Lula: No. It's *like* home but it ain't home. It's different, this and home.
Jay: In what way would you say?
Lula: Well at home you can have some of the things you desire yourself, plan yourself. But here we don't plan nothing. We have to do what they say to do. Whatever they give us to eat, we have to eat what they give us. When you're home, you can plan something of your own, plan your meals. Like if you want a special meal, you can have a special meal. But here you can't. A lot of things they cook I don't like, because I always cooked and I've enjoyed my cooking . . . until here. You got to eat what people cook. A lot of people say they are cooks, but they're not really cooks. But other than that, they're very nice people here. This is a nice place to be. When you don't have nowhere else to go, this is a good place to be. They have some nice help here.

Burton talks at length about the Manor, its "nice help," and the attractive facilities. She even describes some of the help as like family to her and to her sister Lily, noting that the help is not actually kin, but that they're very nice and familylike nonetheless. Burton is careful to mark important distinctions: Homelike is not the same as home; familylike is not actually family.

I ask Burton whether having her sister living with her at the Manor makes a difference in what life is like there. As the discussion unfolds, we learn that the quality of care in the nursing home could never produce the quality of life she once knew, no matter how hard "they" try. The home the Manor is, is a home that Burton and her sister Lily together realize in the memories shared in everyday conversation. Even the seemingly irrational possibility of fishing again continues to be meaningful in the context of a life of common experiences.

Jay: Does it make a difference having your sister with you in this place?
Lula: Oh, there's a difference.
Jay: In what way?
Lula: Well, if they would come in maybe sometime and ask me, "Lula, what would you like to have to eat?" or something like that. That'd be one of the main things. And you don't have no one to talk to here. Maybe the nurse when they bring you the meal or something like that, but other than that, you don't have anybody to discuss nothing with. Lily and I

talk together, we talk. It's much better to be in the room with her than to be with someone I don't know.

Jay: Why is that?

Lula: Well, because we have things to talk about life and the other person. It would be anything we did together. That means a lot to talk about things you've had dealings with and doing together and enjoying things together . . . talk with that, about that.

Jay: So that helps . . .

Lula: There's nothing they can do here to make me love it any more than they have done. But I'd rather be with . . . even if my son was here, I'd enjoy being with him. He can't get here because he's working and he's got a job and he can't get away.

Jay: How does it help to have Lily here with you?

Lula: It helps me because she can talk with me and I can talk with her. We're company for each other. We talk about what we did when . . . right now if we was able to do it, what we would do, like fishing and different things like that. Other than that, we just have to live up life like that. Fishing we can't do anyway, but we talk about it. She won't be able to go fishing unless she can walk. The doctor had to amputate both her legs. She's diabetic like me.

Jay: So you share things and that . . .

Lula: Well, I 'bout done give my best life out in service. Not just working, but helping others. I have enjoyed life and I'm still enjoying life. I'm not sad. I like my life. I enjoy being friendly to people and amuse people and everything. I learned [taught] those girls in that sorority a lot. They liked when I learned them. And one of the main things is that I like to entertain. That's my life.

Jay : Do you miss that?

Lula: Oh yes. I miss that, but . . . I like that. That's life to me. I enjoy life because I've been happy and helped others. I enjoy life because I'm pretty healthy. I don't have a lot of pain and aches and things. That's all in my life.

LILY ROBINSON

I interview Burton's sister, Lily Robinson, in the twin's room, with Burton present and sitting in a wheelchair on her side of the room. Robinson stays in bed throughout the interview, as she does most of the day because of her amputations. She feels more comfortable that way. The curtain separating the two sides, which has been drawn for nursing cares, remains closed. Periodically, as Robinson and I talk, Robinson leans over to ask her sister something. Burton readily responds from the other side of the curtain.

Robinson suffers from diabetes and high blood pressure. Like her sister, she has spent her life in service. She not only was a cook and domestic but has devoted herself, as both sisters put it, to "learning others." Robinson is proud of what she taught her friends, especially the young sorority women who eagerly sought her advice over that of the house mother.

We begin with Robinson's life story.

Well, I don't have much history in my life. It's hard work. I lived on a farm and I was about four miles from town. I had to walk to school. [Elaborates] After growing up, I married and lived on a farm. Then I decided I would try to cook. My mother taught me a lot about cooking. [Elaborates] And then I went out to cook in the neighborhood. I cooked one place here twenty-three years. I consider myself a pretty good cook. I cooked at that one sorority at the university for twenty-three years. After I left there, I haven't worked anymore. I worked in Daytona Beach in a hotel and in St. Augustine I worked in a hotel. I cooked there for four or five years. I haven't done anything but cook. That's all I did all my life. And 'I guess that's about it. I've taken care of children in my home for a while, maybe a year or two for the summer. I worked at a foster home for children for about two years taking care of children. And I . . . after that, I left the sorority because I became ill and I've been kinda down ever since then. I haven't been any good no more. I worked there until I couldn't work anymore. Then I began going to the doctor and I knew then that I was a diabetic. Actually, I worked a long time before I knew I was a diabetic. All at once I broke down. My legs broke down. They had to take them off and that's about it.

I raised one child, raised one girl. Then I adopted her when she was about five months old. I raised her and she started school. Then she had this little girl right here [points to a framed photograph of the granddaughter on her dresser] and I adopted her too. So I don't have any children of my own. I only have two adopted children. That little girl [in the photograph] is ten years old. I had adopted her mother a long time ago and raised her. [Elaborates] Her mother says that she didn't . . . she wasn't married and she got this child and she wanted to give it away. I told her to give it to me. So I adopted her and so she's with me now.

I guess that's about it. I don't know of anything else. Just hard work, that's all, and service. And I'm a Christian. I belong to the Baptist church and I've given my life for the Lord and that's about it . . . service for the Lord. I don't know of anything else. And now I'm in here with these people. I don't know how long I'll be here. But they're all very nice to us. [Nods toward her sister on the other side of the curtain] We're treated nice here.

Continuing to look back on her life, Robinson speaks of youthful desires and what she might have become. The emphasis is less on the actual job than on the service she might have been to others.

I mostly loved people, loved to get along with people. That's my whole desire was in life, was to treat people as I wish to be treated and to live that way, live the way that people would love me. And that's about it. I liked the outdoor life. I liked fishing and things like that, picnics and so on.

I tell ya, I'd love to have been a . . . things I loved to have been when I was growing up, when I was younger. I'd love to have been a schoolteacher so I could teach people something. Oh, I don't know, just learn them the way to live if I could, to the best of my ability. But that's the only thing that I desire, that I didn't get to be a teacher. 'Cause it seemed like I could tell young people what to do. That's about all I had on my mind that I didn't do and I never will do it I guess 'cause I'm too old now.

I know when I was working . . . I was working with young girls. They always came to me for . . . I had ideas, things they wanted to know about. They wouldn't go to the house mother. They'd come to me. So I said, "Why do you all come to me?" They say, "Lily, you always know things." I said, "Well, the reason I know about young people is I was young once myself and I think about telling you all the things that I was used to, how my mother raised me." They said, "Well, we enjoy your talks." That made me feel good. That's about all I can say.

Lula and I both worked in those sororities. But I worked longer than Lula did. We was in different ones, different sororities. I worked at Chi Omega and she worked at Alpha Delta. I think that was it. [Turns toward her sister] Lula? Was it Alpha Delta? [Lula answers yes] Alpha Delta. That was a girl's sorority. We wasn't far apart. She was on one corner and I was on another. We could walk where we worked with each other and things like that. But I worked there, planned my meals. I did my ordering. I did it all, but I enjoyed it.

Robinson recalls her parents, especially her mother and older sister. As twin sister Lula remarked in her interview, Robinson explains that both the mother and older sister were mothers to the twins. Robinson speaks of accepting the sorrow of their deaths, but it is overshadowed by her emphasis on living and service "to make others happy."

The most important one was my mother. That's the only one I can say. Since my mother I haven't really had any important . . . my sister, my oldest sister, she was important 'cause she was just like a mother to us. Other than that, I think that's about all. The only somebody now is my sister. The one right there. That's the closest person I am to now. I don't have anybody closer to me than she is, although my daughter is close to me. But she's not as close to me as my Lula. My sister and I have been so close together and been together all our lives.

I've always been a happy person. I've never had extremely happy things in my life, just from day-to-day things happened. But nothing extremely happy. When I had depression, I never was sad. I'd never dwell on that. I dwelled on being happy and trying to make others happy. So I've always been happy. I've had some sadness in my life. My parents and all passed away. My sisters and brothers. That was pretty sad, but I never dwelled on it because I knew that those days would be. I knew they must go and leave or if I left them. That's why I just accepted it and tried to serve others. Service was the main thing.

Responding to the question about what life now looks like, Robinson conveys her sense of the relation between her incapacity, hope for the future, and living in a nursing home. In the context of her incapacity and being dependent, life is hopeless because she is a burden and can't be of service. According to Robinson, this has little to do with the nursing home. Robinson accepts God's plans for her and looks ahead to salvation. In relation to the possibility of going home, however, there is hope that she again can be of service, especially to her adopted granddaughter.

Jay: What does life look like from you're at now, Ms. R?

Lily: Well, I say it's hopeless, to me. I'm just in other people's way here. I'm no good.

Jay: Being in someone's way— that makes a difference?

Lily: Yes, it do.

Jay: Would you explain that a little more?

Lily: Well, when you can't do anything for yourself, I think you're in other folks' way. If I was up and doing for myself and others, I would enjoy living, but I don't enjoy it.

Jay: So would you say it's the place you're at or you . . . ?

Lily: No, it's not the place. It's just the shape I'm in. That's what I'm talking about. The place is very good to me. But I'm so helpless. I can't do anything for myself. When you're used to doing for yourself . . . and when you get down and can't do nothing unless somebody come and do it for you, that's pretty sad.

Jay: If you could live your life over, what would you do differently?

Lily: I don't know what I would do differently. I don't because I had a good life. Although I worked hard, I had a good life.

Jay: What would you say are the ingredients of a good life? What does it mean to have a good life?

Lily: What I mean is that I enjoyed life. I never had a whole lots, but I've had a comfortable life. What I mean by that is that I was never on the hands of other people. I've always worked and what I wanted mostly I always got at the time. And I think when a person gets the things they want and need in life, that's a good life.

Jay: How would you explain what's happened to you over the course of your life?

Lily: That's hard 'cause I've tried to work it out, but I couldn't really work it out. I wonder sometimes, why this? But God alone knows why this happened to me. So I just accept it as my share and be with Him in time.

But if there would be anything that, if somebody needed help and I could be of service, I would do that. I love to help people. That's my desire, was to take care of people. But I got so helpless that I couldn't help myself. The joy of my life would maybe now be to make somebody happy. That's what I want. I'd like that very much, to make someone happy. The one thing I would like would be somebody to remember me by and say, "Well, Lily did thus and thus before her last day and she seemed happy doing that." That's the thing I know.

I wish I could get out and visit people and talk to friends, have them in sometimes and make a nice dinner for them. And talk about old times and things like that. That'd make me happy. I hope I'll be able to do that one day, hold my own and have a place, and I can have my little girl back with me.

Jay: You had her with you at home for a while?

Lily: I raised her. They just took her from me last year, just before I came here. She went in a foster home. It's been about two months since I seen her. I'm the only mama she has.

Robinson's sentiments about home parallel and elaborate her sister's. While Florida Manor is homelike, it can never be home. The nursing home's quality of care is, simply, nice and "sweet," but never to be taken as part of life. Home belongs to life, the nursing home to a different, more limited domain of experience, the domain of the patient, not the whole person. In regard to the possibility of going home, Robinson points out that as for herself and her sister, they will never "give up," even as they are helpless, because ultimately home is with her Lord in a life everlasting.

Jay: Do you feel this place is part of your life or separate from it?

Lily: Well, I should consider it now as part of my life 'cause I'm here, just 'cause I'm here. But I never will accept it as a . . . really a life for my life. It seem like I'm just visiting here, but not really a part of my life.

There's one or two here that's very sweet and they're like family, not kin, but like family. But other than that, I'm more just like a patient is what I am, someone they have to wait on. You don't be your ol' self here.

Jay: When people go to the hospital, of course, they're patients. But I wonder if it's different here being a patient?

Lily: I think they all seem about just alike. I stayed in the hospital quite a long time when they amputated my legs and the nurses are very friendly, but it's not like home. No place, no hospital, no nursing home is like your own home. Not to me. So I don't think it's like . . . They're friendly, but . . . Peace of mind I think at home makes you different. You run your home. These people here run the nursing home. At home, you're the overseer. You take care of everything and I think that's more like a whole being. Here you're just a part. When you're home, you're whole. You're a whole person. You're taking care of everything and everything comes to you by your means and it makes you feel more at home.

Jay: Do you think it's possible to have a life in a place like this?

Lily: No. I wouldn't want to stay here all my life. I just wouldn't. I wouldn't wish that on anybody. I just come for the rest and somebody to take care of you. Then the family of somebody comes and takes care of you. I think that'll be better. We're not going to, Lula and me, give up to live here. Of course, a lot of people do.

Jay: A lot of people do what, did you say? Did you say, "give up"?

Lily: Yes, they gives up and lives here.

Jay: What does that mean, to "give up"? What does that mean to you, Ms. R?

Lily: I will say give up everything. There's no desire for anything. That's why when somebody gives up just something, you're satisfied, not happy. You just satisfied. It's not the matter of being happy; you're satisfied. I made myself satisfied here. That's all. Nothing with happy. I'm just here. I'm not happy or unhappy. I'm satisfied.

What I'm sayin' is that they come and do us . . . I pray and ask the Lord to take care of me and the people that take care of me, and they do their best. I'm not sick. I'm just helpless, but I'm not sick. And I'm thankful that I'm not sick. And that's a blessing. So many people here that are sick. And I'm thankful that I'm not sick. I get up everyday and I don't feel bad. I get up everyday and I sit up all day long.

I'm just a helpless person. That's all I can say. I'm helpless, but I still have lots to be thankful for. I don't say I'm not. I'm thankful that I'm not in a worse shape than I am. There's many people worse off than I am. So I have so much to be thankful for. I can't go anywhere, but I can sit up and I can be taken all over this place, go to church down there [the activity room] to hear the preacher and singing and what not. I get joy out of staying here, but I don't have a future. The only future I have lies in my end, when I pray and ask the Lord to make me ready, make me ready to have a happy day. That day I'm looking forward to and I'm certainly looking forward to it. I have been admitted to the kingdom and going home to life everlastin'.

Jay: Do you think about death, Ms. R?

Lily: No, I don't think about it. I know it's coming, but I don't think about it because it's not for me to think about. I think that's left for the higher above. I'm here, but I don't think about death because I know it's sure. It's coming for sure. I just want a resting place when I die. I don't wanna be in torment. I want it to be in a resting place.

Since I been here, people do die. I know if I could have kept my mother with me forever and ever, I would've kept her. But she died and left me. I know that I must die. So when everybody I see, people are dying. I know that that day will come. I read in this Bible about death. Death is sure. That's why I know it's coming.

I just look forward to not being here and try to meet each day with a smile. That's the only thing I look forward to. I look forward to getting out of this place one day. I do wanna get out of here. I don't know if I will, but I'm looking forward to get out of here one day. That'll make me happy.

Short of going to heaven, the idea of someday leaving Florida Manor causes Robinson to speak about home and the possibility of again caring for her adopted granddaughter. As she describes the unfortunate events involving her daughter that led to the adoption of the granddaughter, Robinson laments the selfishness of the so-called young race. The young race cares little about anyone but themselves and certainly not older people. To Robinson, it is a generation that has lost the value of prayer and, especially, service. At the same time, Robinson, with her sister, finds solace in memories of a different era and purpose, one committed to others in service and to the Lord.

Lily: It'd make me happy to have my little girl come back to me and stay with me. Just to hear her voice in the house would make me happy.

Jay: So you had her in the house with you until she was about eight years old? Is that right?

Lily: Oh, I had her in the house with me until . . . let's see. I came out here in '89? I came out here in '88. She just left me the first of '88. [Turns in the direction her sister is seated] Wasn't it, Lula? When did she leave?

Lula: She left around, about the last of '88.

Lily: She left me just before I came out here. I remember calling her and telling her I was coming out here. And she said, "Mama, I won't see you no more." I said, "Oh, yes you will."

I don't think there's much joy in growing old. There's so many things you can't do, things you like to do. I think you send good people away when you grow old and you can't do nothing for yourself. One thing people get tired of it when you get old. They don't want to wait on you. Most people don't like to wait on old people. They don't have time to talk with you. Maybe a few years ago, it was . . . years ago people would take time out and talk with you. But now they're going so fast, they don't have time to talk to one another. And old people don't have anybody to talk to no how, except Lula and me, we have each other.

Jay: So you think it's made a difference in that times have changed.

Lily: Oh yes, lots of things changed over time. When I was a child, I loved old people. I loved to be around old people. I loved to talk to them. I loved to see what I could do, what I could do for them. But it's so sad now because people don't have time to do anything for you now. Everything somebody would do for you now they want a lot of pay for it. Used to be people didn't want that. People would do it out of the kindness of their heart.

Jay: Do you think families have changed a lot?

Lily: Yes, families have changed lots. It's not the love in the family that used to be in the family. People used to love their family. Children loved their parents, but they don't anymore. I've experienced that in my own life.

I never was a rowdy person but I liked to go to church and I like to participate in church. I was singing in the choir and all those things I miss. I like to go and visit people. I belonged to a lot of clubs. But I don't have that now. A day come and a day go.

I got a joy out of going to church. I'd cook and take meals. We had some . . . some Sundays we'd have homecoming [at the sorority] and things like that and I'd cook food and take out. Then I'd have our pastor and his wife out to our place for dinners, several times. Well I just loved to take care of the people. I like that. Lula and I got a joy out of doing for other people.

Lula: [From the other side of the room] Sure do.

Lily: Old people can't do the things they used to do and they kind of dread it in a sense. Some people are happier in their old age than they were when they were younger. But I don't care how happy you were, when you get older, you're not the same. You don't get the joy out of life when you get older as you had in middle age. You can't do nothing for nobody else hardly. You got to look for someone else to do something for you. That's kind of hard. You got to wait for someone to do for you when you're used to doing for other people. It makes you happy doing for others and you can't when you get old like this. When people get old and they have to wait on someone else to do things for them, that's takes a lot from 'em.

Jay: What would it be like in old age if you could do things?

Lily: Well, if you could do things and get out and help people, you'd be happier. That's what I know. Get out and try to learn the young people what . . . try to learn them and help them.

I think the young people need more help now than they ever did in life. They're going on this ol' crack and stuff and it's ruining the nation. That's one of the worst things that ever happened. I don't know where it started at. But everybody, all the children . . . what's it gonna be? What's the next nation gonna be like when everybody's turned to crack and drugs and all that stuff. It's bad. It's really bad. I feel sorry for the young race. They're not happy unless they're with that ol' crack or something.

One thing I say, they need to pray more. That's one thing. People need to pray more. A lot of people are not prayin'. They just living each day as it comes and that's it. They don't never take time to thank God for them from one day to the other. They don't thank Him for getting the food. They don't thank . . . a lot of people don't say "thank God" for nothing. That's the thing's destroying the world. Everybody is looking for a dollar. And that's bad. Money is the root of all evil. And it really has taken its toll since that stuff come out.

Jay: You mean since . . . ?

Lily: Since crack and whatever it is, drugs and all that stuff. The dollar bill is all a person want. And that's bad. People are afraid to stand in the store. They're afraid of everything, even in their home. It's really terrible. And I feel sorry for the young race. The parents have done everything to bring them up and since they brought them up, they done turned from their parents. Children have really gone away from their parents. Only thing they want is to get these old drugs and go somewhere to have a good time and that's bad. That ol' crack got my daughter like that.

When I was young, people used to bootleggin,' moonshinin,' making it in the woods out there. Crack's about the same thing. They had wars in the woods. Went to war against each other about that ol' moonshine and stuff and this war now's against people with drugs. They killing one another about that. It's just . . .

Prayer would change things. They need to pray more. I just don't know what it is. I know it's sin. Sin is taking over. The government, the high officials are selling this old crack. They got to make a dollar. They making more than they'll ever spend and they still grasping after money. They say that money's the root of all evil and it's ruining all the children.

It's disturbing, very disturbing. I wish, just wish there's something I could do to change the children, the young race. They have enough in this world to be grateful for. This world has plenty of pleasures and stuff. Why should they go to that crack? I know my days are over but I worry about the young generation. I've had a good life, but I think seriously about what the children are coming to; it makes me sad that I can't learn them. [Turns toward her sister] Don't it, Lula?

Lula: Sure do.

* * * * *

A lifelong conversation can be a valuable resource in the context of nursing home living. Over and over again, shared narrative linkages reclaim the distant and the near past and call out the future for purposes of considering the present. In various and particular ways, the quality of life for the residents of this chapter is conjured up in and through overlapping experiences. The nursing home is a place not only to appreciate the quality of care but to recall childhood on the farm, having fished together, having cooked professionally across the street from one another, having raised adopted children, having lost legs, and most of all having served others and God in common.

CHAPTER

9

Spouses

Like coresident sisters, spouses who share rooms or otherwise find themselves living in the same nursing home bring the horizons of their formerly linked lives with them into the facility. For spouses the horizons are expressly those of marriage, financial support, household management, and relations with children. The horizons of the last chapter's twin sisters approximate this in their having virtually grown up as one and, later in life, having shared the same household for ten years before entering Florida Manor. They were unusual siblings in this regard.

Yet there is a difference. The narratives of this chapter show that in addition to familial sentiments, life together is linked with emotional love. When spouses Jane and Tom Malinger and Sue and Don Hughes speak of what they have meant and continue to mean to each other, they not only convey mutual responsibility and cherished routines but sentiments of physical attraction. The difference comes in talk and interaction cross-cut by affirmations of desire. While husband and wife help and look out for each other, share tastes, and teasingly confirm common preferences, they also express affections different from sisterly or brotherly love.

There are coresident spouses, of course, just as there are coresident sisters, brothers, and others with significantly linked lives, whose narrative horizons are less sanguine. Such horizons provide negative resources for talk and interaction, which arguably is more advantageous than having no communicative resources at all. Sisters who hated each other are placed in the same nursing home because families find that more convenient than placing them in separate facilities. Spouses who lived together as strangers most of their married lives or who continually hurt each other emotionally or physically may find themselves under the same roof and again daily contending with their animosities. These experiences aren't represented here because there were no such cases in the nursing homes contacted who were competent enough to tell their stories. However, such cases are important to keep in mind as we hear the contrasting, positive narratives of the spouses in this chapter.

133

In the years ahead, there may be coresidents who will openly speak of life as gay and lesbian couples, and will have grown old and frail together. They are still rare voices in nursing homes, but they may become more commonplace as a publicly recognized generation of such couples or marriages, as the case might be, comes of age. They will add their voices to the narrative linkages of quality of life and care in nursing homes. This also is important to keep in mind, for spousal horizons can appear in nontraditional forms of long-standing attachment and attraction, adding to the special circumstances from which residents speak of life.

JANE AND TOM MALINGER

Like Sue and Don Hughes, Jane and Tom Malinger are interviewed as a couple. At the time of their interview, Jane and Tom Malinger have been living together for a year at Fairhaven Nursing Home. Their standard double room is packed with household items. Besides the usual hospital beds, nightstands, and tray tables, there is a portable television set, radio, microwave oven, refrigerator, dresser, and smaller objects such as stacks of magazines and framed photographs. Many are the familiar items of a household. Yet, for the Malingers, more important than household items, what makes the room home is that they reside in it together, a key linkage in their interview.

Jane Malinger is a seventy-six-year-old white female who suffers from diabetes and has had a leg amputation. She has been unsteady on her feet, is subject to falling, and remains in a wheelchair. Her husband, Tom, an eighty-two-year-old white male, has cardiac failure, has had several heart attacks, and is in constant pain from inoperable pinched nerves in his back. He is ambulatory.

Tom is alone in the room at the start of the interview. He describes his "short and sweet" life.

> I was born in Turner Hill, New York, and I went to St. Paul's Academy. From St. Paul's I went into Marian College. Then I studied to be a physical thera-pist at a school in New York. I left that and went into respiratory therapy, which was a bit easier work. But I liked it more anyway; I had better contact with the patients.
>
> I wound up here on account of my back and my legs. I'm inoperable. They can't operate on my back. There's nothing they can do for me. So I just have to put up with it. I'm in a good deal of pain right now. That's it. Short and sweet.

At that point, Jane wheels into the room. From then on, much of the interview is a conversation between the three of us. We share details of Tom's career in respiratory therapy and move on to his first and now second marriage. Jane's own first marriage was a success and ended when her husband died. They had had four children. According to Tom, his first marriage was a disaster and resulted in divorce. He never had children of his own. At the time of the interview, Tom and Jane have been married for twelve "gloriously happy" years.

Prompted by questions about what life now is like, the couple discusses daily living at Fairhaven and the meaning of family and home. Home is connoted less by location than by living together. According to Tom, wherever Jane is, is home, the implication being that Fairhaven is now home. This serves to explain how they both came to reside in the facility.

> *Tom:* I've got nobody else outside of my wife. I've got a younger brother still living some place. I don't know if he's living or dead. We just lost track of each other. I've tried to locate him, but he hasn't been in the same city where I tried to contact him.
>
> *Jay:* What about now? Tell me a bit about life now.
>
> *Tom:* Right now, it's pretty good.
>
> *Jay:* Could you tell me a bit more about it?
>
> *Tom:* Well, I get medical care now and my medicine. I don't have to worry about a place to stay, my food, or anything else. It's all provided for me. I don't think I could wish for more than that at my age.
>
> *Jay:* What's a typical day like for you?
>
> *Tom:* In my life now? Oh brother! It's all the same. Isn't it?
>
> *Jane:* I'd say.
>
> *Tom:* You go to bed. You get up. You eat. And you go back to bed. We get out once in a while. It's hard to get out. We don't have a car. She's got one leg and it's hard for her to travel around and get in and out of a van. She lost her leg here [the nursing home]. She stepped on something in the bathroom, in the shower room. She's got diabetes and she got blood poisoning. So they had to amputate. They amputated twice, once below and once above the knee. Outside of that, it's just a question of eat, sleep, eat, sleep, and play bingo on Saturday. That's about it.
>
> *Jane:* You do the same all the time. I'd say it's very monotonous.
>
> *Tom:* You can repeat that again. It's the old sleep-and-eat routine . . . but it's home.
>
> *Jay:* What does "home" mean to you?
>
> *Tom:* Home? Well, Jay, a place where my wife and I could have a place together. Wherever she's at is home for me. But I didn't want to break up the house until I knew she was settled and . . .
>
> *Jay:* How long have you been here then?
>
> *Jane:* Over a year.
>
> *Jay:* You came together?
>
> *Tom:* No.
>
> *Jane:* I came and then he came a month later. He wanted me to see how I'd like it.

Tom: I didn't want to break up the house until I knew she was settled and liked where she was. So I wouldn't move for a month. Then after that, I sold everything out and moved here.

Jay: How did you decide that? I mean how did you feel when you were making that decision?

Tom: The only thing that went through my mind was that I wanted to be with her wherever she was. I don't want to be alone. What was good for her, I figured was good enough for me. But I waited to make sure that she became acclimated to the place and was sure she was going to stay. There was no sense of me going and then turning around and having to leave and start a new life again, another apartment or another home or something else. I figured I'd make sure she liked it. So I came.

She was here a month ahead of me. I missed her. It wasn't home when she was out of the house. I mean if she was there, it would have been fine. I had a good home when she was there. We took turns cooking and baking. I don't feel . . .

Jane: I wouldn't want to be here alone either. I think I'd feel more institutionalized than I would otherwise, I mean if I was alone here.

Jay: You don't feel what, Tom?

Tom: With her I don't feel that way. I feel, well, we've got a home here; we're together. I mean at my age, going on eighty-three, I'm not asking much more than that . . . just to be together with her and love her up. Where she is, is fine with me. You know how it is. Ya got a lot to share, yap about, and all.

While Fairhaven is now home, it has its disadvantages. As the next extract shows, Tom and Jane feel sorry for, but also are irritated by, the presence of the demented. And as others do, Tom and Jane complain about the food. Still, as Jane remarks, "We try to make it a good life." Here and throughout the interview, Tom and Jane seem to be saying that, despite the disadvantages, home is now and their life together is secure for the time being. At the very least, Jane says that she knows this in her mind, if not always in her heart. Both accept the realities of their situations and are grateful that their special circumstance—being together as husband and wife—make it better than it otherwise might be, this quality of their lives overshadowing the qualities of care.

Tom: This is home now. They have very nice people here. We're together. Ninety percent of them [residents] are very compatible. Wouldn't you say that?

Jane: I would, except the ones that are around the other end.

Tom: Yeah. That's a different section altogether, the other end.

Jane: They have . . . what is that . . . Alzheimer's disease.

Tom: God, I wish they'd find a cure for that.

Jane: They can't remember things. You can't talk to them because they don't know what you're talking about. It can be annoying. But there are some here that have their senses. They do talk. They are friendly.

Tom: Yes, on this end.

Jane: On this end, there are very nice people here. And you try to get along, you know, try to be compatible. At least we've got each other for now . . . [endearingly] that big hunk over there.

Tom: I wouldn't be here alone. I wouldn't have come. I would have taken a room some place as long as I was able to take care of myself.

Jane: Like he said, at least in the apartment, we did our cooking and I baked. The food could be better here. But we helped each other. But then I was prone to falling a lot. I fractured three bones up here in my left side. I was always falling. Then he had the heart attack and we couldn't help each other as much as we did before.

So a daughter of mine came down and they knew what the setup was, you know, me falling and all of them worried about it and worried about his heart attack and we couldn't help each other. She started looking around. She suggested a home of some kind, where we could be taken care of. If I did fall, at least I was at some place where we could be taken care of. So this daughter went around looking at different places and we decided on this place.

Like he said, I came here and I stayed a month and it was okay. The only thing I'm against and still am is their food, their eating habits. But, like everything else, you make the best of it, you accept it, and that's all. I mean this is the place when you get old and you have to be someplace where you can be taken care of. So you take the bad with the good. We get our medication. We have a nurse on duty twenty-four hours a day. My doctor comes every twenty-eight days. If I need him before that, the nurse calls him and he comes. So I mean, actually, we have everything. They have a beautiful garden and all outside, where you can sit under an umbrella or just go out and sit. And like he said, we have bingo once a week. And I have PT [physical therapy]. When I put my prosthesis on, I go in there and I walk around and that. We get out once in a while. We have friends here that will take us out to dinner to Red Lobster or one of those places which we like very much to go. And we have each other. So, all in all, I mean we try to make it a good life.

Up here [points to her head], I know it's home. Where else am I going to go? My children are scattered all over Maryland and North Carolina.

Tom: We wouldn't live there anyway.

Jane: And I wouldn't live with them. They'd have to take care of me and all that. It's a big job. My one daughter . . . before she moved to Maryland, she suggested taking a larger home, one that had a smaller home next to it, so that I could have my own place. We were against it because, you know, you get set in your ways and you don't like to be obligated to anybody. You like to be by yourself and be independent.

Tom: We're better off here by ourselves.

Jane: Eventually, we'd have to come to something like this anyway, because, after all, you don't want to depend upon your children to do for you. They have enough taking care of their own needs. So here we are and this is home. We know that.

Tom: Yes, until the black man comes along and takes us away.

Jane: A who man?

Tom: A guy with a Black Maria. The hearse.

Jane: Oh . . . well, here we are anyway.

I was alone a month and I didn't like it no how. I was in with another woman and I was looking forward to him coming. They set us up in this room and it's fine. At least we're together.

Tom: Yep, that's the main thing.

Jane: That's right, you rascal. [Squeezes Tom's arm] So this is home.

Jay: In your mind, what makes a home?

Jane: A home is a husband and love and understanding and just doing for one another. Love of course . . . you've got that more than being just friends. Keeps us going. It counts for a lot.

I help him as much as I can. Like you see he helped me when I was in the bathroom. I can't always manipulate with one leg. So I have to have help. At least he helps me. The girls [aides] can't come in always. They don't answer the [call] light when I put it on. So he helps me. If it wasn't for him, I don't know where I'd be. So he's a lot of help. And we have a lot of love for each other, like I said, and we need each other. I wouldn't want to be here without him, like he wouldn't want to be here without me. So that's it.

But, like I said, if I could only do the cooking myself, I'd get in that kitchen and show them how to cook. I suggested that each resident get a chance in the kitchen . . . one day in the kitchen. Then maybe we'd get some decent meals.

Tom: [Chuckling] They've got a chicken farm on that side [of the nursing home] and a rice paddy on this side. Chicken and rice, everyday. [All laugh]

Jane: It seems that we have a lot of chicken and a lot of rice. You get tired of that after a while.

Tom: We send out and get dinners once in a while, have dinner delivered to us.

Jane: We send out . . . what's the name of that place?

Tom: Lorenzo's.

Jane: Lorenzo's. He likes sausage and peppers. So he gets a submarine and we cut it in half and each has half, and diet Coke or something like that.

Tom: Neither one of us could eat one of those alone.

Jay: Those are big. I don't think I could finish one of those.

Jane: Too big! And sometimes I get an order of spaghetti or something like that. We'll get something else or whatever.

Tom: We've got a microwave and a refrigerator. So we're not going hungry.

Jane: So that's our life. It's our life, period. I mean, where else can we go? We wouldn't go with any one of the children. We can't get an apartment. So once we're out of here, that's it.

Tom: I figure we're a family ourselves, the two of us. Of course, we have our children.

Jane: I had a nice family. I had five children. I lost a daughter in Texas and I have four now. They all took to Tom. They all met him and like him.

Tom: They think the world of me.

Jane: We have a full life, no matter.

Daily, yet minor annoyances are discussed, as are their room's conveniences. Jane repeats the many ways in which Tom helps her—in the bathroom, in the dining room, as she puts it, "just everywhere." Tom tells of the handiness of having a microwave and refrigerator. He's especially fond of salami, which he stores in the refrigerator and snacks on at all hours.

Jane: There're little things like you'd expect that can be annoying. [Elaborates] Things like that. I'll keep the door [of the room] closed all the way because people come by in wheelchairs and look in.

Tom: You'd be surprised. They'll stop and gawk at you. They'll turn around, come right up to the door, and stare right into the room.

Jay: Is that right?

Jane: So we keep it closed and keep the curtain open a little so's we can get some light from that there window. During the night, it's dark, but you do get some light from the outside. If we need anybody, we just press the button over there and the light goes on. Eventually, somebody comes in to see what we need.

Tom: They're not too bad with that, just the times when they're short-handed, they're busy. I've been out in the hall and I've seen these lights lit up all along the hallway like a Christmas tree. Four or five lights at once. You wonder how they can take care of them all at once.

Jane: They have different lights. In the bathroom it's a light that flickers. This light here is just one light that stays on. So they know what that is. If you're in the bathroom and you have the light on, they know you have to have somebody quick. Sometimes I go in myself and I fall. That's why my PT therapist said, "Don't go in the bathroom alone. Don't get off the chair alone. Especially, once you're on the commode, don't get off by yourself."

Tom: I'm here to help you, baby.

Jane: Yes, I know, dear. [Blows him a kiss] He helps me, just everywhere. At least we have each other. We yap about stuff we used to do and things like that. That keeps you going. So we have it made as far as that goes. He helps me quite a bit.

Tom: We have a friend . . . his son has multiple sclerosis and we've gotten to know him real well. So when he visits, he says if we need anything, write it down and he'll get it for us. He's taken us shopping too. We got little cans of stew, spaghetti, hash, and things like that. I can warm it up in the microwave. I have permission to use the microwave. So I can warm it up in there.

Jane: He got two pounds of salami and bread, pickles, olives, and different things.

Tom: The salami kid!

Jane: [Laughing] Yeah. The minute he gets the salami, he's always . . .

Jay: Nibbling away, huh?

Jane: He's what they call a "nosher."

Tom: I love salami.

Jane: He doesn't look it, but he does alright. Except he doesn't eat his meals and that's bad. But he eats what we have in the refrigerator and that makes up for it.

Tom: I'll never starve.

Jane: You sure won't. But I'd sure miss him and his salami.

This soon leads to an affirmation of love, which they describe retrospectively as their having been drawn by fate from their youths. Theirs is an attraction deeper than friendship, something that Tom says gives him "goose bumps." This is their special circumstance, the horizon from which they speak of life.

Tom: [To me] Do you know that all our life we lived a few blocks from each other when we lived in New York?

Jane: But we didn't know one another.

Tom: We shopped at the same stores all our life. I played basketball and she came to the basketball games.

Jane: We went to the same restaurants. We went to the same hotel dancing. We shopped at the same A&P, but we never bumped into each other. I never knew him.

Tom: All our life we were close together, like we were meant to meet someday and here we are finally.

Jane: When he first saw me, he said to himself, "I have to meet that woman." And he did. We met in May and he asked me to marry him in June and July we got married. Twelve gloriously happy years.

Tom: I couldn't let you get away from me, like all those years.

Jane: You couldn't, huh? Why not?

Tom: You still give me goose bumps.

Jane: I still give you goose bumps. That's a good sign if you still get goose bumps!

SUE AND DON HUGHES

Sue and Don Hughes are interviewed by Carol Ronai five weeks after they are admitted to Westside Care Center. Sue Hughes is an eighty-one-year-old white woman with congestive heart failure, chronic back pain, and arthritis that confines her to a wheelchair. Don Hughes is white, eighty-eight years old, and suffers from prostate cancer and heart failure. Don is legally blind but ambulatory. It is their first and only marriage, which has lasted for sixty-three years.

Like the Malingers, the Hugheses live in a standard double room, but without comparable household conveniences. Of course, they are relative newcomers to the facility. It is possible that in time the room may resemble the Malingers' and perhaps in the same way represent home. It is clear from the couple's remarks about what makes a home that such conveniences, personal items, and other concrete markers of one's former life would make a difference. They resent what they perceive as the facility's resistance to the personalization of their premises.

The couple has a negative view of Westside's quality of care. Some of this refers to what they believe are improvable qualities. Some stems from what they admit no institution can do, namely, personalize care so that each and every resident's needs and desires are uniquely met. Sue and Don lament having been placed in the home, but at the same time realize that they could not have continued to make it on their own. Aching to realize domestic intimacy in the context of the nursing home, they confront dead ends at every turn. As their judgments are linked with all of these sources, it is difficult to sort out how Westside's quality of care by itself relates to the couple's sense of the quality of their lives.

As sad as their lives seem to be, the couple has a light-hearted, teasing relationship. They delight and respond with good-humored sarcasm to each other's opinions and sentiments. They even joke about their current situation. This, too, complicates the quality of their lives, just as it enriches their narrative. It is evident at the very start of the interview as Don tells "his" life story, unwittingly ignoring what Sue insists is her part in it, even while she initially helps him along in the account.

Carol: [To Don] I was hoping you'd tell me about your life.
Don: I was a hobo!
Carol: You were a hobo.
Sue: [To Don] Why don't you tell her where you born.
Don: I was born in Minnesota and I left Minnesota when I was 16 years old.
Sue: Go on. So why did you leave?
Don: Just to bum, see the country. So we went, another boy and myself, we went out west on the Northern Pacific Railroad. We was supposed to help put in signal posts. We worked there for a while and then went to Sheridan, Wyoming, and went from there up into the mountains. After that, we came home riding the rails.

   I stayed home for a couple a years and then a buddy of mine says, "Let's go to Florida." At that time, I says, "No." I knew a girl and her father was moving to California and he asked me if I'd drive his Ford there and I said, "Sure." So a buddy and me drove out to California, but when we got to the desert, the car broke down. We fixed it and drove to Sacramento. [Elaborates] We stayed up there for about three months. We moved around and worked in a mine. It was hard work and we finally opened up this old mine and went down in it. After that, we built a two-story garage for a Chinaman. He got all the lumber and bricks from the old California state capitol because they were building a new one.

Just about that time they had hoof-and-mouth disease in California and it was terrible. [Elaborates] So we come back to Minnesota. I stayed home for about a year. I was working on a farm for a rich gentleman. Anyway, he was going to sell the place out to Ford Motor Company and he did. So the superintendent of the farm asked me to take some of the registered Jersey cows up into Massachusetts where he lived. He couldn't find nobody to ride the box car and so I said that I'd do it. It was a fairly nice journey. [Elaborates] So I stayed there for a couple of months. Hunting season in Minnesota was open the fifteenth of September and I wanted to get home. The superintendent gave me the money and I went, took the train home, went hunting, and so on.

That January, my buddy called and says, "Let's go to Florida." That time I says, "Fine." So we left the seventh of January and it was fifteen below in Eau Claire, Wisconsin. We were supposed to sleep in the car. Well, it was pretty cold, but we finally got down into Florida. He had been in the army and the government was allocating homestead exemptions in Florida at the time. He thought he might want one. We looked all over and there was nothing but swampland where we looked. So I came to this part of Florida here and we both were working. That's where I met my wife and that's the end of my life story.

Sue: [Sarcastically] Why don't you tell her that we got married in the meantime? I'm part of it, too, you know.

As Don continues, Sue teasingly insists that the story be based on their life together. While his version initially dwelled on work experiences, the story now includes marriage, house, home, and family living. The nursing home part of their story will be similar. For example, each will differentially collaborate in formulating an answer to the question of why the facility is not home. We return to the interview as Don ends a lengthy description of his many years working as a mason contractor in Milwaukee.

Carol: Was this after the depression?
Don: The depression was . . .
Sue: It was just over.
Don: I walked ten miles to work for ten cents an hour. But you know I had a

family and I wasn't lazy. But, anyway, after I worked for this fella, we
had a big snow storm, eighteen inches of snow in Milwaukee, and it
tied up everything for four days. [Elaborates] So we decided to come
back to Florida. Of course, I went into business for myself and built a
couple of churches and other buildings. [Elaborates] We enjoyed life.
She had penicillin poisoning a couple of times. When I retired, I
thought we had money to last.

Sue: You forgot to tell her one thing, that we built our own home stick by
stick and every nail.

Don: Yeah. Anyway, our money didn't last. I got so's I couldn't work too
much anymore and she got sick two or three more times.

Sue: [Chuckling] Just listen to him. In the meantime we had three more
children. [Sarcastically] Remember that?

Don: Yeah, in the meantime we had three more children. But that's all.
That's it.

Sue: [Laughing] That's it? You're joking.

Don: [Chuckling] This much I can tell ya. We've been married sixty-three
years and enjoyed every bit of it. We worked together and never left.
For instance, she had a bunch of girlfriends and she never went out at
night. And I had boyfriends and I wouldn't go out at night. If we
went to any place, we went together.

Sue: We traveled together. We went all over the country together. We
didn't have such a bad life. We loved to camp. We loved to fish. We
loved to do all kinds of outdoor sports. We like baseball, football.
Name it. And we did all the things together. We never went to one
place and let the other fella go another place.

The conversation turns to economic hard times, the money they
thought was adequate for their retirement years, and the rude awaken-
ing that frailty and sickness brought along. Yet, as Don notes, aside from
this, theirs was a "perfect marriage." Nursing home placement, however, soured this, even beyond the hardships of the depression, according to Sue.

Don: But inflation come along and, uh, I don't know if you know about it,
but it was tough. I don't mind telling you that we had our home and
over $50,000 and I thought, well, we can live on that. But with infla-
tion and the way we was used to living, it just went.

Sue: And sickness. My sickness alone has cost us a fortune.

Don: Well, you wasn't sick any more than I was.

Sue: Yeah, but yours was little compared to mine. I was sick from so far
back, it wasn't funny.

Don: I had a prostate operation and I had an operation on my heel. I fell off
a ladder and broke it. I had an operation for kidney stones . . .

Sue: And on his eyes.

Don: She finally ended up in here and I'm trying to get up to the idea of being up here with her and accept the idea that I can't stay at home. But, other than that, we had a perfect marriage. And we're still in love, let's put it that way. We gab, too. So that helps pass the time. And that's the story.

Sue: We had a lot of fun together—the traveling, the fact that we had four nice kids, fourteen grandchildren, and twenty-four great-grand-children. There's a bunch of us.

Carol: That does sound perfect.

Don: Until we came up here. They don't do anything for you. You ask them to do something and they ignore you like a dirty shirt.

Sue: No, they say, "In a minute." Yeah, this is different. Before this, we had the life of Riley.

Don: [To Sue] After the depression don't forget.

Sue: Yeah, well, living through the depression wasn't bad. We had some-thing to eat. We had a place to sleep. It wasn't the pleasantest in the world, but we were happy. We had fun. We loved to play cards together. We did all kinds of things together. What more could you want? Right now, if you were to compare everything with what we had during the depression, I don't know . . . I believe I'd take the depression.

Don: Yeah.

Sue: At least we were free to come and go.

The nursing home's quality of care and the quality of life are dis-cussed. The depression continues to be used as a negative baseline for placing the home's quality of life lower. The Hugheses are disappointed and angry that Westside does not offer a better living environment. At times, their view, especially Sue's, of what would be desirable comes close to being a description of the Malingers' living situation at Fair-haven, which has the conveniences of home right in their room. At other times, complaints about the quality of care are about institutional living in general, not Westside in particular. This extends to the ailments that caused them to be placed in a nursing home in the first place.

As the following extended extract suggests, quality of life for Don more nearly references freedom to come and go, while for Sue it falls in the area of household conveniences, reflecting both earlier life experi-ences and their differential concerns with family living and home life. It would seem that the difference is as much historical as it is individual in that the Hugheses' is still a generation of couples in which men worked outside the home and women tended the household and saw to the family. Future generations of nursing home residents are likely to show less clear-cut differences in narrative linkages between spouses.

A further complication comes in what initially appears to be a racist attitude toward the nursing staff. According to Don and Sue, the black nurses and aides don't much care about the residents. But we also are told that the staff is "there to making a living," which underscores the fact that institutional caregiving is as much a job as it involves caring, race notwithstanding. Indeed, we soon learn that black staff members can be especially caring, enhancing the quality of daily life in the facility.

We return to a discussion prompted by questions about the typical day of the nursing home resident and about everyday life a year from now.

Carol: Describe to me a typical day in your life now.

Don: Oh, boy. I go to bed with the chickens and get up with the chickens. That's about the only thing. There's nothing to do. We get television . . . This is not for us. We're not used to something like this. We're not used to being cooped up.

Sue: We're not used to eating somebody else's food. We like our own.

Don: I never . . . she had surgery on her back.

Sue: My spine.

Don: Four years ago. It's going on four years and four months. It didn't prove successful. She's been practically an invalid all that time. In the meantime, she got arthritis in both hips and so on. We were home. I done the cooking and that ain't my cup of tea, but I done the best I could. When it comes to salting something, I couldn't see how much salt I put in because I was declared legally blind. We got along fine, but we kept getting worse and getting sick and going to the hospital.

Sue: I was allergic to everything. And I was in intensive care. Believe it or not, I swallowed all of my teeth.

Carol: Oh for goodness sakes.

Don: They just fell out, broke off. Yeah, that happened.

Carol: What do you think life will look like a year from now?

Don: I don't think I'll be here. I don't think she will be either. Because I have a rapid heartbeat and when that comes, it's bad. And she had cardiac, allergies, and back trouble and so on. So I don't think we will live . . . especially if we're up here [in the nursing home]. If we could be home together, which the kids don't want us to do, I think it might last a little longer, but I doubt it. I'm living on borrowed time.

Carol: You say that so fearlessly.

Don: Oh, it don't scare me. I know I'm living on borrowed time.

Sue: Listen, if you have lived as long as we have and had as much fun as we've had, death you know is coming.

Don: Well, it's like I said. We've had a wonderful marriage and death doesn't bother me at all. I don't know if it bothers her.

Sue: No, it doesn't.

Don: It don't bother me. So I'm ready to go. We got our cemetery lots out there in Clarkston and . . .

Sue: We don't owe anybody anything. [Pause] But we'd be happier if we could be out at home.

Don: But they [the children] won't let us out. My son says, "No, you got no business out there."

Sue: We can't afford to have somebody to stay with us. So we can't be at home.

Carol: What does the word *home* mean to you?

Don: Everything in the world. Her home is our home and [sings] be it ever so humble, there's no place like home.

Carol: Is this at all like home?

Don: No. No way. This is just like a prison.

Carol: What could they do to make it seem more like home?

Sue: Put a little icebox over there so's we could have some Coke. If that isn't silly, but it would help. You could put Coke in there. You could put fruit juice, tomato juice. We're used to having that at home. If they'd allow us to have . . . well, they're just small iceboxes, refrigerators . . . right there in that space.

Don: They told us this morning that the state wouldn't allow it. So I told my son not to get it.

Sue: I think it's stupid.

Don: Well, really, I tell ya, the way I look at it, this is . . . a place like this is nothing but a place to die. Everybody's in a wheelchair. So you can understand my position. If I was home, it'd be a whole lot better . . . and she was with me.

I didn't like the idea of coming here, but our son, he put in a lot of time and a lot of work to finding this for us and we didn't want to disappoint him. He said that he couldn't see us everyday either because he lives down in Norris.

Sue: I resent what they [nursing home staff] pulled on us last week.

Don: You ask the nurse for something and she says, "Maybe we'll call the doctor." They don't call them. I asked the next day, "Did you call the doctor?" She says, "We couldn't get him." Well, I know they could if they tried, but they just don't take the time to do it.

Sue: We're not allowed to use the phone. You got to go and ask for permission. Another thing I resent when we came in here was the first week we came in here, they came and gathered all our clothes.

Don: Yeah, they took them down and washed them and we never got half of them back.

Sue: No, they didn't wash them. They took them down and sterilized them. They stripped us and put a hospital gown on. He sat five solid hours in a chair with no clothes on. He couldn't even get in his bed. It wasn't made. They sterilized the bed.

And that's not the worst part of it. They took our clothes out of the closet. They took them downstairs and they put 'em in three bags. I saw them when they did it and marked the bags "Hughes." I'm not going to wear them damn things like that.

Don: Don't get yourself worked up. Take it easy now. It's not *that* important.

Sue: They were satin. They're gone. And they've marked everything. They got no business taking our stuff and marking them up like that.

If they could tape them, I'd go along with that. Put it inside the collar or sew it in. If they had given me the tabs, I would have written on them and sewed it in. But you can look at them [her clothing]. They're up there. If I was to replace those housecoats today, they would cost me $50 a piece.

Don: And this morning I asked for towels and they didn't get them. When I asked them at noon, they still hadn't got them. So the nurse went out and got them.

Sue: I asked her for two cups of hot water . . .

Don: . . . and she hasn't got it yet. I tell you, to be honest with you, it's a prison. It's just a place to come up here and die, by the looks of all the patients.

Sue: It's changed our way of living.

Don: It's free living but I don't like that at all. I never was used to something like that and never will be. Even when I was on the bum, it was a whole lot better than it is here.

Sue: You know, I wouldn't mind them cleaning my stuff if I thought it was necessary. But why did they have to mark the stuff up like that on the corner and let it sit there hour after hour. They ruined our clothes. My pillowcases too; I had them all embroidered. And there were two satin housecoats I'll never get replaced.

Don: It's bad. All those people in wheelchairs. I hate to knock the place, but you ask some of these black ladies [aides] for something and they ignore you like a dirty shirt. And there's very few white people on the floor.

Sue: There are some real nice ones here. Don't misunderstand us.

Carol: Do you see that as part of the problem, the race thing?

Sue: No.

Don: No, no. I was always a champion of the black man, but in the last ten years I've changed my mind.

Sue: The best friend we ever had was a black, but that isn't it. It's the fact that they just don't care here. They're here to make a living. I know that. You know it too. If somebody don't call their crane, then they just don't do it, regardless. The best one is Sylvia and she's black.

Don: Yeah, but that little girl that's on . . . Saturdays I believe . . . she helps.

Sue: I think she's a nurse's aide. She's black and better than the white ones. They can be when they try . . . and that can help.

Don: Well, anyway, Sue hadn't had a BM movement for four days and she's [the aide] the only one that would help. She told the rest of those nurses, white and black, "We'll see about it. We'll call the doctor." Another day goes by and Sue hasn't had a BM. But this little girl, she really helped out, didn't she?

Sue: Yes, she did. It was kind of ridiculous the way it happened anyhow. She actually had to pull it out by hand. Well, I had gone seven days.

> Don: These places are all alike
> Sue: You're right about that.

As the interview winds down, the mood lightens. Don and Sue tease each other, conjuring up their respective foibles and confirming their mutual affection. In this framework, quality of care is marginal to the "sassiness" they call out in each other. Now they are not as much nursing home residents attuned to caregiving as they are the Don and Sue they have delighted in over the years.

> Don: I'm a hellcat.
> Sue: [Sarcastically] You can complain, but you ain't no hellcat. He's lying in his teeth.
> Carol: What do you mean by being a hellcat, Don?
> Don: Well, I loved to chase around. I wasn't a woman chaser, but I just loved to go, be on the go.
> Sue: [Scoffing] I couldn't prove he wasn't a woman chaser.
> Don: [Chuckling] I was a no-good bum.
> Sue: He's no bum. We're just as close as we were before and I love him. He's the only thing that makes this place tolerable. But he gets sassy sometimes and I have to knock him down a peg or two, but other than that, we still have fun together. He plays cribbage and cheats, but we still manage to get by. We gab and blab, about the old days, you know. That keeps us goin'.
> Don: But this isn't the place for us. That's all I can say. It's too much like prison. If I didn't have her, I'd go crazy and so would she. [Elaborates] At least we have each other.
> Sue: I know, dear. We've had a good life, but now we're bitching like the devil. [Chuckling] I hope *that* isn't on the tape.
> Carol: Well, it is.
> Don: [To Sue, sarcastically] You mean to say you're not "itching" now?
> Sue: [Chuckling] I didn't say "itching." I said "bitching." We still manage to giggle.

* * * * *

Once again, we hear complex narrative linkages being made between shared meaning and the qualities of care and life. The marriages that are a couple's special circumstance are a horizon that can, in the Malingers' case, retroactively extend the meaning of the statement "as long as we are together" into early life. According to the Malingers, being together in their room, intimately living out their days in the nursing home, is a relationship with very old roots. The Hugheses narratively link the qualities of care and life in their facility with their room's lack of domestic amenities and the shoddy staff treatment, but still manage to joke about their respective complaints. The couple resents, but understands the reason why they have had to be placed in a nursing home. Positive, negative, and even humorous linkages make it impossible to understand the subjective quality of their current lives in terms of better/worse, either/or, more/less, and similar binary descriptors typical of conventional assessment.

10

Disabled

Three elderly white women with long-standing disabilities present another special circumstance. One of them, Grace Wheeler, now seventy years old, has been afflicted since birth by spastic paralysis, a form of cerebral palsy. The second woman, Opal Peters, who is seventy-six years old, has been disabled by rheumatoid arthritis for thirty-five years and is unable to walk. Celia Turner, the third woman, is sixty-four years old, has had multiple sclerosis for forty years, and sits in a wheelchair when she's not in bed.

The women have brought their experience with disability with them into the facilities where they now live. Disability is a central horizon of their everyday lives, significantly mediating the subjective meaning of being a nursing home resident. For Grace Wheeler, the meaning of being a nursing home resident is articulated in linkages with the security of supportive and caring parents and siblings, who in Wheeler's view made it possible for her to live a normal life except for her disability. She speaks of the future in similar terms, looking ahead to, and yet being worried about continued security. Opal Peters views herself as on a mission for the handicapped. Peters hosts a radio program called "Perspectives of the Handicapped," the purpose of which is to inform listeners that one can "fight" a disability, not let it win, and make contributions to life. Celia Turner likewise has a mission, partly informed by a lifetime of writing and similarly rooted in the need to show that even frail nursing home residents can realize new meanings, "reinventing" themselves in the process.

While, for these women, nursing homes have both their good and bad points, which affect the quality of care, the homes are viewed mainly as a base of support for other concerns. The facilities enable them to attend to lifelong interests and long-standing goals. It is not so much the quality of care that is at stake for them in discussions of institutional living, as it is the ability to carry on as before, for which the facilities seem to provide adequately.

GRACE WHEELER

Grace Wheeler's paralysis usually keeps her sitting awkwardly in a wheelchair. During the interview, she was lying in bed because she had hurt her back from the strain caused by the coughing of a cold. According to Wheeler, her muscles tighten excessively at times and this puts pressure on her spine, which is worsened by coughing. Wheeler never married, was raised in a rural area of Ohio, and was family tutored.

Wheeler's mother, Lucy, is ninety-three years old, widowed, and shares her daughter's room in the nursing home. Lucy suffers from high blood pressure and emphysema. No longer able to care for daughter Grace on her own, Lucy nonetheless continues to do "little things" for her, such as getting Grace a glass of water and soothingly wiping her face with a damp cloth.

I interview mother and daughter together in their room at Bayside, the facility in which they've lived for a year and a half. Grace's life story is a narrative of happy times spent in the company of friends and family members. When Grace recounts the sacrifices her disability caused, she is remorseful, as if to tell me that while she cheerfully made the best of her handicap, she does recognize what she missed in life. The support of family members and the security of home are narrative linkages throughout.

> *Jay:* Why don't we start by your telling me about your life?
> *Grace:* Well that was quite a many years ago. I was born in Brinton Station, Ohio.
> *Lucy:* She was a seven-month baby.
> *Grace:* I was a seven-month baby. That's what it was. Anyway, my childhood, I guess, was as happy as it could be under the circumstances . . . I had two younger sisters that played with me a lot and an older brother that took care of me like a girl. He was wonderful. They've all been wonderful.
> *Lucy:* They taught her . . .
> *Grace:* And they taught me as well as my mom and dad. And then when radio and television came to the farm, why I learned from them. I loved the quiz shows.
> *Lucy:* She types with a stick in her mouth.
> *Grace:* I type with a stick in my mouth. I paint with a brush in my mouth. I turn pages of the book . . . I read with a stick in my mouth. And I've been to Oregon, on a trip with my sisters. That was quite a flight. I flew over there in . . . what was it . . . 1952.
> *Lucy:* I don't remember.
> *Grace:* I think it was 1952. And then we left the farm and moved to Wooster, Ohio.

Lucy: Down where Wooster College is.

Grace: Yeah. And I'm a great [Cleveland] Indians fan, too! I love baseball and I love the Indians. For football, I love the Miami Dolphins.

Jay: So you're a real sports fan.

Grace: Yes.

Lucy: Yes, she is. That television's on . . .

Grace: I love it!

Lucy: That television's all sports to her.

Grace: Well, sports and shows. [Giggling] I love animal shows, too. I love animals.

Lucy: Game shows.

Grace: Game shows, animal shows, detective stories. I like to read detective stories. My favorite author is John D. McDonald.

Jay: That sounds enjoyable. [Pause] You were telling me about Ohio before . . .

Grace: Well, after I grew up, then the rest of the family . . . It was just Mom and Dad 'cause the rest of the family moved out and got work, got jobs. They got married. We moved down to Fort Lauderdale [Florida] and Mom and Dad bought a little home for us. When we couldn't handle it any longer, why we moved in with my sister and brother-in-law. They were wonderful to us.

And I've had a lot of friends. I make friends easy. And I love to be with people. I love people.

Jay: Yes, I can see that.

Grace: And I really like my sense of humor. If it weren't for my sense of humor, I don't think I could get through this life.

So, as I was telling you, we moved into with them, with my sister and brother-in-law.

Lucy: No, we didn't move in with them. We moved in the cottage behind their house.

Grace: [To Lucy] No, no, no, Mother! I'm talking about Jack and Kitty.

Lucy: Oh, Jack and Kitty.

Grace: That was after Daddy couldn't do it anymore. Jack and Kitty gave us three of their rooms for our own place, like our own place. We ate, we took meals with them, but we had our own quarters. See, my daddy had to have his left leg amputated. So we moved in there with them. And then we lived there until my sister passed away. So then we moved in with my brother and his wife. From there, we moved up to South Carolina with my youngest brother and his wife. He had a little cottage back there, a two-bedroom cottage that we lived in, my mother and I. Dad had passed by then. We didn't care too much for it there because it was . . . [chuckles] it was out in the boonies. And then we moved in here. We came here. We thought this was the best place for us.

Lucy: Two years in June.

Grace: Now nobody has to worry about us too much and we are well taken care of here and, well, I like to be, as I said, I like to be with people. Mother doesn't too much. She stays and does what she can for me. She can't do too much for me yet. Does little things for me like give me a drink or, you know, things like that. [Pause]

Jay: Grace, if you were given a chance to write the story of your life, what would the chapters be about? Let's say the first chapter . . . what would that be about?

Lucy: Growing up.

Grace: Well, I'd have to think about it. [Pause] The first chapter . . . the first thing I remember real distinctly is parading around the . . . riding with my mother and my grandmother up to the next town to get some feed ground.

Jay: Some what?

Grace: Some feed ground for the animals.

Lucy: Grain ground for feed.

Jay: What about the second chapter?

Grace: My teenage years, I guess. That wasn't very funny, seeing all the other girls going out and having fun and I couldn't do it. But we had some good friends anyway. They would take me riding, roll me down the streets in my wheelchair. We had a lot of fun that way. And I guess the next chapter would be Florida.

Jay: What about the last chapter?

Grace: I don't know what the last chapter will be.

Lucy: The last chapter would be here.

Grace: Yeah, here so far. They've been wonderful till I hurt my back. I don't know how I did it.

Lucy: You know how you did it.

Grace: When I get tightened up real tight, my muscles have spasms. When they tighten up, it hurts my right hip so bad that I can't sit up in my chair. I had an awful cough, too, and that made it worse. I like to be up. I don't like to be in bed. When I get rid of this back problem, it'll be back to normal. I can get up and type and read and enjoy myself again. I've gotten over the cold pretty well but it did get me down a bit.

We discuss her recent convalescence and talk about sports, especially baseball and football, which are Grace's passions. She laughs and jokes about certain television programs, everyday matters that strike her as funny, and the hilarious things that other residents and the staff do. Her humor is contagious; I find myself laughing with her.

At one point, as Grace explains how fond she is of singing, I ask her what she would have done differently if given the opportunity to live her life over again. Looking back in those terms, she considers how things might have been had it not been for her paralysis. She recalls her hopes, several dashed. She would have liked to become a singer. Yet she is thankful for the support that made possible what she was able to realize.

Grace: What would I do differently? Let's see. I'd get a good education. I always thought I could . . . before when I was younger. I could carry a tune and I thought I would like to be a singer. But, you know, in time you know you can't. I always wanted to be a mother, get married, and have children. I love children. [Pause] Just have a normal life I guess, well, maybe different than I did have. Oh, I think I'd be living in Oregon instead of Florida. I like Oregon better than I do Florida, but Florida was the best choice.

Lucy: We wasn't there long. You don't know whether you liked it or not.

Grace: I did, Mother! I loved Oregon. I didn't want to come home. But, Mother and I are inseparable. Aren't we, Mother? [Chuckles] Inseparable and insufferable, too.

Lucy: I've been her hands and her feet.

Grace: Mother is very, very important to me. My whole family has been really. Some friends, too. Jim Malloy was wonderful. Right, Mother? [Lucy nods] And Pete Sikorski taught me to paint.

Lucy: The man was a painter and taught her to paint. You know, how to mix the colors around and all that. She's done all these paintings. [Points around the room]

Grace: Yesterday, I was typing . . . at the new typewriter. I'm going to type today when I get up . . . type a note. I'll do it this afternoon. [Pause] No, I won't do it this afternoon either 'cause I'll have the Browns to watch play ball. The Cleveland Browns; they're in the playoffs. I love television. I'll go down and have breakfast with my mom and then we'll come back here and watch television. In the afternoon, I watch TV all the time because I watch soap operas. I've got three of them: *Days of Our Lives*, *Another World*, and *Guiding Light*. Then I watch Oprah or I watch Geraldo or one of the others.

As we talk, Grace begins to look ahead. She expresses worry over her security and remarks that supportive family members have passed from her life. She worries especially about how much longer her mother will be with her. It is in the context of continued support and security that the nursing home takes on its meaning, a place where she hopes to remain living in the way she has become accustomed. As Grace mentions at one point, as old as she is, she knows no other way.

Grace: If I'm still here, I hope I'll be doing just about the same thing I'm doing now, only with a better back I hope. [Looks at her mother] I don't know how long my mother's got to stay with me. She's been a lot of security for me, love . . . the whole family has, really. Right now, I'm all right. We're at home here.

Lucy:	Anywhere's home when we're together and have a roof over our head and eat. We used up all our resources taking care of her. I had to have help to take care of her, which is . . . used up everything. So we're here, to be taken care of. I don't know how long. They're good to us. We're taken good care of and people are nice. The nurses are nice.
Grace:	The aides are very nice.
Jay:	What makes this feel like home to you?
Grace:	Security, especially knowing that maybe soon no one will be around to take care of me, except this place will be here.
Lucy:	They know that after I'm gone nobody will take care of her. So if she feels like this is her home, she needs to feel like she likes it here.
Grace:	So this is my life now. But I still have a good sense of humor and I like a good laugh. I like to give somebody a good laugh. And I have a temper, too.
Lucy:	She's a little more independent than she used to be. She used to depend on all of us for help for what she needed. Gettin' so's she's kind of being a little independent now. Tells me what to do.
Grace:	Well, I've been told to watch out for my mother.
Lucy:	Yes. She was . . . she led a normal life just like anybody would, except for she has to sit in a wheelchair all her life. But we all helped her one way or another.
Grace:	The way I see it, you've got to make the best of what you got . . . doing the best you can with what you have to do it with. You know what I mean?
Jay:	I think so.
Grace:	And I had my mouth and I used it. [Laughs] In more ways than one. [We all laugh] Sometimes it gets me in trouble. Sometimes you can find my feet in it. My condition is funny, too. I used to take this thing here [supportive bandage] and throw it around and around and if Mother didn't duck, it'd hit her in the head. Or I'd trip her up with my feet. [Chuckling] Just spastic, you know. I have a weird sense of humor.
Lucy:	She's been that way and pretty healthy all her life. She's had a normal life as far as that's concerned . . . except for her condition. Even now that she's older, she's pretty much the same.
Jay:	Is there anything you dislike about your age, Grace?
Grace:	No, because I don't know any other way.

OPAL PETERS

Opal Peters has been at the Oakmont Nursing Home for four years and lived at several other homes before that. Her disabling arthritis relates to a different way of speaking of life. Peters is an admitted fighter, who relentlessly acts against her disability to prove that life goes on despite the handicap. She brings the fight into Oakmont, where she continues to broadcast her weekly radio show. For Peters, the nursing home represents one more link in a long chain of insults to her independence, which she weekly exhorts those similarly afflicted to struggle against.

Carol Ronai conducts the interview, which, among other things, features Peters's parents' missionary activity in China. In the following extract, Peters recalls her early years, the sister whom her mother favored, Peters's ambition to be a singer, and her developing arthritis. In later extracts, the parents' mission will be linked with Peters's own struggle.

I was born in New York City in 1914 and Mom and Dad at that time were in the dry cleaning and laundry business. They had returned from China where Mother and Dad met and were married. Mother was from Norway and Dad was from Hungary, but they were both born in New York City and they both went to China with separate groups, missionary groups. They met out there, and married out there.

My sister was born out there in Jungdeng Fu, just as some Chinese bandits were trying to kill off all the missionaries and Americans that they called "foreign devils." And so my parents ran across Northern Siberia over to Norway where Mother was from and got sanctuary there. Then they sailed over to New York on a boat and I was born a year and a half later after my sister. A year and a half after me, my brother was born in the same hospital and the same room, but not the same bed.

When I was about six months old, my auntie came from Norway after her mother died. Auntie lived with us and she was our grandma. She did all our sewing and cooking and cleaning and everything while Mom and Dad were doing their missionary work.

Well, in nineteen-something (I can't remember the year) we all sailed to China and while we were over there, Mother did the business work in the mission house and Daddy went out and did the preaching. Then, after the First World War, he was called over to France to clean up after the war. They had imported a bunch of Chinese coolies and Daddy could speak the language. So he was sent over there under the YMCA and I was, I guess, about five or six when we came back to New York.

Then Daddy came back from that and in 1925 he and Mother heard about Florida and the big boom. So, leaving us with Auntie, they all came down to Miami and they fell in love with it. Mother came back and sold the house lock, stock, and barrel and everybody moved to Florida. I've been here off and on ever since. Miami's been my home for sixty years. I remember when it was a nice little resort town. It's different and everybody thinks it's "Miami Vice." But I still remember Miami nice.

I got married when I was quite young because my mother doted on my sister and my sister went away to four Bible colleges during the depression under Mother's sponsorship. There wasn't enough money left for me. So when I was young, about eighteen, I got married and then I started having my children. So I couldn't do what I wanted to do with a career, like singing, which was my wish. I had taken lessons. [Elaborates] So when I got married and the children came, they were all a handful and then later on, their father (their biological father) just left and I married again. My second husband adopted the children and gave them his name. During the Second World War, he had a contract to drive these trucks and things for the government. He couldn't get the help he wanted because all the good guys were in the service. They were either too young or too old. So I was it. I had to help and we took the children right with us and traveled the road.

Then I started to contract rheumatoid arthritis, first in the left knee. We were taking a trip to California and I started to limp before we even got there. In Phoenix, Arizona, I went to a doctor and he said you've got rheumatoid arthritis, which I didn't know beans about and my family didn't either. But we soon found out and over a period of about thirty-five years, it's been up and down. I've had seven operations, an artificial knee, a fused right leg, and things like that that are not easy to live with. And so I've been in nursing homes up and down. I had my own home for a while in Miami and sold that because I couldn't do the yard work and so forth anymore. So, after my husband died, why now I'm here and I've gone from one nursing home to another.

Ronai prompts Peters to continue with her narrative by asking about the chapters of Peters's life story. It is now more decidedly a story of Peters's struggle against arthritis, its ostensible source in the hard work she did in her husband's trucking business, and advice to others based on her experience.

Carol: Let me ask you this. If you were writing a story of your life, what chapters would you have in your book. Like what would the first chapter be about?

Opal: Fighting arthritis.

Carol: Fighting arthritis? That'd be the first chapter in your book? Okay. What would the next one be about?

Opal: How to handle it. How the family can handle it and what is arthritis and what makes it do like it does and a lot of medical questions that I've asked doctors over the years and they have given me answers to. I was too late to prevent it because of the work I did. I'd say how people can prevent it by not overdoing like I did working in my husband's business.

Carol: Other chapters?

Opal: Well, other chapters would be, as you realize it's getting worse, you have to see the limitations coming on . . . to accept them. Don't run away from them. The limitations are what are hard to take, especially when you've been able to do everything. Not let the family get a feeling of guilt that they have to do it. And not letting the children overdo and do what they can't do but try to help anyway. My mission was to prevent them from getting what you've got and so forth and so on.

Carol: What about the last chapter?

Opal: The last chapter? Well, I think it's not a terminal disease. You can never get better but it doesn't happen like cancer in a hurry. So just make your years as enjoyable as you can. Fight it! I have my radio program, "Perspectives of the Handicapped," which I take an interest in and I love to do and think it's keeping me going. I've been doing that now since '72, off and on. So the last chapter is living with it and doing the best you can. Don't give up. Whatever you do, don't give up.

Carol: I'm curious. I've asked some other people the question, you know, about chapters and most of them started out with things like their childhood. I noticed you went right to the arthritis. Why do you think you did that?

Opal: Because I've lived with it a long time and I'm so familiar with it. I know what it could do to you if you let it, which I did for a while because I didn't know how to fight it. It affects how you see your whole life, straight through. Also because I think other people should be acquainted with it.

Carol: So it's been a huge thing in your life?

Opal: Oh yes! There have been times that I've had to cater to it. Just lie there and feel your bones disintegrate and you can't do anything about it. You lay there and cry and cry and cry. You don't want to put that on other people because it's not their fault. But I didn't let it win. That's my mission in life.

Ronai and Peters discuss the ups and downs of the disability, how it affected Peters's family life, and the various goals she had set for herself, all of which her handicap hampered in some way. According to Peters, her religion sustained her and now, supporting her mission, allows her to help others who are similarly afflicted. At one point, following Peters's remarks on the power of prayer and faith, Ronai asks Peters what part God plays in her life. Peters's response appropriates to her mission related images from her parents' missionary activity.

Carol: So God plays a big part in your life?

Opal: Definitely! I think that stems from my childhood. I was raised in the church. We used to go to church three times a week and twice on Sunday. We went to every Wednesday night service and I went to choir practice. My parents were missionaries and that was part of everything. It was just part of growing up.

Carol: What does all of that mean to you?

Opal: It means to me that when I need Him and even when I don't, I find myself singing hymns to Him. It's sort of a way of thanking Him for being with me and keeping me strong for what I have to do with the [radio] program and all, like it did for my parents when I was a child, it helped them in their missionary work. I hope I don't disturb my roommate but I just sing along and every Sunday I have church on the TV from 8 A.M. or from 7:30 until noontime. That's the way I spend my Sundays. I can't go to church; so it comes to me.

Carol: What does life look like from where you're at now?

Opal: I think that God has been with me and seen me through an awful lot and helped me get out on top of the last . . . because the radio program has meant so much to me. He gave me that talent where I can talk to people, try to help those that listen in, if possible.

Ronai and Peters discuss possible sponsorship for the radio program. Peters had been asked by the local radio station to get a sponsor to help with production costs. She is worried that lack of support might mean the end of the program, but also knows that she can depend on the faith that has sustained her, just as it sustained her parents.

The discussion turns to daily living at Oakmont. Peters has been resident in a number of nursing home over the years, either postoperatively or because of her arthritis-related dependency. While in Peters's opinion, Oakmont is among the better homes she's been in, none has been of central concern to her, displacing her mission in life. Peters's responses suggest that Oakmont, under the circumstances, is something to be adjusted to as a way of getting on with living, which in Peters's case is her mission.

Carol: You've lived here since September '88. Is this home?

Opal: Right now, it's all I can call home. I have a room. Didn't think I'd ever be reduced to that.

Carol: Does it feel like home?

Opal: I guess it's all I can expect. As I said, you learn to accept. It doesn't make that much difference anyhow. I've got to do what I've got to do, no matter where I am. I've thought if I won the lottery I would buy a van with a hydraulic lift and I would have somebody capable to help me up and down. [Elaborates] And I would continue with my program, but I would have it spread all over Florida. I would try to get it syndicated, something like the "Oprah Winfrey Show." I would gear it only to the needs and activities of the handicapped and try to get some kind of a transportation system so we're not prisoners in our own homes. That's the way I felt when I had my own home and I couldn't get anywhere. Then they started transportation in Miami, which was a real blessing.

Carol: Do you feel that living here is part of your life or separate from it?

Opal: Oh, it's part of it. I've learned to accept it. They do things their way and I just accept it. I remember a long time ago, Tip O'Neill, who used to be speaker of the house in Washington for years . . . he made a wise statement one time. He said that to get along, go along. I never forgot it. I had to learn to just go along.

But not for things that count! You know there have been a lot of cutbacks by the government for the handicapped and for the senior citizen. A lot of cutbacks! We don't have the help we need and some of the food, I've noticed, isn't what it should be. That shouldn't be. Instead of sending the money across the waters or up in the air, we should do something for our own, the people that put the money there. We paid for it all these years. So what are they doing with it? Pardon me for getting on the soapbox. Gotta spread the word.

CELIA TURNER

Celia Turner is fairly young as far as nursing home residents go, being sixty-four at the time Carol Ronai interviews her. Turner has been a resident at Greenfield Nursing Center for six years, since the facility opened in 1984. Born and raised in Florida, Turner formed her career as a playwright and magazine writer in New York City. She moved about the country from south to north and back again. As she became increasingly incapacitated by her multiple sclerosis and unwilling to have family members care for her, she settled in a Florida nursing home.

The self-realization of the writing process is a central narrative linkage. It is the means by which she casts her identity earlier in life, continues to define who she is, and now searches for who she can be as a woman and as a handicapped nursing home resident. Her story is imbued with the meaning of writing, as the following extract begins to show. In the last paragraph, there are hints of self-realization.

I was born here on March 8, 1928. My great-grandparents were one of the first doctor couples I guess in this country, certainly in town. My mother was a third-grade teacher and was one of the first members of the textbook committee of Florida. My father was a postal servant then. They were very active in community affairs.

I graduated from [the local] high school and went immediately to Columbia University. I had a fellowship and I went to New York with a one-way coach ticket on the train and $25 cash. My mother says that she still gets nightmares thinking about it. New York in those days was not quite as scary as it is now. That's where I met my husband.

I hit New York just at the right time because they were really trying to develop new talent. I had some plays done off Broadway and really was on that track when I had multiple sclerosis. That kind of slowed me down a bit. But the lovely thing is that a good friend became a nanny to our children. I would go to work and then come home and be there. I've always had pride in work. So I worked all the time. I guess you would say that I was sort of a nonstop writer.

Ask my kids, I was a nonstop mother, too. The kids all turned out great.

One of them, my oldest daughter, sort of followed in my footsteps, if that's the word. I had worked at *Cosmopolitan Magazine* and, a generation later, she did too. She's now the editor of her own publications in Chicago. I had five kids in all.

I worked at *Mademoiselle*. That's where my first job was. Then I worked at *Good Housekeeping* and *Cosmo*. The last was *Bride's Magazine*, where I expanded my horizons from fashion to homemaking.

Talking about myself, I think the most flattering thing I can say about myself . . . oh, I can tell you what I'm gonna have on my gravestone! Really, that's important. It was something one of my kids said, Dennis. He was taking the trash out at night, you know, putting it out on the curb and he went out and then came running back in with his eyes wide like that. He said, "Come on, Mom! Let's go take out the garbage and look at the stars." So that's going to be on my gravestone: She's going to take out the garbage and look at the stars.

Turner talks about her five children, their schooling, careers, and their own families. She's proud of them, repeating earlier remarks about the daughter who followed in her footsteps. Turner describes in greater detail the onset of her multiple sclerosis, how she managed motherhood, and developed a writing career in the process. Bringing her life story up to date, she recounts current writing projects, suddenly speaking of the potential of writing for the self.

Now it's writing, writing, writing, writing. I've got something out in two magazines now. I've published articles . . . you know I'm very ambitious. At this point, I've written five, actually six, plays. I have one, which is about a dying man. Another one, *End Time*, is about nursing home relationships, between people who work in a nursing home. I'm now working on a diary called . . . oh, I forgot to tell you that I did a cookbook, a bride's magazine cookbook. [Elaborates]

But the older I get and this handicap gets me, the more writing makes me what I am. Through writing, you make yourself up, write yourself down . . . we invent ourselves that way. Of course, the older we get, the more we have to invent. I wanted to write a book and it's going to be called *Making Myself Up and Writing Myself Down*. That's one title; the alternative title is *Entitled*, which is also a play on words. What I'm excited about is that it's a kind of self-revelation. It's very exciting. I'm on the cutting edge . . . or on the crushing edge of being able.

[Shows Ronai a magazine article] I was fascinated to find this article, which is about the way older women in this women's writing workshop wrote about life and about themselves and, in their way, put differences and similarities together to relearn who they were. I hope I can give a little something to everybody else by writing that way. I can't put my finger on it. I've begun to mysteriously come together as I read and think about what I've written about myself. I feel more useful than I have in a long time because, like perhaps I'll work on this way of writing. You know, you're inventing yourself, you're new again even if you're old.

I'm a bit of a maniac. I don't know how much of this is the old Presbyterian still wanting to make a contribution or it's a way of still finding new meaning, that you're not just used up. I don't really know what it is, but I would like to write something that would help someone besides myself to realize that.

Ronai asks Turner about the quality of daily life at Greenfield. Turner looks to her writing for the answer, her way of laying claim to what a long line of southern women before her has accomplished and that now serves to develop her own identity despite the odds. She speaks relatedly of the concrete shape of her immediate environment, particularly the appearance of her room, casting her mission accordingly, as virtually "rippling" through, time and again, what she is and intends to be, despite her MS (multiple sclerosis).

I've tailored my life here to fit what I'm about. I come from a long line of southern women—I guess you'd call them "thriving women"—who pretty much made their mark on life, regardless. You should hear my children tell it, about my life here. The minute they saw my room, they said, "Mom, your room always looks the same no matter where you are." And they don't mean that it's cluttered. They mean that I have things that I love around me, that I have them arranged in a protective way so that I can sort of nestle in them and nest them. Back there by that wall is . . . the bookcase . . . well, the books. The phone is reachable and the typewriter and the computer are here. Everything sort of works for me, all around me, where I write myself.

It's been that way all along, typical of me at any age. It represents the way I see life, like dropping a pebble in the water and the ripples go round and round. Or you drop a planet in the sky and the gases go around. Well, I'm very good at ripples and gases. I don't tend to go backwards and forwards much in time. I kind of ripple. I mean that I kind of drop that stone there and let the ripples go where they go, which makes me the stone, I guess.

I'm trying very hard to make myself understand the occurrences . . . of MS. [Elaborates] It gets in the way but it's also a background thing, the MS, that I work around, that's not going to keep me from doing what I have to do. [Pause] But I love the tactile business of hitting the keys on a typewriter or computer. I know it's there and it comes out through that. So it's all here, all around me. Wherever I am is where I live . . . I mean it's my room, my home . . . my MS. I really think this is really all I need. I've got space enough for me.

There is a long digression away from matters of daily living, to the collages and poetry that Turner has placed around her room. Turner describes the collages as "self-serving," not completely artistic, explaining that they are her way of arranging on paper, with images and poems, the way she feels about herself and life. The collages concretely renew her awareness that she is ageless, not a useless thing that has ended but one who capably continues to make meaning.

Something in the room causes Turner to giggle as she refers to the way Julia Child, the famous television cook, charmingly fumbles through food preparation and still manages to triumph in the end. The lesson is in the whole, not its parts. It is a whole whose parts, linked together creatively, can invent meaning time and again. Turner offers these final comments.

> Life is a huge and wonderful question. Me, I'm hokey, kind of a word person. I seize on what I need. So the meaning of life is looking for more little words in that great big world. I don't know how I can . . . I put everything in writerly terms. I'm sorry.
>
> One needs to grow. You have to find something, even here. You know you have the seed and you need to look around somewhere to grow up through the ground. It must hurt like you know what, to pop open. But everybody, I'm convinced, has a way that they can grow up. For me, it's through writing and everything around.
>
> I'm aware that potential in a lot of cases isn't really great. But there are people out there doing things that, every so often, I get glimpses of. I realize that what's important to me is not really the most important thing to them. There are people doing crafts. There are people playing cards. That represents to me some of the things that people can do to grow.
>
> But I can only give you subjective answers. Basically I'm egocentric and my main thing is always gonna be to try to do it my way, the way I know, to write myself.

* * * * *

For all three residents of this chapter, being disabled looms prominently in their narratives, further diversifying how the past is linked with the present and future. For Grace Wheeler, disability is a horizon that has organized the meaning of her life from the start, even while she had what is said to be a "normal" upbringing. Now in a nursing home, the quality of care is a concern that questionably links with the security family members had provided. Opal Peters's mission further articulates the horizon. For Peters, the nursing home is mainly a place to engage a life goal, which is to speak for and on behalf of the handicapped. In the context of the mission, the nursing home, notably its homeyness, "doesn't make that much difference anyhow." Celia Turner's narrative linkages center on writing, making it possible for her to invent herself in a world contained by her own immediate surroundings. All told, the special circumstance of these disabled women link the qualities of care and life in ways unaccountable by conventional assessment.

11

Knowledgeable

Karen Gray, a divorced white woman now confined to a wheelchair from multiple sclerosis, spent ten years of her career as a nurse being what she calls a state "surveyor," inspecting nursing homes, hospitals, and home health agencies for quality of care. She also participated in the certification process. In addition, Gray worked professionally as a public health nurse and nurse educator. Her former husband, a doctor whom she helped through medical school, was in private practice until a stroke forced him to retire.

Gray began to have symptoms of multiple sclerosis when she was twenty-five years old and pregnant with her first child. Now aged fifty-five and our youngest respondent, the last few years of her life have left her so disabled from MS that she has been, as Gray puts it, "floating around in nursing homes." One of the homes was a facility where her own father convalesced and eventually died. As she points out, that home was "as good as any other for me," the only difference being that her father was resident there, which, she adds, "really didn't make that much difference, except that I could look in on him every so often."

Gray's special circumstance is that she is knowledgeable about nursing homes in a way most residents are not. Her adult working life dealt with matters of primary concern to this book. She not only has considered the quality of care as a professional, but has lived the subject matter of her professional considerations, personally experiencing nursing home living.

Gray is interviewed twice by Carol Ronai, the first time as a resident of Fairhaven Nursing Home, where she has lived for two months, and the second time six months later in the apartment to which she has been discharged. Her narrative shows her views of nursing home life to be mediated by two related horizons of meaning—professional and personal—which affect her judgments about all nursing homes' quality of care. As Gray puts it, when she wears her "professional hat," she orients to nursing home living in terms of state and federal "regs" (regulations), straightforwardly and unemotionally. Wearing this hat, Fairhaven for her is more nearly a health care facility than a home and leaves much to be desired. Wearing her "personal hat," Fairhaven represents a daily living environment, something narratively linked with home. When Gray is interviewed in the apartment and is asked to compare apartment living with Fairhaven, the quality of life for her in the apartment pales in comparison. While the quality of care at Fairhaven left much to be desired when she resided there, six months later Gray says that life in the nursing home "wasn't all that bad." The two hats' perspectives highlight the complex ways in which horizons of meaning can link quality of care with quality of life.

THE FIRST INTERVIEW

Initially, Gray's story is a litany of straightforward opinions, which we learn in a later extract is her way of speaking while wearing a professional hat. As many do, she organizes the story chronologically, although Gray will remark in the second interview that she might have preferred to have organized her story thematically.

> I'll try to sort of pull it together and try to do it sort of chronologically. I was born January 15, 1935, in Massachusetts in an upper-middle-class household that I detested thoroughly. I went to an assortment of schools. I started out in public school. I was diagnosed as having rheumatic fever, but I don't know if this is really, truly true. My parents ran me into a really weird, private situation. It [the school] was sort of a little concentration camp for several years. I came out of that and I was in public school for a couple of years. My parents didn't think that the people I was running around with were appropriate. So I ended up in one of the best girl's schools in the East, where I did grade eight through twelve. I was reasonably miserable. But I had a love of horses that was always with me. Oh golly.
>
> When I was eighteen, we had a college decision to make. I was turned down at Duke. I was accepted at Middlebury. And out of total desperation, I got accepted at the University of Mississippi. My father was Mississippian; my mother was from Kansas. She floated around. So I moved down to Mississippi at eighteen, married some of the local talent in '55. I ended up in nursing school the summer of '59. Then I was pregnant with my child and was diagnosed with MS, you know, big deal. I worked while I was in school. I supported, basically, my husband Jake, and I had a fairly decent allowance. I sent half to him; he was busy flunking out of medical school on a fairly repetitive basis. He finally went through and it was in his senior year that our son Jim was born. I laid out for a little while and then went back to work.
>
> Later on, Jake started to get funny on me. I was doing public health nursing at that point. He was making fairly good money, but he decided he wanted to do his internship in a residency in Richmond, Virginia, because one of his friends went there. So he took off, actually on our anniversary,

and left me with two kids. After a while, I followed him. We eventually got settled. [Elaborates] I was teaching nursing after a while, med-surg. Then Jake decided he wanted to go into private practice. So we moved back to Mississippi and I had probably one of the worst periods of depression in my whole life because all my friends at this point were in Virginia.

So here I am with two kids, no job, confined to a house, and not adjusting. I got a little obstinate and decided I was going to go back to work. Jake went a little crazy with that. I got hired as the director of nursing services at a nice little hospital. It was the sixties and you didn't need a 100 percent education to do stuff back then. I worked there roughly ten years. They had a change of administration, some serious politics, and I ended up not working there. So I went to work for the State of Mississippi and surveyed nursing homes, hospitals, and home health agencies, just about everything that moved. I worked with that agency for as long as I could continue to work with the MS.

The kids had done relatively normal things. By the time I quit, they were both married. But my daughter Lynne was soon divorced and, later on, Jim got divorced. My husband was playing around with my friend that worked in his office and she decided she wanted the goose that laid the golden egg. So she got him, which sort of devastated me. I was surprised (a) that he was screwing around and (b) that he would divorce me. But it was the way things worked out. It was all right because—I'm not a nice person—see, he had a light stroke and isn't practicing medicine. His wife has two jobs. So I don't really feel bad, although I hurt at times.

There was an old fellow that was extremely kind to me, a World War II vet and below-the-elbow amputee. Jerry was sort of my feet and I was his hands. We lived together from '78 until a few years ago. That relationship went down the drain. He had sleep apnea and I was not sleeping well. Then he had some sort of cerebral changes. He was sexually oriented before, but he got extremely inquisitive about my body. We'd been living together and that's all right. But when you get to the point where you're sitting on the commode and somebody is enjoying watching you, it's not any fun. So I backed out of that one, using my illness as an excuse, and I've been floating around in nursing homes, basically, ever since.

Ronai asks Gray about the chapters of her story. As Gray proceeds to answer, the main linkages of a life narrative are conveyed: her "cruddy" childhood, her love of horses and other animals, nursing and nursing homes, and MS.

The first chapter would probably be about my cruddy childhood. I have spent some serious psychology time at the psychologist over the last six months roughly, trying to sort it out. As she [the psychologist] says—and I agree with it—she says that basically my parents should have never multiplied. They were not loving, caring, feeling people. I was basically a status symbol. Everybody had two cars, one child, a dog, and, you know, a living room, a parlor, a kitchen, three bedrooms, two baths, you know, and I was part of the inventory. I didn't like it. I didn't like it as a child and I resent it now. I perceive them being very egocentric and self-centered. At the expense of an only child, who had basically no peer group because they were older parents, I was jerked around between schools. I felt very much like a pawn and I was resentful of it. [Elaborates]

Let's see. I'd probably have a chapter about . . . do a horse and a dog one. I would definitely do a nursing home one. I am thinking very seriously of getting myself a word processor and doing an interesting analysis of nursing homes. I've surveyed them. I've lived in four or five. I'm acquainted with the federal regs and I'm acquainted with state regs in two states fairly thoroughly and I'm working on my third one. I think I would spend some serious nursing home time.

The last chapter is a hard one. If we're doing it chronologically, we're gonna have to deal with terminal things. We know how MS ends. It is not a great disease and it might be about MS. If I was gonna write it now, I would probably do that.

She discusses the history of her MS, how she dealt with it as she followed her husband's career from Mississippi to Virginia and back, and the kinds of sacrifices she made because of the affliction and the moves. It's an admittedly sad tale of truncated opportunities, which Gray continues to tell while wearing her professional hat, that is, in a straightforward, mainly unemotional manner. In an extract from an exchange following the discussion, Gray's manner becomes focal as she describes how she's made important decisions in her life, hedging on her professional self.

Karen: I very hardheadedly decided that I was not going to live in Massachusetts, but I ended up a nursing major instead of something else. I had to deal with it when Jake started sleeping with what's-her-name, or maybe when we lost the ability to talk to each other. I've always had a certain amount of paranoia, and he himself was not without problems, but I think had I not been set up . . . well, maybe not . . . my mother possessed me. I was an object and I was set up for Jake, because he was in charge. I think that had I had the wisdom . . . the wherewithal . . . to fall in love with somebody who would not fall into the control game, you know, that things might have been different.

Carol: You seem assertive to me. You don't seem like someone who would find herself in that fix.

Karen: I'm assertive about some things and not in others. I can . . . I think that, basically, professionally I am assertive, when I have my professional hat on. But when I get down to personal stuff, my personal hat . . .

Carol: Relationships?

Karen: Relationships. I have trouble doing that. I think I'm doing a professional thing with you right now and the stuff we talked about earlier.

Carol: Okay.

Karen: This is a person that can talk to you straight, basically. I think that if we got down to the "me" sort of stuff, I would be sitting here being embarrassed or getting real mushy. You know, I can totally back off into myself and I'm not doing this like that. I don't think that this is one of your goals.

They move on to discuss nursing homes in general and Fairhaven in particular. At first, Gray chooses to convey her thoughts and feelings about Fairhaven while wearing her professional hat. Gray judges Fairhaven to be worse as a nursing facility than many, but at certain points it isn't clear whether, professionally speaking, she is perhaps defending Fairhaven or describing nursing homes in general. This will be cast differently six months later when she thinks back on the Fairhaven experience from the vantage point of the isolation of apartment living. The discussion is prompted by a mention of the lack of a support system, the result of a recent disagreement with her daughter Lynne.

Karen: So I'm a bit miffed at Lynne and she's not too happy with me right now. So I've got less of a support system than I thought I had.

Carol: You mean from the point of view of living in this place?

Karen: Oh golly. I seriously avoid this place as much as I can.

Carol: But you live here.

Karen: Yeah. I go ahead and have breakfast in my room. I have got a pretty vigorous bowel control program. I take care of that, basically take a professional orientation. I find a book and go out and sit here or outside or, you know, spend some serious time scattered here and there.

Carol: Yeah. I noticed that you've had some sun on your chest. So I figured you'd been out.

Karen: Right, right. I'm basically a real kind of pale sort of person. But I've taken some serious outdoor time up here and at the last facility. The noise and confusion disturb me. The lack of privacy . . . not physical privacy . . . but quiet and not being able to go off and sit down and talk with somebody for thirty or forty minutes. [Nods toward her roommate's side of the room] I mean, you know, it is her room, too, but I've been using it. I just haven't had to use it when she did before. The lack of a place to go; that's a problem. But we're getting into the warmer weather cycle and I'm gonna have to find a place to sit where I can stand it.

Carol: What do you think your life will look like a year from now?

Karen: I hope I've got better digs. I don't think I'll be marketable. MS is sort of slow unfortunately, or fortunately, and I imagine that physically I'll be about where I am now, you know, unless something really disastrous comes around. I think I'm sort of stuck in this time warp for a while.

Carol: Before you came to live here, what'd you think it would be like?

Karen: Well, professionally, I knew what it was gonna be like. I mean I had been surveying these suckers for ten years. I knew some of them were better than others. I didn't know how bad the bad ones were.

Carol: Oh?

Karen: I have learned, were I still surveying, where to look. I am finding things that I didn't know to look for. I would have looked more thoroughly at infection control. I would have sure looked . . .

Carol: You think that's a problem here?

Karen: I think that cleanliness is a problem. I think here roaches are a problem. We are having a roach war here, okay? They are trying to kill the roaches. I myself am not a roach person. I don't like them. I used to write out nursing homes for roaches all over. And this place has probably got as good roaches as I have ever run into.

Carol: Ugh.

Karen: I mean, I was sitting with Harry [another resident] last night talking and one of them walks up the leg of the chair. In my room, one of them walks up the back of my dresser. I do not keep loose food in my room, okay? An experienced surveyor knows this. We have got a really, truly, serious, bad roach problem. We have, you know, the age group that hoards, like food, and we have some real hoarders here and they cleaned them out a couple of weeks ago and hopefully things are better. That's what you've got to do in these places if you're going to keep the roaches down. I've seen it in all these nursing homes.

Carol: They're all like that?

Karen: Well, really, yeah. I would look at bathtubs, too, because I got bathed this morning and you know that funny scaly stuff in bathtubs? Yeah, and were I surveying, I would run my finger in every damn bathtub. I wasn't smart enough to do that back then. But now that I've lived in them, you'd look at stuff like that.

Carol: I see. So you generally knew what you were getting into, for the most part though, when you moved here?

Karen: For the most part.

Carol: So you're not surprised living in 'em now, relative to what you thought when you were surveying them?

Karen: I am sort of repulsed. I have been in facilities better than this for sure. The rudeness and the ignorance of the aides, I have now experienced. As a surveyor walking into a facility, everybody is always so nice and polite and lovely. And everybody is always busy taking care of patients and, believe me, that ain't the way it is. They need to walk in on [shift] three to eleven and you'll find the nurse out somewheres and you'll have three aides sitting at the nurse's station. I'm sure they can cough up a good excuse of why they're doing that. That's the way these places are. The lack of caring. The lack of involvement. The lack of a place for me. I've made friends with other nursing services. This particular one is very remote and exclusive. I don't really know what's going on internally, but we practically never get the same three to eleven nurse. We have some consistency. I think I've had three or four baths since I have been here, by choice, but I think that a different person is doing it every time.

Nobody knows my routine. They are terribly rude about moving your crap around so that they can paint or paper or whatever they want to do and not putting it back. Then when they put it back, everything's out of place. I need some accommodation, you know, with a wheelchair and the transfers and all that stuff. Nobody knows my routine.

We had a care planning conference and they were kind enough to invite me, which is one of the federal regs, that if you are able, you are supposed to be included. They did do that here. But the little girl that was doing the conference was concerned with my hemorrhoids, which were a problem prior to my surgery a year ago, and I've got some needs that are really a lot greater than that . . . the fact that I have a catheter and really don't want to pick up any more strange bacteria; the fact that I've got a bowel problem related to my illness. The bowel problem is important to me because I don't want to be in the position where I shit in public, excuse me.

Carol: Right.

Karen: So I'm very compulsive about the darn thing because I know if I am taken care of in the morning, I will probably not have a boo-boo in the afternoon, and I have done this on occasion. These are the things that are important to me. And they're talking about my hemorrhoids!

Carol: I see what you mean.

Karen: I think that I need some recognition as an individual. Any patient does. I think that people should be aware of my needs and fit them into the routine. I think that if we had the same staff working, with all in the same way, basically every day, we could get a routine. These things would help these suckers.

Carol: Do you think of this place is part of your life or separate from it?

Karen: Basically, it is part of my life . . . because I worked with nursing homes so intensively for the ten years prior. I worked for ten years with them and then I ended up in them. I don't feel it's that hard. I feel like I got a lot to contribute. I'm frustrated because they have their system and I have no input.

Carol: Is there anyone in here that you feel close to?

Karen: At this point, not particularly. We've got a couple of older gentlemen that have a little bit of sense. I sort of assume almost a professional role with at least one of them, Alec. He is telling me about his sexual problems and I'm sitting there studiously not being turned off and I really don't care whether he can have a hard-on or not, you know.

But he's gonna have a [penile] implant and he's gonna tell me about the implant. It makes him happy. So, you know, what the hell.

I find it frustrating here because I've got more desires than I can physically accommodate. You know, I would be retiring in ten years and I could, you know, get loose and do some really neat things. I was thinking that Jake and I could travel and do things. Of course, he and Kitty [Jake's present wife] are traveling and doing things. 'Course he had a stroke. This is not a 100% great existence.

Carol: But you can still read and everything.

Karen: But you need a little more than that. You need some serious personal contact, besides listening to Alec's problems. You know what I'm saying? I guess I'm sorta getting personal now. Let's change the subject.

THE SECOND INTERVIEW

Six months later, discharged to an apartment, Gray feels isolated. The loneliness calls out a different persona, not the straightforward, professional surveyor of health care settings, but the sedentary, disabled woman whose personal hat now frames daily living. Speaking of Fairhaven, the framing serves to contrastingly portray the quality of the facility's care at the time she was resident.

Carol: Looking back at where you were when we last talked, how do you feel about it?

Karen: It's been an interesting experience. There've been a lot of problems. Discharge planning is not something that I think any facility is good at, and we made a bunch of mistakes.

Carol: Like what?

Karen: I did not manufacture an adequate support system. I have imposed on my daughter enough that we are now estranged. I have gone through a period of real insecurity. I didn't like a lot of reg stuff that was going on at Fairhaven, but at least I felt secure there. I guess you might say that there's more to life than regs. I haven't gotten enough help, I think, from the home health agency. I should have probably signed up for the aide services with those people. Except, basically, I'm able to pay for it and I feel like I'm cheating the government if I take something at the price they charge. I can hire it for a third on my own.

Actually, I'm planning to move back to Mississippi. I have an old lover there, Jerry, who has got a lot of physical and emotional problems. I think that if I say I want something, that he will manage to get it for me. I've got another friend, too, who's a nurse practitioner and I'm planning on using her general practice group. I feel like I can ask Sharon for anything.

Carol: How does living here compare with being at Fairhaven, where we talked last time?

*Karen:*Different.
*Carol:*Would you say better or worse or anything like a value judgment of any kind?
*Karen:*Oh golly. There are pluses there. It wasn't all that bad. Basically, in a nursing home, you have three hots and a cot. You didn't have to worry about that sort of thing. Over there, there were families coming in that you could chat with. There were staff members that were pretty yucky, but you pretty well avoided those. There were others that I really got to be pretty fond of. You could complain a lot, you know, professionally, which I did, but it was more secure in a certain sense. And there was some companionship. The isolation here has been real bad. I guess I didn't perceive my disability as great as I now know it is.

The conversation turns into a lengthy discussion of Gray's cat, which she adores, and Gray's relations with her daughter. Evidently, living in the apartment would not be half as bad if relations with the daughter weren't strained. Gray remarks that while "a lot of little things" sparked the estrangement, much of it can be attributed to the fact that Lynne can't fathom the extent of Gray's helplessness. Gray explains didactically what she means in the following extract, ending the lesson with a positive reference to her most recent nursing home stint at Fairhaven.

While I was visiting in Mississippi, there was an MS support group that had probably about a dozen people. I was just sort of sitting in. It was a little, local group, you know, and they sorta knew each other. I was there for just one meeting, so I mostly listened. The thing I heard over and over again was that their kids wanted them to be normal. One lady had two little stepsons and, you know, it was, "Where ya going? Why are you doing that? Why aren't you? Why? Why?" They didn't understand. There was a lovely Dutch lady who writes letters, apparently to everybody, and the kids are saying, "But Mom, we can't read it." And she says, "It's not my writing. It's . . . I mean it's not my MS. It's the way I learned to write in Holland." A younger woman was saying that she finally made it over to the couch and she laid down, and her little kid wanted a glass of water. She says to him, "Run and look and see if there's one in the refrigerator. I knew there wasn't, but at least he could leave me alone while he went and looked." And then he comes back and he says, "It's not there." There was a young girl who looked as good as you look, I promise you, wearing a sweatsuit. Believe me, any MS person with a sweatsuit is pretty all right. Heat tolerance is limited. And her mother is saying to her, "But Carrie, you would feel so much better when you came home from work if you didn't go to bed and if you got up and got out with your friends like you used to." And Carrie is saying, "And I'm dead at the end of the day." Things like that that Lynne can't seem to get, like you didn't have to think twice about at Fairhaven. At least there they understood dependency.

Mention of Fairhaven leads Gray to recollect her father's death in a nursing home and her move there to be with him. Gray wears her personal hat as she recounts her experiences there and in other facilities. In the process, she speaks of what nursing home life is like in general, despite differences in the quality of care.

Carol: You were in the home with him [Gray's father]?

Karen: Yeah. That was after the other two.

Carol: And how long did that last? The one you were in with your father.

Karen: December until he expired, like the end of either April or May. I've forgotten. I'm bad on times. We lost him in April. After that, Lynne brought me down here.

Carol: I'm curious about the experience with your father. How was that, living in the same place? Did it make being in a nursing home easier for you, him being there and all, or more difficult?

Karen: I don't think it made much difference either way. It was as good as any other for me. A nursing home is a nursing home. There was some nice people there. The food was particularly good. The care was not bad. Some of his friends visited, which tended to make it easier. The fact that he was down the hall dying was just one of those things. It really didn't make that much difference to me, except that I could look in on him every so often. When you live in those places . . . well, there are the differences you can list out, like that . . . but it's still a nursing home, right? You take the bad with the good, you know what I mean? It's like living any other place. Shit happens wherever.

Carol: He was aware of you and everything?

Karen: Yes, he knew I came. Yes, at times, he knew I was there. But I remember, one day, he was insisting that I was not his daughter, you know, just off-the-wall sort of crap. Initially, he was maybe aware that I was there. He didn't regard my presence as a love offering, which was basically what it was. For the first time in my life, I realized what a really egocentric, self-centered person he was. I mean just a lot of kinda pointless self-pride. I was really, really upset . . . excuse me . . . to find out what a son-of-a-bitch he was, 'cause I always thought he was great. He not only was not so great, but he wouldn't ask for help when he needed it. [Elaborates] They're still trying to straighten out his taxes, which he messed up so bad because he thought he could do everything himself.

Carol: So it had more to do with him than that place.

Karen: Oh sure. Ya got a lot on your mind anywhere you are, right? I had a lot on my mind: him, him dyin' and all, and what he got to be like.

Carol: So those kinds of things affect your judgment about these places?

Karen: Sure they do. Hell, you've got a life, too. Don't get me wrong. That last place [Fairhaven] I was in wasn't all that bad. Yeah, they had roaches, but you name any place down here and it's got roaches.

Carol: So how does life look like to you from where you're at now?

Karen: Well, I'm looking ahead to moving back to Mississippi. I see my life as a pretty knotty situation at this point. I don't really have a place to live that suits my needs. I'm walking away from this soon and walking into a new situation. I don't know what I'm gonna be dealing with. I don't know if we're gonna find digs that are appropriate. I don't know if I'm gonna get a bed in a nursing home. I don't know a lot of things. If worse comes to worse and I can't make it out of here, I can go back and live in that nursing home [Fairhaven]. Personally speaking, it was not *that* bad. I think I can survive it. I've survived others.

Carol: What do you think you're life will look like a year from now?

Karen: Hopefully, I'll be in Mississippi. I've got friends there. Jerry's there [the old lover]. I'll have some sort of assisted independent living facility or a nursing home. At least I won't have the isolation I've got here. I maybe can lean on somebody for a ride to church, you know, to help me out and feel like he's getting brownie points with God. And I'll have the pleasure of being out with some people. I'm not sure whether that's an appropriate or inappropriate use of the church.

The interview moves back and forth between Gray's present living situation, being resident at Fairhaven, and future options. Gray recounts her life story chronologically, but comments that it might have been better told thematically. Certain themes "really" stand out, she remarks, such as MS, her childhood, and nursing homes. As the interview winds down, Gray's current living situation is considered. Gray speaks of it metaphorically and eventually uses the metaphor to convey the meaning of her Fairhaven experience. While Gray's comments might be interpreted as retrospective nostalgia, embellished by her present situation, one thing is nonetheless clear: The subjective meaning of her nursing home experience is drawn from the different linkages that articulate narrative, from her two hats to her past and current troubles.

Carol: Living here. Is it part of your life or separate from it?

Karen: Well, personally, it's part of the continuum, but it's like a narrow place on the ribbon, if you will.

Carol: A narrow place on the ribbon?

Karen: A detour on the highway, if you will.

Carol: I'm not sure I'm picking up that metaphor. It's a detour on the ribbon or a narrowing of the ribbon? Which or what?

Karen: I think that life is a continuum.

Carol: Uh huh.

Karen: And I think that a continuum, that ribbon, has got a certain width as well as an unknown length.

Carol: Right.

Karen: I think there are times in your life when it isn't very rich and the ribbon is pretty narrow, although it continues.

Carol: Uh huh.

Karen: And the ribbon can spread out. It's like you're knitting a sweater and you get real tense and it gets real tight in that particular area.

Carol: And narrows.

Karen: Uh huh. You're with me. So now we're in one of the tight places.

Carol: So was living at Fairhaven in one of those spots?

Karen: It was part of the continuum.

Carol: Was that tighter than this part?

Karen: No, no. It's different, because, you see, there were people in and out, and there were families, and there were patients that were . . . that you could talk to.

Carol: So the ribbon was wider there, looser knit?

Karen: Yeah, sure. This here is the tightest.

Carol: Because of the isolation?

Karen: Yeah and the estrangement from Lynne. So I'm looking for it to loosen up, either here or in Mississippi or back in that nursing home.

*   *   *   *   *

Being knowledgeable as Karen Gray is, is fairly rare among nursing home residents. But rarity does not detract from the fact that an additional horizon serves to articulate the subjective meaning of the qualities of her nursing home's care and life. The horizon informs her comments in complex ways, narratively linked with the role (hat) she chooses to take in making comparisons and offering judgments, as well as with the MS and her history of interpersonal relations with her daughter, her former husband, friends, and her parents. From Gray, we learn how fine-grained the meaning of the qualities of care and life can be, actively linked as the latter are with contrasting biographical categories.

12

Lessons

The narratives presented in the preceding chapters are a slice of those collected in the study. There were other residents whose orientations to the quality of life only hinted at being worried to death, possibly making a new home, or "taking no lip" only if push actually came to shove. There were some who seemed to make a frenzied job of being worried, who were so emotionally distraught that they were hardly interviewable. Some residents combined these horizons, such as making a new home and taking no lip from family members about the life they had formed in their new environs. A few linked being worried to death with "lovin' the Lord," aching for the afterlife as a way of leaving dire straits behind.

Other special circumstances also presented themselves. Some spouses and siblings resided in the same nursing home but not the same room, as Karen Gray from the last chapter did in the facility she moved into to be with her dying father. There were residents who had relatives, sometimes a husband, a wife, or a parent, living in nursing homes distant from their own. Some pined for the relative whom they felt might never again be seen alive; others seemed to care less, not knowing whether the relative were alive or dead. There were those whose special circumstance was that they could not speak English or who were otherwise incommunicable, but who were nonetheless alert, ambulatory, and available for interaction.

That there are horizons and diverse narrative linkages across the variety conveys general lessons about subjective meaning. Some lessons are conceptual and instruct us about how to understand the subjective contours of lives. Some are methodological and offer guidelines for studying subjective meaning and, specifically, its relationship to the quality of care and the quality of life. There also are lessons for us as fellow persons, about what any one of us might very well become in years to come—nursing home residents. This concluding chapter presents the lessons, returning us to matters raised at the start.

CONCEPTUAL LESSONS

As a way of orienting the reader to the interview material at the end of Chapter 1, I distinguished the life history from the life narrative, noting that the life history is an objective record of the person's past, while the life narrative is the subjectively constructed life. Life narratives are offered in response to what sociologist Brandon Wallace (1992, 1993) calls "narrative challenges" or occasioned requests to recount life. When Carol Ronai and I asked our respondents to tell us their stories and subsequently discussed with them their pasts, presents, and futures, together with related matters of home, family, and the qualities of institutional life, the narrative challenge was for residents to offer up accounts in response to the requests. The occasion itself—the interview, its participants, and the topics—was part of what ensued, making residents' stories narrative collaborations.

One lesson of this regards how to conceive of the way in which the lives that are the subject of narration fit in the flow of experience. The life is not something distantly set in stone, which the researcher more or less accurately retrieves and records. Rather, the life is a narrated entity, a constructed whole served up against horizons, in relation to which matters of various kinds such as the quality of care are given voice. The narrated entity that is a life is current and practical. When Roland Snyder, Jake Bellows, Lula Burton, Grace Wheeler, and others speak of life, linking it with particular versions of home and institutional living, it is life articulated out of its narrators' present situation as nursing home residents. Yet the situation is not subjectively homogeneous, complicated as its meanings are by different orientations and special circumstances. "Distant" lives are as recent as the present and its perspectives.

The constructed life informs us that what is told is pertinent to the here-and-now, indeed cannot be separated from the here-and-now (Gubrium et al. 1994). The constructed life only makes sense when we consider it in relation to the situation in which it is conveyed. In a manner of speaking (or writing), the constructed lives of nursing home residents Snyder, Bellows, Burton, Wheeler, and others are conceptually hyphenated lives: versions-of-life-subjectively-pertinent-to-the-nursing-home-situation. How the lives and their linkages would be articulated in other situations would need to take the situations' respective orientations and special circumstances into account.

The meaning of the past in relation to the present is neither narratively uniform nor unilinear. As travelers, Jake Bellows and Peter Rinehart orient to their nursing homes as hotels, the facilities virtually being two more resting places along well-traveled roads. Lovin' their Lord, Julia McCall and Mary Carter orient to an altogether different world, marginally concerned with the comforts or discomforts of the present. Bellows, Rinehart, McCall, and Carter hardly accord to the quality of care the significance that, say, Bea Lindstrom does, who is vigilantly attuned to the quality of care and will "take no lip" from her caregivers. Moreover, as the longitudinal aspect of the project showed, narrative linkages change in a complex manner over time. The change is not stepwise or generally unilinear, akin, say, to a process of adjustment, but change that relates to the shifting and varied linkages of the present in relation to life as a whole.

Another conceptual lesson concerns how to think about the related roles of everyday life. Pertinent here is the role of the nursing home resident, although other roles such as family caregiver and significant other are implicated. The life narratives of residents indicate that the role of nursing home resident cannot be defined separately from the horizons of meaning brought to the definition. The role means something personally positive for Martha Gilbert, who admittedly never had a home to speak of. It means something quite the opposite to Rebecca Bourdeau, who left a lovely home to recover at Oakmont, the nursing home in which she now resides. For spouses Amy and Tom Malinger, home is wherever they are together. Fairhaven finds them as much *home* household occupants as registered residents. Twins Lula Burton and Lily Robinson continue the sisterly conversation at Florida Manor they have had all of their lives residing and working a mere stone's throw from each other.

The category "role" does not stand isolated from biographical activity (Gubrium 1988). Knowing that Martha Gilbert and the others are nursing home residents gives us a certain, broad fix on their lives, but it does not inform us of subjective meaning. For that, we need to turn to narrative, in which, say, Myrtle Johnson, a resident of Westside Nursing Center, wonders audibly how it could possibly have come to this, referring to how the meaning of life and destiny could be reduced, day in and day out, to forever being sick, incapacitated, and staring at four institutional walls.

A third conceptual lesson derives from the contrast between the biographically active idea of role and its official organizational understanding. Officially, there are relatively few roles in nursing homes. There are staff roles, administratively distinguished into aides, nurses, dietitians, social workers, and physical therapists. There are resident roles, which are commonly classified into personal-, intermediate-, and skilled-care. In some nursing homes, certain residents are called "patients" to differentiate them from the more able-bodied or "residents." There also are family roles, although they border on the unofficial.

The workings of organizations, evident in their daily shifts and rhythms, job descriptions, and surveillance functions, tend to homogenize the lives within them into official classifications. Residents who orient to the nursing home experience in dramatically different ways, or whose special circumstances articulate particular horizons, officially are more or less simply residents, albeit with varied care needs. While the aide has a past, a home life of her own, and distinct ambitions, she is officially just an aide. As Diamond (1993) shows in his book *Making Gray Gold*, if anything, these subjective matters intrude on organizational rationality, which, as Diamond argues, shortchanges the profit motive.

From a formal organizational perspective, official roles fully penetrate the nursing home experiences of staff and residents. As far as "the" resident is concerned, he or she not only is housed in a room, has a bed, and is served three meals a day, but thinks and feels like a resident. The subjective contours of the resident's past and future are relevant only to the extent they are periods of life pertinent to the official present. Biographical particulars, such as the residents' view of life, are ultimately marginalized in organizational processing, even while enlightened administrators and staff try to take them into account. In the care planning conference, for example, short- and long-term care goals are set and biographical particulars mainly accorded meaning in terms of care needs and service provision (Gubrium 1975).

The idea of the biographically active resident is a conceptual defense against this. Residents are viewed as articulating their roles in different ways, only some of which convey thoughts and feelings appropriate to official concerns. The idea allows us to recognize that, within the parameters of their situations, residents construct and live in worlds of their own making as much as they participate in or forebear the official nursing home world and its roles. Conceiving of residents in this way could provide the rationale for establishing institutional structures for displaying and regularly affirming subjective meaning.

METHODOLOGICAL LESSONS

Methodological lessons relate to the study of subjective meaning, particularly researching the quality of care and the quality of life. I put these in the context of the interview as a research tool, considering interviewing as a narrative collaboration with the respondent.

Social research methods books commonly describe the interview as a technique for gathering information from individuals about their thoughts, sentiments, and activities. The interview involves someone called the interviewer asking questions of someone else called the respondent, who in turn answers the questions out of his or her experience. The ideal interview is one in which respondents' answers convey what was in the respondents' experiences "all along," as it were.

The life narratives presented here warrant another approach. Its point of departure is that the interview is a meaning-making occasion; results cannot be conceived as completely separate from the occasion's narrative challenges. The interviewer is not a passive inquirer. While the interviewer may work from a set of orienting questions such as those contained in our interview guide, he or she participates with the respondent in considering the kinds and versions of questions the respondent deems pertinent to particular concerns. The interviewer attends to how the respondent narratively organizes experience in the process of linking elements of the past, the present, and the future, and from that targets meaning. This allows the respondent to set his or her own horizons of meaning for the matters under consideration.

Not just anything goes. The interviewer encourages the respondent to construct a sense of experience based on the assumption that horizons organize subjective meaning and a working commitment to trace linkages from the broader context of the respondent's life as a whole. This is not an interviewer who passively inquires from an interview schedule or is bound by the topics of an interview guide, but someone who nonetheless remains assiduously sensitive to the respondent's biographical activity. The procedural understanding is that horizons and their narrative linkages guide the active interviewer.

Research methods books commonly assume that the respondent is whoever he or she is designated to be, in our case, a nursing home resident. In the research process, designated respondents remain narratively fixed from start to finish. A sample of nursing home residents is taken to respond as nursing home residents. They are not viewed as differing so much in orientation as to lead the researcher to raise questions about the subjective relevance of the role of nursing home resident. Nor do respondents shift identities in the course of their interviews. The idea that the respondent puts on different hats during an interview, as Karen Gray did in hers, confounds the assumption.

Yet this is precisely what horizons of meaning and their narrative linkages do from respondent to respondent or during a single respondent's interview. In my experience as a field-worker doing both participant observation and ethnographic interviewing, it wasn't unusual for respondents to specify the capacity in which they were addressing a particular question or topic. Sometimes, they simply stated the capacity. For example, in field research on Alzheimer's disease caregiver support groups (Gubrium 1986), caregivers prefaced remarks about their home care experiences with statements such as "Speaking as a wife, I feel [such and such]" and "Putting my caregiver's hat on, I think [thus and so]." They then went on to describe how they felt or what they thought, in those capacities. Some would turn about midresponse to convey sentiments and thoughts from another vantage point. Capacities could even represent preferred thoughts and feelings, as when a caregiver stated, "Right now, I prefer to think of myself as a wife, not his caregiver, because a wife naturally feels more."

The contrast between the designated respondent and narrative capacity presented itself poignantly in one field site. Caregivers had completed a standard burden-of-care questionnaire as part of their participation in a hospital-based study of related stresses. A few days later, in a support group, the caregivers recalled their thoughts and feelings in completing the questionnaire. Some mentioned that they didn't think of themselves as being burdened, but just doing, as one of them put it, "what I feel I have to do." According to a caregiving adult daughter, it hadn't even crossed her mind that caring for her mother should be framed in those terms—burden, stress, strain. The daughter always considered what she was doing for her mother as part of what the daughter owed to her mother in return for the mother's devotion to her daughter over the years. The daughter had come to the support group to learn how to be a grateful daughter, as it were. In contrast, other caregivers felt that the tone of the questionnaire captured matters well, clarifying for them what had been vague thoughts and mixed emotions. In their case, the tone served to crystallize the narrative capacities required to make responses meaningfully those of *caregivers*. Unbeknownst to the administrators of the questionnaire, the questionnaire itself was biographically active, which also remains unrecognized in nursing home quality assurance assessments.

Using a questionnaire, interview schedule, or interview guide for purposes of inquiring about the thoughts and feelings of the respondent without attending to the capacity in which the respondent gives voice to experience puts the procedural cart before the horse. As we try to understand respondents' experiences, we must make sure whose voices speak to us. Nursing home residents' life stories and related responses suggest that narrative horizons must be discerned in order to sort the variety.

There are specific methodological lessons about quality-of-care and quality-of-life assessment in the nursing home. While research on quality of care and quality of life has burgeoned in the last decade, especially as applied to frail elderly, the concepts' methodological underpinnings remain muddled and tentative (Birren et al. 1991).

As far as the nursing home is concerned, quality of care usually has referred to the cleanliness of the premises; the kinds of nursing, medical, therapeutic, domiciliary, and ancillary services offered; staffing patterns; the physical and psychosocial status of residents; and compliance with regulations. Emphasis is on the actual care given, the availability and qualifications of professional caregivers, and care and treatment outcomes, all of which are taken to be objectively assessable conditions.

At the same time, it has been noted that there is more to quality than concrete care provision, especially in the context of the nursing home (Estes and Binney 1989; Kane 1989; Institute of Medicine 1986). In contrast to the nursing home, hospital stays are relatively short and pose fewer problems of life-style adjustment for patients. Short stays mean that patients can virtually put their lives on hold or temporarily leave their lives behind as they undergo treatment and initial recovery. In nursing homes, except for brief periods of convalescence following acute care or physical rehabilitation, stays are lengthy and present significant life-style challenges to residents. The term *nursing home* not only connotes a hospitallike venue providing nursing cares, but a homelike setting offering shelter and sustenance, in many cases for years or for the rest of one's life.

Long-term stays bring lives along as well as ills and disabilities. For some, such as those who are worried to death, what is brought along figures distressingly into personal outcomes. For others, such as those who love their Lord, personal outcomes are subordinated to something of much greater value. A variety of lifelong concerns is at stake in the nursing home experience and affects adjustment. These subjective concerns are a diverse configuration, far broader, more complex, and less immediately concrete than the specifications regularly taken to make up the quality of care.

Psychologist Powell Lawton (1983) has written that quality assurance, especially in the nursing home setting, includes residents' life-styles and perceptions of the value of life—features of what Lawton calls the "good life." He explains that quality of life is a general, multidimensional concept and suggests that what it means to be a long-stay nursing home resident cannot be understood without taking this into account. Most researchers agree that quality of life is a key ingredient of quality assurance and many, but not all, think of it as something distinct from, if not unconnected with, standardized quality of care (see Birren et al. 1991; Institute of Medicine 1986).

Significant as quality of life is considered to be, the concept is not easily rendered into the restricted operations of measurement. Psychologists James Birren and Lisa Dieckmann state that

> for many years the concept of quality of life was viewed as abstract, "soft," and difficult to operationalize. Consequently, this concept was overlooked, particularly by psychology and other disciplines intent on achieving "hard science" status. More concrete health measures, such as

mortality, morbidity, restricted activity days, and functional status typically have been used to evaluate the cost-effectiveness of interventions or
to assess quality of care, and social scientists have relied on related but less
complex concepts, such as life satisfaction, to elucidate the subjective aspects of life. (1991, p. 344)

The statement conveys a disturbing irony. On the one hand, it is
agreed that, while abstract, quality of life is highly significant in its own
right, if not also in connection with the quality of care. On the other
hand, there is notable handwringing over how to measure it. Because
the concept is recalcitrant to "hard science" operationalization (which
confuses science with technology), the concept either has been ignored
or thought too methodologically complicated to research, something like
starving for lack of a particular eating utensil and not thinking to use
one's hands. As the front-page article entitled "Quality of Life" states in
a recent issue of the newsletter *Network*, published by the New England
Research Institute, the specific instance of "health-related quality of life"
or HQL

generally denotes aspects of life most likely to be affected by health, such
as physical functioning, physical health, mental health, cognitive functioning, social functioning, intimacy or sexual functioning, and productivi-
ty. Although HQL has gained widespread acceptance as an important
medical outcome, its measurement is riddled with conceptual and methodological issues. What constitutes HQL? What factors moderate HQL?
Should HQL be represented by a single overall score or by scores on
different dimensions of functioning? Should measures be generic or
disease-specific? Should measures reflect patients' perceptions of HQL or
objective assessments of functioning? The array of instruments and complexity of approaches to measuring quality of life can seem overwhelming,
even to those in the field. (1992, p. 1)

The preference is for measurement scales, quality of life scores, or the
like, the idea being that life and its qualities can be described arithme-
tically. The article goes on to list criteria for the ideal instrument, among
which are that it should "require less than 15 minutes to complete" and
be suitable for telephone as well as other forms of administration (p. 2).
It is explained that some existing instruments are completed by the
physician, which assumes that the physician or, as is more often the case
in nursing homes, a nurse can effectively assess that "holistic" entity
called quality of life. This is the way in which information in minimum
data sets is to be collected (see Morris et al. 1990). While lip service is
paid here and elsewhere to the validity of assessment—namely, that
assessment be about that which it claims to be, in this case quality of
life—efficiency is the name of the game.

The idea of efficiency bandied about in such discussions centers on four criteria. First, measurement or, more broadly, assessment is efficient if it can be completed in short order, such as in ten to fifteen minutes. A quality of life assessment instrument that would take longer to complete would be considered inefficient because, among other things, it would take too much time away from other activities for which those who administer the instrument are responsible. Second, assessment is efficient if the information gathered can be readily coded for data processing. On this criterion, the precoded response categories of a staff-administered, survey instrument would be more efficient than the transcribed narrative of an open-ended interview. Third, efficiency is productive of concise data, usually meaning numeric data. Results reportable in the form of a single, overall score or individual scores for particular components of quality of life are preferred. Fourth, efficiency has a scientistic tenor. Assessment that sounds "scientific," presented in a vocabulary replete with terms such as measurement, reliability, statistical analysis, and indexes, is more acceptable than the so-called soft and "unscientific" vocabulary of narrative. The criterion is scientistic because it capitalizes as much on the rhetoric of popular science as on scientific rigor.

But rigor in science would seem to center ideally on the relationship between method and subject matter. If quality of life concerns the qualities of the subject's life, the concept ostensibly would pertain to whatever might be included and evaluated in the life by the experiencing subject whose life it is. Psychologist Torbjörn Svensson specifies what he would take this to mean.

> There seems to be general agreement that quality of life is a global measure or concept. At the same time, it is agreed that quality of life is built upon other concepts, which have been described as domains or attributes. . . . [I]t is proposed that these domains are qualities *in* life. Qualities in life are defined as the specific areas a person perceives to be vital to the ability to enjoy life and to feel that it has meaning. It can also be said that these qualities are areas into which an individual puts high meaning and involvement. As such, involvement and meaning are important aspects for measurements that seek to discern what is perceived as a quality in life. Meaning in life particularly must be considered since it involves a global evaluation of the entire life situation, with former, present, future, and perhaps transcendent aspects of the individual's life content. (1991, p. 257)

The last sentence, especially, not only would extend the concept to the life and the qualities described by nursing home residents Karen Gray, Rita Vandenberg, and Jane Nesbit, but also to those conveyed by Myrtle Johnson, Alice Stern, Julia McCall, and Mary Carter, whose narrated

lives have borders and qualities taking them beyond the official parameters of their immediate situation and its time frame.

Truly rigorous assessment requires a different sense of efficiency, one
directing us to draw out and convey whatever a concept validly references, however resistant to arithmetic representation that might be. This
expressly links efficiency with validity, enhancing efficiency's scientific
status even while reducing its scientistic tenor, which in part has moti-
vated the narrative character of the research reported in this book.

A lesson to be drawn from this is that quality of life can be revealed to
be something quite distinct from the quality of care, even while some
narrative linkages, such as Bea Lindstrom's, immerse the quality of life
in the quality of care. This does *not* mean that, in the context of some
horizons, the quality of care provided by the nursing home doesn't need
to matter. What it does mean is that lives and care are not necessarily
understood by their subjects in terms of the administratively defined or
scientistically attributed conditions of immediate situations. As the horizons, narrative linkages, orientations, and special circumstances of our
nursing home residents show, there is far more to life and its qualities
than the multidimensional components of a measurement scale.

A related lesson is that we need to take on board entirely different
methods of procedure to study the subjective meaning of the quality of
life and the quality of care than those customarily used in assessment.
Required is a methodology attuned to life as a broad and narratively
assembled entity, guided by an analytic orientation that recognizes stories to be invariably situated. It is a methodology centered on subjects as
active agents in determining whatever is meaningful and valued in life,
a methodology whose narrative purview extends beyond the immediate
present because subjects make meaning from lifelong experience.

I don't mean to suggest that standardized quality assessment is irrelevant. Such assessment is useful for helping to maintain minimum levels
of care for what might be called the "objective" conditions of residents'
daily lives. But we need to remind ourselves, too, that residents live as
much in subjective worlds as in relation to objective conditions. Indeed,
while I have argued that horizons and narrative linkages meaningfully
and collaboratively assemble the subjective qualities of care and nursing
home life, minimum data sets and the like are also meaningful collaborations in that they are constructed out of what we as a society believe
objective standards of care should be (Pifer and Bronte 1986) and their
facts are generated out of the descriptive contingencies of assessment
occasions (see Cicourel 1964). It all suggests, on the contrary, that meth-
odologies pertaining to the study of lives and their qualities need to be
most inclusive.

PERSONAL LESSONS

I have been personally instructed by the narratives. One lesson, precious to me, is how narratively rich lives can be even as their subjects suffer from pain, are severely restricted by disabilities, have lost most if not all of their loved ones, and have little or no chance for recovery. Theirs are faces *with* stories, who under the most trying bodily conditions are still able to make meaning, to link together semblances of explanation and understanding for life and living. Their stories have taught me that, even with dreadful insults to one's body or being near death, varied horizons communicate meaningful differences. Experience does not necessarily coalesce around immediate afflictions, their cares, their trials, or dying.

I cherish the memory of the many residents who readily spoke of their lives, who in many instances I actually could see breathing with difficulty or aching from pains in their backs, chests, legs, and elsewhere as we talked. Most went on, wanted to go on, despite the difficulties. Their will and stamina amazed me. In a few cases, it was more than I could bear, knowing that they were succeeding in presenting to me what their lives had been like, what life had become, and, perhaps most significant, what a life could still be.

Here I was, a man in his midforties at the time of the research, concerned with the completion of the interviews, the management of the narrative material, and the emerging results. And here in front of me during the interviews were persons near the end of their lives or in intractable pain. What was I hearing as they conveyed their experience? Data? Stories? Responses? Meanings? Interviewees? Narratives? I was hearing all of this, of course, but placed side by side, the resulting polarities shocked me. Data versus stories. Responses versus meaning. Interviewees versus storytellers. It shocked me because, on the one side, I was aiming to complete a study and, on the other, I was witnessing what the suffering and dying were telling me, were conveying *for me*. It was a gift, really, and it shocked me that I had to remain committed at the time to listening, recording, and going about research business, respondent after respondent. It was a gift I could not return then, having to remain satisfied that only later could I give something in return by telling their stories in the best way I could.

Another lesson relates to the idea of the end of life. Residents Julia McCall, Mary Carter, and others seemed ready to die, but only bodily. They loved their Lord and were set to go on to another world, a life they imagined in the beyond. For them, the end of life signified the end of life in this world, not the end of life altogether. Roland Snyder, Rita Vanden-

berg, and Rebecca Bourdeau were worried enough to want to die, because this world was too bodily or spiritually painful. Spouses Amy and
Tom Malinger and Sue and Don Hughes were in it together until the
end, which would seem to come when a spouse died. Other residents
construed death in still different ways: as the eclipse of security, the
demise of imagination, the loss of home and significant others, or in
terms of the unfathomable place of fate in life.

In their narratives of life and death, living and dying, the residents
taught me that endings are made, constructed, and reconstructed, even
at the very end, as it were. Having heard their stories, their thoughts
and feelings about living in relation to dying and to pasts, present conditions, and futures, I am hard pressed to think of the final years of life as
years of "life review," as psychiatrist Robert Butler (1963; Butler and
Lewis 1977) puts it, that is, as a time of final reckoning or stocktaking.
The longitudinal material gathered from residents interviewed more
than once indicates that the very idea of a course of adjustment at the
end of life shortchanges its variety, complexity, improvisations. There is
little overall evidence that affairs are ultimately settled, sundered ties
finally repaired, transgressions at last righted or accounted for, or prepa-
rations for the future or afterlife completed. While some residents, of
course, do speak of waiting for heaven, buying cemetery plots, and
making funeral arrangements—points of information that indeed may
hold considerable value for them—these do not necessarily signify terminal horizons.

Finally, I draw a lesson from reflecting on certain aspects of my own
life. As I look over the residents' stories, I read about significant others. I
have twin daughters, now college sophomores. As I read the transcripts
of twin sisters Lula Burton's and Lily Robinson's remarks about the
lifelong conversation that continues to sustain them at Florida Manor,
do I hear what my own daughters, fifty years hence, might call upon to
give meaning to those years? Looking back on my own, still developing
research career—seemingly filled with important research, momentous
decisions, and academic achievement—what do Myrtle Johnson and
Alice Stern tell me about destiny? That it all could come to "this"? And
what is "this" in any case? Certainly "this" could be part of a new life or
the life to come, even a life that isn't so bad after all if one removes a
professional hat. The stories and narratives are about *our* lives, whose
horizons and linkages can form in many directions to give meaning to
the years ahead.

Appendix

LIFE NARRATIVE PROJECT—INTERVIEW GUIDE
(Probe for Thoughts and Sentiments)

Life in General

1. Everyone has a life story. Tell me about your life, in about twenty minutes or so if you can. Begin wherever you'd like and include whatever you wish.
2. What were the most important turning points in your life?
3. Tell me about the happiest points in your life.
4. What about the saddest points?
5. Who've been the most important people in your life?
6. Who are you closest to now?
7. What does your life look like from where you're at now?
8. If you could live your life over, what would you do differently?
9. How do you explain what's happened to you over your life?
10. If had the opportunity to write the story of your life, what would the chapters be about? Chapter 1? Chapter 2? . . . What about the last chapter?

Daily Life

11. Describe a typical day in your life now. People here. Others. Quality of care/life.
12. How is a typical day now different from before you came to live here?
13. What do you think your daily life will look like a year from now?
14. Before you came to live here, what did you think it would be like?

Home

15. What does the word *home* mean to you?
16. Now that you've been here for _____, does it feel like home?

17. What would it have to be like here for it to be like home?
18. Do you feel this place/living here is part of your life or separate from it? Why is that?

Family

19. What does the word *family* mean to you?
20. Right now, in this place, is there anybody who's like family to you?

Self

21. How would you describe yourself when you were younger?
22. How would you describe yourself now?
23. Have you changed much over the years? How?
24. What is your philosophy of life? Overall, what is the meaning of life to you?

Aging

25. How do you feel about growing older?
26. What do you like about being your age?
27. What do you dislike about being your age?
28. Do you think about the future? Make plans?
29. What do you look forward to now?
30. Do you think about death?

References

Atkinson, Paul. 1990. *The Ethnographic Imagination*. London: Routledge.

Bauman, Richard. 1986. *Story, Performance and Event: Contextual Studies of Oral Narrative*. New York: Cambridge University Press.

Berger, Peter and Hansfried Kellner. 1970. "Marriage and the Construction of Reality." Pp. 50–72 in *Recent Sociology No. 2*, edited by Hans Peter Dreitzel. New York: Macmillan.

Bertaux, Daniel (ed.). 1981. *Biography and Society*. Newbury Park, CA: Sage.

Bertaux, Daniel and Martin Kohli. 1984. "The Life Story Approach: A Continental View." *Annual Review of Sociology* 10:215–37.

Birren, James E. and Lisa Dieckmann. 1991. "Concepts and Content of Quality of Life in the Later Years: An Overview." Pp. 344–60 in *The Concept and Measurement of Quality of Life in the Frail Elderly*, edited by James E. Birren et al. New York: Academic Press.

Birren, James E., James E. Lubben, Janice Cichowlas Rowe, and Donna E. Deutchman (eds.). 1991. *The Concept and Measurement of Quality of Life in the Frail Elderly*. New York: Academic Press.

Blumer, Herbert. 1969. "Science without Concepts." Pp. 153–70 in *Symbolic Interactionism*, Herbert Blumer. Englewood Cliffs, NJ: Prentice-Hall.

Bruner, Jerome. 1986. *Actual Minds, Possible Worlds*. Cambridge, MA: Harvard University Press.

Butler, Robert N. 1963. "The Life Review: An Interpretation of Reminiscence in the Aged." *Psychiatry* 26:65–76.

Butler, Robert N. and Myrna I. Lewis. 1977. *Aging and Mental Health*. St. Louis: C.V. Mosby.

Charmaz, Kathy. 1991. *Good Days, Bad Days: The Self in Chronic Illness and Time*. New Brunswick, NJ: Rutgers University Press.

Cicourel, Aaron V. 1964. *Method and Measurement in Sociology*. New York: Free Press.

Clifford, James and George E. Marcus (eds.). 1986. *Writing Culture*. Berkeley: University of California Press.

Clough, Patricia Ticineto. 1992. *The Ends of Ethnography*. Newbury Park, CA: Sage.

Coe, Rodney. 1965. "Self-Conception and Institutionalization." Pp. 225–43 in *Older People and Their Social World*, edited by Arnold M. Rose and Warren A. Peterson. Philadelphia: F.A. Davis.

Diamond, Tim. 1993. *Making Gray Gold*. Chicago: University of Chicago Press.

Estes, Carroll L. and Elisabeth A. Binney. 1989. "The Biomedicalization of Aging: Dangers and Dilemmas." *The Gerontologist* 29:587–96.

Frank, Gelya. 1980. "Life Histories in Gerontology: The Subjective Side to Aging." Pp. 155–76 in *New Methods for Old Age Research*, edited by Christine L. Fry and Jennie Keith. Chicago: Loyola University Center for Urban Policy.

Gadamer, Hans-Georg. 1993. *Truth and Method*. New York: Continuum.

Garfinkel, Harold. 1967. *Studies in Ethnomethodology*. Englewood Cliffs, NJ: Prentice-Hall.

Geertz, Clifford. 1988. *Works and Lives: The Anthropologist as Author*. Stanford, CA: Stanford University Press.

Goffman, Erving. 1961. *Asylums*. Garden City, NY: Anchor.

———. 1974. *Frame Analysis*. New York: Harper and Row.

Gottesman, L. E. and N. C. Bourstrom. 1974. "Why Nursing Homes Do What They Do." *The Gerontologist* 14:501–6.

Gubrium, Jaber F. 1975. *Living and Dying at Murray Manor*. New York: St. Martin's.

———. 1986. *Oldtimers and Alzheimer's: The Descriptive Organization of Senility*. Greenwich, CT: JAI Press.

———. 1988. *Analyzing Field Reality*. Newbury Park, CA: Sage.

———. 1991. *The Mosaic of Care: Frail Elderly and Their Families in the Real World*. New York: Springer.

Gubrium, Jaber F., James A. Holstein, and David R. Buckholdt. 1994. *Constructing the Life Course*. Dix Hills, NY: General Hall.

Gubrium, Jaber F. and Robert J. Lynott. 1985. "Alzheimer's Disease as Biographical Work." Pp. 349–67 in *Social Bonds in Later Life*, edited by Warren A. Peterson and Jill Quadagno. Newbury Park, CA: Sage.

Gustafson, Elisabeth. 1972. "Dying: The Career of the Nursing Home Patient." *Journal of Health and Social Behavior* 13:226–35.

Henry, Jules. 1963. *Culture Against Man*. New York: Vintage.

Institute of Medicine. 1986. *Improving the Quality of Care in Nursing Homes*. Washington, DC: National Academy Press.

Johnson, Colleen L. and Leslie A. Grant. 1985. *The Nursing Home in American Society*. Baltimore: Johns Hopkins University Press.

Kane, Robert L. 1989. "The Biomedical Blues." *The Gerontologist* 29:583.

Kane, Rosalie A. and Robert L. Kane. 1981. *Assessing the Elderly*. Lexington, MA: Lexington Books.

Kaufman, Sharon R. 1986. *The Ageless Self*. Madison: University of Wisconsin Press.

Kayser-Jones, Jeanie. 1981. *Old, Alone, and Neglected*. Berkeley: University of California Press.

Lawton, M. Powell. 1983. "Environments and Other Determinants of Well-Being in Older People." *Environment and Behavior* 17:501–19.

Maines, David R. 1993. "Narrative's Moment and Sociology's Phenomena: Toward a Narrative Sociology." *Sociological Quarterly* 34:17–38.

Maines, David R. and Jeffrey T. Ulmer. 1993. "The Relevance of Narrative for Interactionist Thought." *Studies in Symbolic Interaction* 14:109–24.

Morris, John N., et al. 1990. "Designing the National Resident Assessment Instrument for Nursing Homes." *The Gerontologist* 30:293–307.

New England Research Institute. 1992. "Quality of Life." *Network* (Winter):1–3. Watertown, MA: Author.

NHCMQ Training Manual. 1991. Natick, MA: Eliot Press.

Pastalan, Leon. 1970. "Privacy as an Expression of Human Territoriality." Pp. 37–46 in *Spatial Behavior of Older People,* edited by Leon Pastalan and Daniel Carson. Ann Arbor: Institute of Gerontology, University of Michigan.

Pifer, Alan and Lydia Bronte (eds.). 1986. *Our Aging Society.* New York: Norton.

Rubinstein, Robert L. 1988. "Stories Told: In-Depth Interviewing and the Structure of Its Insights." Pp. 128–46 in *Qualitative Gerontology,* edited by Shulamit Reinharz and Graham D. Rowles. New York: Springer.

_____. 1989. "The Home Environment of Older People: A Description of the Psychosocial Processes Linking Person to Place." *Journal of Gerontology* 44:S45–S53.

_____. 1990. "Personal Identity and Environmental Meaning in Later Life." *Journal of Aging Studies* 4:131–47.

_____. 1992. "Personal Meaning and Acts of Interpretation." Paper presented at the annual conference of the Gerontological Society of America, Washington, DC.

Sarton, May. 1973. *As We Are Now.* New York: Norton.

Savishinsky, Joel S. 1991. *The Ends of Time: Life and Work in a Nursing Home.* New York: Bergen and Garvey.

Schutz, Alfred. 1967. *The Phenomenology of the Social World.* Evanston, IL: Northwestern University Press.

Shield, Renee Rose. 1988. *Uneasy Endings: Daily Life in an American Nursing Home.* Ithaca, NY: Cornell University Press.

Skolnick, Arlene S. 1983. *The Intimate Environment.* Boston: Little, Brown.

Stannard, Charles I. 1973. "Old Folks and Dirty Work: The Social Conditions for Patient Abuse in a Nursing Home." *Social Problems* 20:329–42.

Svensson, Torbjörn. 1991. "Intellectual Exercise and Quality of Life in the Frail Elderly." Pp. 256–75 in *The Concept and Measurement of Quality of Life in the Frail Elderly,* edited by James E. Birren et al. New York: Academic Press.

Van Maanen, John. 1988. *Tales of the Field: On Writing Ethnography.* Chicago: University of Chicago Press.

Vourlckis, Betsy S., Donald E. Gelfand and Roberta R. Greene. 1992. "Psychosocial Needs and Care in Nursing Homes: Comparison of Views of Social Workers and Home Administrators." *The Gerontologist* 32:113–19.

Wallace, J. Brandon. 1992. "Reconsidering the Life Review: The Social Construction of Talk about the Past." *The Gerontologist* 32:120–25.

Wallace, J. Brandon. 1993. "Life Stories." In *Qualitative Methods in Aging Research,* edited by Jaber F. Gubrium and Andrea Sankar. Newbury Park, CA: Sage.

Ward, Russell. 1979. *The Aging Experience.* New York: Lippincott.

Watson, Wilbur and Robert Maxwell. 1977. *Human Aging and Dying.* New York: St. Martin's.

Zusman, Joseph. 1966. "Some Explanations of the Changing Appearance of Psychotic Patients: Antecedents of the Social Breakdown Syndrome Concept." *Milbank Memorial Fund Quarterly* 64:363–94.

Index